# WRITING INDIANS

A VOLUME IN THE SERIES

Native Americans of the Northeast
Culture, History, and the Contemporary

EDITED BY

COLIN G. CALLOWAY AND
BARRY O'CONNELL

HILARY E. WYSS

# WRITING INDIANS

Literacy, Christianity,
and
Native Community
in
Early America

✝ ✝

✝

University of Massachusetts Press

AMHERST

Printed in the United States of America
LC 00-036384
ISBN 1-55849-264-X
Designed by Dennis Anderson
Set in Adobe Garamond by Graphic Composition, Inc., Athens, Georgia
Printed and bound by Sheridan Books, Inc.

Library of Congress Cataloging-in-Publication Data

Wyss, Hilary E.
    Writing Indians : literacy, Christianity, and native community in early America /
Hilary E. Wyss.
        p. cm.—(Native Americans of the Northeast)
    Includes bibliographical references and index.
    ISBN 1-55849-264-X (alk. paper)
    1. American literature—Indian authors—History and criticism. 2. Indians of
North America—New England—Biography—History and criticism. 3. Christian
converts—New England—Biography—History and criticism. 4. American
literature—New England—History and criticism. 5. Christianity and literature—
New England—History. 6. Indians of North America—Missions—New England.
7. Literacy—New England—History. 8. New England—In literature. 9. Indians in
literature. 10. Autobiography. I. Title. II. Series.

PS153.I52 W95 2000
810.9'897—dc21

                                                                    00-036384

British Library Cataloguing in Publication data are available.


Portions of Chapter 2 are reprinted from *Early American Literature,* Volume 33, 1998.
Copyright © 1998 by the Department of English, University of North Carolina
at Chapel Hill. Used by permission of the publisher.

A portion of the Epilogue is reprinted from *American Indian Quarterly,*
Volume 23:3/4, 1999. Copyright © University of Nebraska Press. Used by
permission of the publisher.

To James and Anna

# CONTENTS

# CONTENTS

# ACKNOWLEDGMENTS

I OWE thanks to a great many people and institutions for making this book possible. Financial support was provided by the John Carter Brown Library, Auburn University, and the University of North Carolina. Polly Pierce at the Stockbridge Town Library and Frank Lorenz at Hamilton College were enthusiastic supporters of this project, and I am grateful for their individual attention and helpful suggestions. Norman Fiering at the John Carter Brown Library provided an extraordinary opportunity not only to engage with a wealth of primary materials but also to interact with colleagues whose interests overlapped with my own; I shall always be grateful. My thanks also go to the staffs at the Connecticut Historical Society, the New-York Historical Society, and the Massachusetts Archive.

Without my writing group in all its forms this book simply could not have been completed. My thanks go to Erin Lang Bonin, Amy DeRogatis, Keith Zahnisser, David Zercher, Sandy Bardsley, and Tim Spaulding. My thanks also go to Philip Gura, Joy Kasson, Robert Johnstone, Robert Cantwell, and Laurie Maffly-Kipp, all careful readers whose enthusiasm and generosity helped keep me going forward. His book *John Eliot's Mission to the Indians before King Philip's War* was published too late for me to include it in this book, but I want to thank Richard Cogley for his generosity in reading my work and sharing his expertise. Other readers who provided important insights as well as much appreciated encouragement include David Hall, David Murray, and Laura Murray. I want to thank my colleagues in the English Department at Auburn University for their friendship and support. I am particularly grateful to Paula Backscheider for sharing her wealth of knowledge and patiently answering my endless questions. Colin Calloway, Barry O'Connell, and Clark Dougan at the University of Massachusetts Press have been a pleasure to work with. I also want to thank the Wysses, the Eingorns, and the Trumans for support, encouragement, love, and babysitting. And, finally, how can I possibly express my gratitude to my dear husband, James Truman, friend and colleague, who gave time from his own work to make mine possible?

H. E. W.

# A NOTE ON THE TEXT

A FEW words are in order to explain some of the editorial decisions I made in this book. Quoted texts are represented exactly, which means that spelling, grammar, and even spacing are erratic throughout. My point is to show the idiosyncrasies of seventeenth- and eighteenth-century printing and orthography—idiosyncrasies that are by no means limited to Native writers. Also, I capitalize the racial/cultural terms "Native" and "White" (except in direct quotes from other writers), as well as the more obvious "Indian" and "Anglo-American," in an effort to maintain consistency in the confusing and often contradictory quagmire of racial language.

# ABBREVIATIONS

BL      Beinecke Rare Book and Manuscript Library, Yale University, New Haven

CHS      Occom Papers, The Connecticut Historical Society, Hartford

DC      Dwight Collection, Norman Rockwell Museum, Stockbridge, Massachusetts

DCC      Dartmouth College Collection, Dartmouth College, Hanover, New Hampshire

HC      Hamilton Collection, Hamilton College Archives, Clinton, New York

MA      Massachusetts Archives Collection, Massachusetts Archive, Boston

MHS      Pickering Papers, Massachusetts Historical Society, Boston

NYHS      The New-York Historical Society, New York

STL      Historical Room, Stockbridge Town Library, Stockbridge, Massachusetts

# WRITING INDIANS

# WRITING IN THE MARGINS

## Christian Indian Identity, 1643–1829

†

> I, Nathan Francis, this is my writing at this time.
> September 6, 1738. This is my writing, Zachary Hosueit.
> I am Matthew Seiknout, this is my Bible, clearly.
>
> —Bible marginalia, translated and transcribed by
> Ives Goddard and Kathleen Bragdon

IN 1663, after years of labor, the New England missionary John Eliot and Native translators John Sassomon, Job Nesuton, and James Printer produced and printed a Bible in the Massachusett language. The Bible was the basis for Anglo-American Protestantism, but the edition printed in Massachusett was inaccessible to most English settlers. It was also inaccessible to most Native speakers of Massachusett, since the language did not exist in written form before Eliot and his Native co-workers created it.[1] The Bible in this indigenous language, printed in hundreds of copies, became the most visible artifact of the emerging bicultural community of Christian Indians in New England.

As the Bibles came into their hands, individual Native owners created an alternative "text" in the margins that marked each copy as an extension of their own particular identities. The marginalia of the Massachusett Bibles contains a wealth of information that sometimes responds to the text of the Bible itself and often converses with an entire community of Native Christians. Scrawling sideways, upside down, on any bare space, Native readers of these Bibles not only marked their own presence but also left a record of their interactions with the text. And those interactions were extraordinarily varied. In their collection of Native writings in Massachusett, Kathleen Bragdon and Ives Goddard report seeing written alphabets, single letters, and numbers, all of which indicate that the Bible was used to practice penmanship or orthography.[2] Repetition of sentences or words further suggests that the Bible was a textbook in which individuals rehearsed and perfected their writing. For these individuals, the practices we would today call "literacy" were intimately linked to the Bible, both as the physical site in which to perfect these skills and as the basis for the phrases repeated over and over.

Some writers recorded their responses to particular biblical passages. One proudly remarks in the margin of the Old Testament book of Nahum, "This chapter I read, the first chapter of Nahum" (Goddard and Bragdon 379). Writers also included cross-references to other biblical passages, quotes from elsewhere in the Bible, religious messages, warnings, and reminders. "You, Thomas, remember: do not fornicate" (Dan. 1.2) (377), says one writer to himself or perhaps to someone else. Another writer, probably Joseph Papenau, a Native preacher at Falmouth and Bourne in the mid-eighteenth century, writes, "Remember you people, this book is right and You (people) should do good in all your times" (Lev. 8.1) (417). He also writes, of Exodus "This truly is so among all of us" (Exod. 7.1), and "It was true in former times" (Exod. 7.2) (417). Writers thus maintain an extended conversation with one another and with the larger community through their textual annotations.

Native writers also used their Bibles as records of events. One writer records his departure from his community: "I Josiah Attaunitt made this on March 18, 1716. I am going to the ocean" (449). Another Bible records the death of two sachems: "Ephraim Naquatta died on July 7, 1731" (4) and "Joshua Seiknouet died January 22, 1716" (5). Some less auspicious events are recorded as well: in the margin of Jer. 2.1–3 one writer gleefully writes, "I Banjmon Kusseniyeutt caught a Negro man and a white woman" (451). One writer proudly announces his brief possession of the Bible: "This is Papenau's book. I am looking after it" (417). Sometimes writers recorded little more than their names and the fact of their presence. "I, Nathan Francis, this is my writing at this time" (377), says one writer, while others write, "I Jamesasabh" (385), or "I, Mantooekit, (x) This is my hand" (391). Others stress their ownership of their Bibles, and in the process give clues about what such a possession might imply. One announces, "I am Matthew Seiknout, this is my Bible, clearly" (463); another, "I, Nanahdinnoo, this is my book, and . . . I Nanahdinnoo, own this forever. Because I bought it with my money" (397). As these individuals use writing to record their thoughts and even their particular identities, they participate in the structures of colonial society. At the same time, their use of their Bibles to mark both the mundane and the profound departs from the Anglo-American norm, suggesting a different relationship to the sacred, and perhaps even a particularly Native sense of spirituality. After all, though many family Bibles have records of the births and deaths of individuals, few have practice alphabets and numbers. The marginalia of the Eliot Bibles suggests some of the ways Native Christians used writing to create and maintain a community that is a product of colonialism but is at the same time rooted in a traditional Native identity.

As we are drawn to the stories in the margins of various copies of the Bible, the commentary accompanying Goddard and Bragdon's translations takes on an elegiac quality. For some copies, they report simply: "The margins of the pages were cut down during the modern binding affecting the text of the marginalia in some places" (374). That is, in some preserved versions, though the printed Massachusett text of the Bible remains, the marks of the lived experience of those who read it have been cut away. And with those marks, the identity of these colonial subjects, proudly proclaimed again and again in the margins of those pages, is cut away. More broadly, in our longing to find an "authentic Native voice" speaking to us from the past, we have ignored those who wrote and thought from a Native perspective that included a sense of their colonial position. This problem of authenticity has haunted literary studies. And in the search for the "real" Indian, such valuable resources as the Massachusett Bible marginalia have been overlooked or downplayed because they do not have appropriately "authentic" pedigrees. The result is a resounding silence in the canon of Native American literatures until the nineteenth century, and often until well into the twentieth century, when linguists and translators explored the possibility of recording authentic voices though sophisticated and complex techniques that often had the effect of exoticizing Native Americans.

To gain access to early Native American cultures, critics have generally focused their attention on the published narratives of Euro-Americans, since the assumption was that Native Americans were not literate before the end of the eighteenth century.[3] Relatively speaking, literacy among Native Americans was indeed low, since it was limited to converts to Christianity, who would have had access to missionary schools. But though opinions vary over whether missionary efforts in New England should be considered successful,[4] according to R. Pierce Beaver "by 1674 there were 14 towns of 'praying Indians' with a reported population of 2,200 on the mainland and 1,800 to 2,600 on [Martha's Vineyard]" (431), numbers which suggest a significant literacy rate among Natives. Still, the assumption persists among certain historians and literary critics that Native Americans were not literate, and thus little work has been done on the writing of all but a very few Native Americans before the nineteenth century,[5] when William Apess published what recent critics have called the first significant Native American autobiography.[6]

Although literary critics consider Apess's 1829 published narrative, *A Son of the Forest,* the first significant Native autobiography, I maintain that in fact there is a tradition of Native American life writing that precedes Apess by almost 150 years. This writing takes the form of letters, journal entries, and religious confessions. It is also often embedded in the published tracts of colonial missionaries who quote Native converts at length. Taken together, these materials, including sermons and even cultural histories, define the unique identity and cultural position of the Christianized Native American in colonial American society. To borrow Mary Louise Pratt's term, these texts are "autoethnographies . . . in which colonized subjects undertake to represent themselves in ways that *engage with* the colonizer's own terms" (*Imperial Eyes* 7). Pratt continues, "Autoethnography involves partial collaboration with and appropriation of the idioms of the conqueror" (7). But though such autoethnographers use the language and structures of the colonizers, they do not eliminate their identity as Natives but rather come to a distinct understanding of what Nativeness means in a colonial order.[7]

For many critics, Christianized writing embodies the loss of traditional values to the dominant culture. Two important critics perhaps best represent the view that Native American autobiography has an extensive (albeit quite unorthodox) Native American past that has been distorted in its translation into a genre more familiar to Anglo-American readers. H. David Brumble identifies six preliterate forms: "the coup tales, the less formal and usually more detailed tales of warfare and hunting, the self-examinations, the self-vindications, the educational narratives, and the tales of the acquisitions of powers" (22–23). For Brumble, such forms are at the core of Native American autobiographies, even those which have been heavily edited by White editors. Hertha Wong expands Brumble's definition of preliterate autobiography. She extends that label to pictographs, narrative wampum belts, quillwork, and even to naming practices, all of which she claims "have generally been examined . . . from routinely Eurocentric assumptions with which they were never meant to conform, [and therefore] they have been devalued or overlooked" (25). For such critics, Nativeness is distorted or tainted through the intervention of Anglo-Americans, but, they suggest, a careful reader can find marks of authentic Nativeness within certain texts.

For others, "Native American autobiography" is by its very nature a contradiction in terms and can exist only as a bicultural artifact. A. LaVonne Brown Ruoff claims that such autobiography "represents a break with oral tradition because the personal narrative is not part of American Indian oral literatures" ("Indian Authors" 192). Arnold Krupat, too, sees the autobiography as a primarily European form. He distinguishes between autobiographies by Indians and Indian autobiographies (the latter form including "as told to" books), but emphasizes that both forms necessarily involve biculturalism (*Voice* 133), since "Indian autobiographies are not a traditional form among Native peoples but the consequence of contact with the White invaders-settlers, and the product of a limited collaboration with them" (*For Those* xxvii).

I too maintain that written narratives by Native converts are necessarily bicultural products. Simultaneously, however, I contend that autobiography has a place in traditional Native cultures. But my project is aimed less at identifying what is authentically Native than at pointing out the cultural influences that define and are in turn redefined by Christian Indians in particular. Brumble briefly points to the useful convergence of preliterate traditions of autobiography and Christian confessions in respect to intensive self-examination (33). I argue that such cultural convergences—I call them "transculturations" and "reculturations"—provide an opportunity not only to preserve Native traditions but to develop and expand them. Literacy was for many Natives the means through which they acknowledged their participation in the larger colonial world. By writing their own narratives of conversion, Natives were defining their place in a newly forming colonial structure, positioning themselves simultaneously as Native Americans and as colonial subjects. Early Native writers syncretically joined what at first glance seem to be incompatible conceptions of selfhood.[8] Thus the concept of the autoethnography better captures the complexity of these Natives' writing than does the term "autobiography," as the former hinges on a politically active and ongoing redefinition of multiple cultural traditions, while the latter suggests a more personal endeavor.

The autoethnographies of Native converts in the seventeenth and eighteenth centuries reveal the crucial role of literacy in forming a colonial Native subjectivity. While critics of Native American autobiography such as Brumble, Wong, and Krupat look elsewhere for the origins of Native life writing, my study argues for the importance of the Protestant Christian tradition in this genealogy. Rather than trying to look past the "salvationist discourse" (Krupat *Voice* 142) of converted Natives, we should see it as central to asserting a particular subjectivity. New England Protestant missionaries believed that only through literacy could true conversions take place, and thus much of their religious work with Native Americans involved teaching them to read and write. In turn, Native converts attempted not only to acquire literacy but also to create an identity through literacy that marked them as different from missionaries as well as from other Native Americans. This identity is neither strictly "Native" nor purely assimilationist but rather a hybrid of Anglo-American and indigenous cultures.[9]

The acquisition of literacy was no small task for Native converts. Though critics disagree about the specific consequences of literacy on non-literate societies, most do agree that it could have a profound effect. Advocates of the "strong text" perspective such as Walter Ong and Jack Goody emphasize the fundamental alteration that occurs in the newly literate individual's orientation to the outside world, including the shift to abstract thinking, social isolation, and the rise of impersonal "bureaucratic" social and political structures. Though this approach has provided useful ways to think about the possible consequences of literacy, the anthropologists Sylvia Scribner and Michael Cole warn against a too facile application of these ideas. They stress, instead, the importance of the social context of literacy. Documenting a range of literate activity based on specific social situations, they argue that there can be no universal consequence of literacy; instead, each situation will produce its own set of practices and characteristics, all of which are contingent on the larger social system in place (237). In a similar vein, Marilyn Cooper proposes an "ecological model of writing," in which "writing is an activity through which a person is continually engaged with a variety of socially constituted systems" (6). She emphasizes that such systems "are inherently dynamic; all the characteristics of any individual . . . piece of writing both determine and are determined by the characteristics of all the other . . . writings in the systems" (7). In the case of Anglo-American missionaries and their Native American converts, vestiges of their unequal power relations remain embedded within their texts and provide a key to the conflicting cultural assumptions of those involved in the acquisition of literacy.

By carefully examining not only the writings themselves but the particulars of the social and political situations in which they were produced, we come to a better understanding of the cultural position of the Native American convert. The assumptions of the missionaries and their approach to education had a profound effect on Native writers. New England Protestantism in the period spanning the late seventeenth and the eighteenth centuries structured itself on the principle that only literacy could provide a true understanding of God, since his truth was contained in the Bible. According to David Hall, "Every household in New England was affected by the premise, originating with the Reformation, that all godly people should be literate" (*Worlds* 34). David Cressy notes the link between literacy and civility in seventeenth-and eighteenth-century sermons. He explains that contemporary ministers connected "rudeness, licentiousness, profaneness, superstition and any wickedness" with the inability to read and write (24). In addition, he writes, both in the colonies and in England there was a firm belief that "literacy and education could combat 'misorders' and 'disobedience' and could promote 'policy and civility'" (25).

Historians and sociologists agree that there is clear evidence for an increase in literacy practices throughout the eighteenth-century colonial world. But Deborah Keller-Cohen points out that what we think of as "literacy"—the ability to read and write—was not a single, coherent process for most colonial people (170). In fact, as David Hall points out, "literacy" could refer to "the Latin-based world of academic learning" that was a sign of "the politics of privilege," or it could refer simply to the act of reading or writing in the English language (*Cultures* 152). Thus, David Cressy warns, when speaking of the American colonies "it is important to talk of the margins of literacy, gradations of literacy, and of the uneven incidence of literacy in a partially literate society, rather than a simple dichotomy of literacy and illiteracy" (27). Keller-Cohen prefers to speak of a "web of relationships among reading, writing, and speaking" (158).[10]

Protestant missionaries in particular emphasized the importance of reading and writing as integrated practices leading to proper religious conversion. This attitude had important implications for the orally based cultures of Native American converts, which were dismissed by missionaries as inadequate for a true understanding of Christianity.[11] Some of the earliest missionary efforts involved not only reaching out to Native Americans themselves but also "bring[ing] the Indian language to rules" (Eliot, *Grammar* 1)—the implication being that Indian language was innately incoherent until Anglo-American grammatical rules transformed it into a written language more suitable for spiritual matters.[12] The New England Protestant missionary effort to impart literacy presumed not only the theological superiority of the Christian faith but also the cultural superiority of Euro-Americans as a rational, literate people; missionaries believed that their religious work necessarily involved literacy training, which in turn involved a redefinition of the cultural traditions of Native peoples.[13] Though problematic in many ways, the belief structure of these missionaries has left a rich source of writing by Natives that gives us a sense of their experience and shows how they redefined "literacy" to suit their own purposes.

In analyzing the textual productions of both Anglo-American missionaries and Native converts, I examine the ways in which these individuals participated in a highly contested process of Protestant identity formation in the period spanning the late seventeenth to the early nineteenth centuries. Although their texts share rhetorical patterns and structures that mirror each other in the formation (and affirmation) of a Protestant religious identity, texts by Anglo-American missionaries and their Native converts diverge in important ways. From early colonial Puritanism to the fervor of the mid-eighteenth-century Great Awakening through the expansive early nineteenth-century Second Great Awakening, American Protestantism was constantly redefining itself. These changes redefined individuals' agency over their own salvation, increasingly opening space for Native Christians to voice their own particular relationships to the divine.

For over twenty years now, advocates of the "new Indian history" heralded by Robert Berkhofer in 1971 and practiced by scholars such as James Merrell, Neal Salisbury, Richard White, and Daniel Richter have incorporated writings by Native Americans into their studies.[14] But literary critics have generally shied away from this material for a number of reasons, the main one being the foreignness of the writing. Though some early documents are quite literally written in a foreign language,[15] many are not; the main issue for literary critics is that "translating" such documents must occur on a cultural level, not simply linguistically. A glance at early documents written by Native Americans confirms that they are not always easily accessible as literary acts, since they often convey a cultural reality that is quite foreign from our own. Thus the translation issues that complicate direct access to specific meanings can seem overwhelming. Complicated by an anxiety over identifying an "authentic" Native voice (one conveniently recognizable to literary critics of all stripes), the project of understanding Native writing seems all but impossible.

The caution of most literary critics in tackling these materials reflects a highly charged political issue. David Murray and Eric Cheyfitz both argue that the act of translation is aggressively and consistently resisted by dominant groups, for to acknowledge it is to acknowledge powerlessness, or at least the inability to communicate. These critics suggest that by always putting Natives in the position of having to translate their languages into English, early colonists perpetuated their own sense of power while confirming the inferiority of Natives, who were forced to communicate in a language not their own.[16] By refusing to acknowledge or engage in the act of translation, modern critics extend a practice with a long history, ignoring or effacing the words of Natives that are not immediately transparent. In the process, they affirm their sense that somewhere out there is an "authentic" Indian voice and until we find it we need pay no mind to any other.

And the problem is still more complex. Translation of texts written by Native Americans is necessarily twofold, since readers must also "translate" the agendas of those for whom and by whom such tracts are written. The words of Native writers are generally embedded in other texts such as colonial histories and missionary tracts, whose writers had their own purposes: proving the cold-heartedness of Native warriors, as did chroniclers of King Philip's War such as Increase Mather and others, or gaining benefactors by showcasing Native writing ability, as Eleazar Wheelock often did. In particular, Wheelock's effort to control the representation of missionary fieldwork was characterized by the masking and erasing of mundane details. He tells Samson Occom at one point: "Don't fail to write nicely . . . write with care and all the acuracy you [can], Suitable to be sent abroad[ ], if you want to write yt which is not suitable to be sent abroad write it on a different paper" (June 27, 1762 CHS). The deeply hierarchical structure of missionary culture involved constantly shifting axes of power, and, as Laura Murray has indicated, power did not move in a single direction. Anglo-Americans used the words of Native Americans to prove points that had no relation to the words themselves: Wheelock urges Occom to write neatly so that he can send his letters along to benefactors, not because what he is trying to say matters but because as long as the handwriting is appropriate and the English is refined, Occom represents Wheelock's success as a civilizing agent. And Natives at times manipulated the expectations of their readers to make their own points, as when one writer brandishes his "worthlessness" as an Indian to emphasize English losses in King Philip's War, saying, "You must consider the Indians lost nothing but their life; you must lose your fair houses and cattle" (Gookin, "Historical Account" 494). Reading early Native American texts, then, involves a double translation in the sense that the words of Native writers must be understood not just as isolated texts but as part of their larger context. The modern critic must recognize that the possibility of something getting lost along the way is very real, but not to attempt any translation at all seems worse.

By reading the words of Christianized Natives, one does not get access to the ideas and values of indigenous peoples—or what Gayatri Spivak might call "the subaltern."[17] In large part, Christianized Natives were rather tenuously connected to traditional tribal structures, and they lived in communities where social and cultural structures were constantly being renegotiated and redefined. Their words do not constitute a record of "authentic" Native American identity in the sense that Euro-Americans have defined it—an identity that Spivak would argue is finally unknowable and is so invested with nostalgia as to be unintelligible. There are no written records of "authentic Native communities" because the act of writing and the possibility of recording the authenticity of nonliterate peoples ultimately contradict each other.[18] But what we can find in the writings of Christian Indians is a record of the experience and world view of Native Americans who are participating in a newly developing culture which threatens to exclude them entirely if they do not accept its terms. Never fully accepted by the Anglo-American community whose values they incorporated into their lives, and often hated by other Natives who saw them as betraying traditional ways, these converts nevertheless show through their writings an impassioned commitment to the idea of a Native American community that incorporated elements of the various cultural traditions around it. The acculturation of Christian Indians gave them the tools by which they could be understood by Euro-Americans; unfortunately, this identification with the dominant group also means that such Indians are rejected by Euro-American scholars as not quite authentic enough.[19]

By focusing on the cross-cultural mediations, appropriations, and translations that are inherent in the early texts of Native Christians, I challenge any essentializing assumptions we may have about either the term "Native" or the term "Christian." Specifically, I examine the ways in which works such as the missionary tract, the captivity narrative, and various writings by literate Native Americans all help define the cultural position of the Christian Indian. Though in some senses these forms of writing would seem to be at cross-purposes, I maintain that in fact they mirror each other in ways that have significant repercussions for both Native converts and the Euro-Americans who interact with them.

To fully appreciate the interplay of the various texts, we must clearly define certain genres of writing. The *missionary tract* is a form that encompasses a range of stylistic features and performs multiple rhetorical tasks. Though some are single-author documents with a carefully controlled narrative, often they are collections of seemingly random information in the form of letters, contracts, citations, and anecdotes that all point to the efficacy of a certain missionary or missionary group. Primarily, these tracts have a persuasive function, as they are written to convince benefactors of the worth of their ventures; the key to the missionary tract, then, is its potential financial impact. The assumption behind many of these narratives is not only that the missionary has the Natives' best interests at heart, but also that he knows those interests better than the Natives. Often, the premise of the missionary endeavor is that Natives must be saved from themselves; thus missionaries felt free to pass judgment on the "national traits" of the Natives they worked with.

Tensions arose, however, between the job of conversion and the act of fundraising. Occasionally missionaries based in the colonies and missionary societies in England or Scotland were at odds with each other. For example, despite the regular support Eliot received, his relationship with the New England Company was at times strained because his individual fundraising got in the way of the company's own fundraising (Kellaway 32–34). And Eleazar Wheelock was not above acquiring money from whatever sources seemed willing to give, while Samuel Kirkland at one point was drawing a salary from two different missionary societies.[20] Poor communication as well as funding agencies' distance from the needs of missionaries and their converts further raised suspicions about uses of funds. For example, Wheelock never actually went out to visit any of his missionaries, but got his information through their letters, so they were perpetually underfunded at least partially because he never fully understood their needs.[21] Letters from missionaries are filled with pleas for such basics as clothing and food; responses from funding agencies often dismiss or downplay such requests as frivolous.

The missionary tract was rhetorically connected to another colonial literary form: the *captivity narrative.* Many captivity narratives, including Spanish and French narratives, were written and transcribed before the Puritan version. Though these are certainly important works in their own right, I focus on the genre that emerged from the Puritan experience, with its particular typological significance. Originating in seventeenth-century New England, the Anglo-American captivity narrative is a devotional work that uses a lived experience as a metaphor for religious experience. In the introduction to their collection of Puritan captivity narratives, Alden Vaughan and Edward Clark point out that the form emerged as a "separate and distinct literary genre" only in the seventeenth century (2), although it incorporated features of existing literary strands. In particular, the Puritan captivity narrative borrowed heavily from the spiritual autobiography, with its deeply personal spiritual message; the sermon (including the lay sermon), with its emphasis on moral lessons and its use of biblical citation; the Jeremiad, an attack on backsliding; and of course the secular adventure story, with its melodrama, action, and excitement (4–10). The captivity trope, as inflected by a ministerial voice, reflects Calvinist theology in its most essential form: God's incomprehensible plan is made manifest through seemingly random events, and it is only by trusting entirely in his will that one can be saved. Human suffering, in this context, is a sign of God's will; paradoxically, the more one suffered, the more one felt God's saving power. In captivity narratives, such Biblical precedents as the Babylonian captivity, Job's sufferings, and the parable of the prodigal son were adapted to a particularly American experience (Slotkin 101–3). Tara Fitzpatrick and Slotkin both argue that the captivity narrative exists at the center of a particularly American archetype: "the imperiled but chosen pilgrim alone in the wilderness braving the savage 'other'" (Fitzpatrick 2).[22]

The Puritan captivity narrative has as its central premise the disruption of racial or cultural identity; through a violent separation from family, friends, and community, captives must come to terms with their identity in opposition to the Native community that has taken them. The missionary tract of the same period chronicles a somewhat parallel situation in which the Native must separate himself or herself from family, friends, and community to appropriate an altered (Christian) identity. As the captivity narrative details the (failed) possibility of a descent into savagery, the missionary tract chronicles the rise of the Native to Christianity. Thus the two forms are part and parcel of the same project: to redefine the Puritan family—and by extension a larger sense of Puritan identity—in the face of potentially devastating cross-cultural interactions.

Both the missionary and the captive struggle in isolation to maintain their moral and spiritual superiority over the uncomprehending yet strangely seductive Natives who surround them. Captivity and conversion are thus closely tied to each other even as they are inversions of one another—the missionary being the vehicle through which God's word is made available to the Indians and the captive understanding God's word through his or her Native American captors. But though the captive retains his or her moral superiority through victimization, the missionary is alone in the wilderness specifically through his desire to be there. The missionary structures a community of believers around himself and therefore must constantly fight the possibility of his own tyranny.

Captivity narratives, like missionary tracts, are the post-facto accounts of individuals faced with extraordinary and often incomprehensible moments in which their faith in God and in their own cultural superiority is constantly being challenged. In the retelling, these moments serve to confirm the superiority of the captive or missionary who has withstood chaos. Conceptually impossible, David Sewell notes, is the independently written captivity narrative of someone who stayed with the Indians—impossible because a necessary part of the definition of the genre is that what is unstable and culturally foreign is rendered coherent for the dominant White culture. Thus the captivity narrative must always be the story of one who returned—one who resisted the temptation to cross over, to change into the "other."

As the captivity narrative and the missionary tract glorify endurance, the *conversion narrative* is a story of surrender. The conceptual base of the religious conversion narrative is the rejection of one's previous identity following a transformative moment that grants a new religious experience. The convert must surrender all that previously defined his or her life as coherent and embrace the terms of the new religious system to which he or she has converted. And despite a moment or two of doubt or confusion, that life change remains permanent. Virginia Brereton outlines the five stages of the classic conversion narrative. Following a period during which the narrator more or less ignores the question of salvation, he or she becomes acutely aware of his or her sinfulness and of the possibility that he or she would be damned forever. The next stage is the surrender to God's will in conversion proper, during which the convert feels the oppressive sense of sinfulness lifted and gains confidence or at least hope that he or she is saved. With this comes a description of the narrator's changed behavior and attitudes and an account of periods of discouragement and low spiritual energy followed by renewals of dedication (6). Daniel Shea and Edmund Morgan both stress the particularity of the American Puritan conversion narrative, which was a "regularly stipulated . . . qualification for church membership" (Shea 91) in American churches but was not required back in England. The conventionalized, ritualized forms of conversion narratives, captivity narratives, and missionary tracts coexisted uneasily in a politically charged dance of surrender and endurance as each in its own way attempted to define the parameters of proper Christian living in colonial society.

The subject of this book is vast, and I have had to leave out much that is potentially of interest. I have not attempted to write a definitive history of missionaries or of White captives. Nor have I attempted to uncover all writing by Native Christians. Instead, I have focused on five specific situations that range from the late seventeenth to the early nineteenth centuries in the northeastern United States.[23] I examine writing communities that are each formed and perpetuated in distinct ways, but that all balance between maintaining a Native identity and finding a place in the colonial world. Looking at various scenes of writing, I hope to show the ways in which Protestant Christian Indians simultaneously define and are defined by the writing produced within such communities.

I begin with an examination of the documents by and about Christian Indians in King Philip's War. These include letters by such Christianized

Indians as James Printer and Job Nesuton and narrative accounts by Mary Rowlandson, William Hubbard, and Increase Mather. Scholars of early American literature have focused on dramatic accounts such as Rowlandson's, but the words of Native writers of the period offer an alternative story of captivity and redemption that is as compelling as hers. By comparing John Eliot's missionary tracts to ransom letters concerning Rowlandson that were written by apostatized Natives allied with King Philip, I conclude that Natives were actively defining the terms through which they accepted Christianity.

In chapter 2 I move to Experience Mayhew's 1727 biographical history of Native American conversions on Martha's Vineyard, *Indian Converts,* which contains autoethnographic narratives of converted Indians. I investigate the ways in which the multiple voices of Mayhew's text characterize the Native Christian community of Martha's Vineyard. Through this text, as well as related textual fragments such as land deeds and Bible marginalia, I examine the ways in which literacy transforms Native structures of identity while also providing a means of maintaining cultural integrity.

Chapter 3 examines alternative accounts of Native conversion in Stockbridge, Massachusetts. I begin with the writings of John Sergeant, missionary to the Mahican Indians along the Housatonic River. Sergeant adopts the language of the captivity narrative in his journals, and in the process reveals his limited understanding of his converts. In particular, Sergeant's journal entries on Native alcohol consumption indicate the sometimes painful struggles of Native converts as they come to terms with mission life. I relate these writings to several works by Hendrick Aupaumut, a Native American writer and diplomat educated by missionaries. Aupaumut was a devout Christian as well as a political leader of his tribe, and his writings, which include letters, a journal, and a tribal history, emphasize the connection between his personal history and the history of his people. The writings of Sergeant and Aupaumut define the Native community of Stockbridge in very different ways, and by doing so reveal divergent conceptions of Native Christianity and community.

Chapter 4 examines Brotherton, a Native community in upstate New York created by several of Eleazar Wheelock's former pupils from Moor's Charity School. Through the writings of Wheelock and his Native American pupils (Samson Occom, Joseph Johnson, and David Fowler), I look in more detail at the tensions between Anglo-American and Native American conceptions of Native conversion. Though Anglo-American missionaries' rhetoric often stressed Native inadequacy and incompetence, Brotherton's Natives suffused their own rhetoric with a countering language of Native agency, potency, and manliness. Deeply affected by the rhetoric of the American Revolution, the language of Brotherton manipulates concepts of liberty and independence as it articulates the desires and perspectives of the community of Native converts, becoming in a certain way the "auto-biographical act" of the community.

I conclude with a discussion of William Apess, examining first his missionary biography/autobiography, *The Experiences of Five Christian Indians of the Pequot Tribe,* in which he integrates his role as a missionary into his role as a member of a particular Native community. I briefly discuss what is considered by many to be his most famous piece, "Eulogy on King Philip," touching on the uses of revolutionary rhetoric and various uses of history, and then look closely at Apess's 1829 autobiography, in which he has absorbed and appropriated the contradictory discourses of captivity, Christianity, and savagery. Rejecting what he sees as the repressive conventions of the Congregational church of his youth, Apess links the religious enthusiasm of the Second Great Awakening to a renewed sense of himself as a Native American. However, his identities as a Native American, a Christian, and a "captive" of White society from his early youth are constantly in flux and ultimately serve to problematize each other in many ways.

Christian Indians emerged from a brutal and culturally devastating process in which Native identity was threatened with annihilation. Rather than producing pacified, anglicized Christians, however, the sometimes violent convergence of cultural systems enabled Natives to carve communities out of an active engagement with both colonial and traditionally Native structures. Native converts' words reveal the complexity of the process of acquiring and adapting literacy. In the face of overwhelming cultural pressures, Native writers formulated narratives of community using theological language that differed significantly from that of Anglo-American missionaries. Replacing such missionaries' condescending language with language that emphasized personal agency, action, and control, Native community leaders reconfigured Christian theology to meet their own political goals. In the process, something was produced that was reminiscent of yet distinct from all that came before.

# CHAPTER ONE

# LITERACY, CAPTIVITY, AND REDEMPTION

## The Christian Indians of King Philip's War

✝

Because wee pray to God, other *Indians* abroad in the countrey hate us and oppose us, the English on the other side suspect us, and feare us to be still such as doe not pray at all

—*Clear Sun-Shine* of the Gospel . . .

His information (because it had an Indian original, and one can hardly believe them when they speak truth) was not at first much regarded

—Increase Mather, *Relations of the Troubles* . . . , in reference to a Christian Indian's disclosure of the Native plans to attack Lancaster

THE colonial New England experience has been scrutinized from the perspective of the colonizers, but little has been done to examine the Christian Indians' written record in the seventeenth century. As the English grudgingly accepted Natives into their colonial order, they demanded from them wholesale changes in religion, customs, and social practices. In particular, John Eliot, missionary and founder of many "praying towns" (communities of Christian Indians modeled on English towns), set the limits of Algonquian participation in English society. Insisting on their physical distance from the English, Eliot also demanded the rejection of most Native cultural practices.[1] As Algonquian converts encountered Eliot's rules, they struggled with the idea of a written language, unfamiliar religious concepts such as sin, redemption, and monotheism, and Puritan rules about the relationship between surface change such as hairstyles and clothing and deeper change—conversion, or the acceptance of God's grace. Rather than becoming the Anglicized proselytes that Eliot desired, these Christian Indians adapted Eliot's practices to their own lives, and in the process produced new and different versions of both Christian and Native identity. Through their confessions, carefully recorded by Eliot in the missionary tracts he sent to the Society for the Propagation of the Gospel in England, we can begin to see the ways Native Christians made places for themselves in the colonial order.

As New England Algonquians faced the encroachments of the increasingly dominant Anglo-American colonial settlements, they made choices about how they would incorporate various features of that culture into their lives. Through "transculturation" (an ethnographic term marking the ways in which subjugated peoples appropriate materials transmitted to them by the dominant culture), Algonquians determined for themselves the boundaries of ethnicity and acculturation. At times, notes Kathleen Bragdon, the result was actually a "strengthening or reaffirmation of traditional identities, redefined in new institutions and symbolic forms" ("Native Economy" 28). Even as missionaries such as John Eliot spent their lives attempting to eradicate Native culture by transforming it into a reflection of Anglo-American culture, the Algonquians who converted to Christianity probably operated on a very different set of principles.

As long-standing tensions between Algonquians and Anglo-American settlers culminated in King Philip's War (1675–76), Eliot's Christian Indians, conversant with the practices of both English and Native cultures, became a pivotal force. In particular, Christian Indians played an important role in one of the most famous events of King Philip's War, Mary Rowlandson's captivity and release. Invisible but crucial as couriers, spies, informants, and scribes, Christian Indians, existing only in the margins of Rowlandson's captivity narrative, played central roles in both her captivity and her release. The wife of a minister, Rowlandson has been seen as having produced "the archetype of a kind of official mythology in which the colonial experience was symbolized by the peril of a white Christian woman in the Indian-haunted wilderness" (Slotkin and Folsom, *Dreadful* 302). In her version of the events of her captivity, she downplays the role of Christian Indians, preferring instead to demonize and marginalize the very individuals who made her redemption possible. By seeing her narrative together with letters of those Christian Indians involved in her release, however, we can come to a clearer understanding of the terms through which Christian Indians participated in colonial New England.

## John Eliot and the Christian Indians of New England

When Puritan missionary John Eliot first reached out to a local Algonquian community in 1643, he set in motion a process that was to have far-reaching repercussions. Even though the English had been living in what they presumed to call "New England" for over twenty years, before John Eliot little had been done to extend what Puritans believed was the only possibility of salvation to their Algonquian neighbors. Despite the overtly missionizing message of the Massachusetts Bay Colony seal, which depicted a Native figure saying, "Come over and help us," most colonists were reluctant from the start to include Algonquians within their elect community on any terms. Indeed, long before King Philip's War, the greatest obstacles to early missionary work were not just the leaders of the Native communities but also the colonists on whose behalf missionaries such as Eliot were ostensibly reaching out to "save" the Natives. Most settlers dreaded an organized Native presence—Christian or otherwise—and furthermore were reluctant to part with land they saw as their own to establish praying towns.

Though Eliot in many ways tried to fight this Anglo-American suspicion of all things Native, distrust was central to his own missionary work. Eliot's work has received a great deal of attention from historians and other students of early American culture, in large part because he left an abundant written record of his goals and activities. Eliot is most famous for his translation of the Bible into Massachusett (1663),[2] as well as for other translations including the *Indian Grammar* (1666), the *Indian Primer* (1669), and the *Logic Primer* (1672). He also authored or was featured in a series of tracts collectively known as the "Eliot Tracts," New England Company publications that recorded "the progress of the gospel," or missionary work, under the sponsorship of the company.[3] Taken together, these writings establish patterns of conversion and set up the expectations and cultural assumptions of the missionaries under whose guidance conversions were to take place.[4]

Eliot believed, as did the vast majority of his compatriots, that "if anything at all was to be done about converting the Indians they must first be civilized" (Kellaway 8). This process involved, as James Axtell has pointed out, the paradoxical notion of "reducing them to civility"—that is, eliminating their "false pride" and instilling in them a proper sense of humility and submission by awakening them to their insignificance in God's eyes (*Invasion* 178). Such humility and submission would initiate them into more appropriate—or civilized—living. Sensitive about the difficulties of such a task, Eliot and his colleagues were at times defensive about the slow pace of conversions. The very first of the Eliot tracts explains in 1643, "Wonder not that wee mention no more instances at present: but consider . . . their infinite distance from Christianity, having never been prepared thereunto by any Civility at all" (*First Fruits* 1). And later: "We are oft upbraided by some of our Countrymen that so little good is done by our professing planters upon the hearts of Natives; such men have surely more spleene then judgement, and know not the vast distance of Natives from common civility, almost humanity it selfe" (*Day-Breaking* 15). The links were clear: Christianity was central to civility, which was essential to humanity. Eliot's task, then, was to make Natives more human by introducing them to English manners and customs.

Eliot's missionary work complemented but probably did not initiate a process of acculturation that was already under way. Several Native communities had already expressed interest in learning more about Christianity by the time Eliot began his missionary work, although this was by no means the Algonquians' universal response. Native interest in Christianity undoubtedly had pragmatic roots. For some, conversion to Christianity may have seemed a necessary step in maintaining a legal, social, and economic status specifically as a Native American community. The historian Hugh Amory notes, "They thus gained protection against other Indians, especially the Micmacs; secured a legal basis for their continuing existence; and received a small part of the lands they had formerly ruled *back* from the English" (29). It was quite possibly to perpetuate rather than to eradicate their difference from Anglo-Americans as well as from other Native American groups that certain Natives may have gravitated toward John Eliot's teachings.[5]

At least on their surface, Eliot's teachings seem to provide little opportunity for Algonquians to maintain their sense of identity. According to his plan, converts were to live in solid English houses, not wigwams; they were to be subject to scripturally based laws, not government by consensus; they were to wear English-style clothes, farm in English style, and restructure their families in the patriarchal style of the English colonists. There were fines for maintaining such customs as "pawwowing" (using a traditional healer), keeping long hair, having more than one wife, biting lice, using bear grease, and isolating menstruating women.[6] At the same time, however, and with no apparent sense of irony, Eliot felt that the best way to convert Natives was to keep them at a physical distance from the English while transforming them into as close a resemblance to English people as possible. To accomplish this, he explains, "a place must be found . . . some what remote from the English, where they must have the word constantly taught, and government constantly exercised, meanes of good subsistence provided, incouragements for the industrious, meanes of instructing them in Letters, Trades, and Labours, as building, fishing, Flax and Hemp dressing, planting Orchards, &tc." (*Glorious Progress* 8). Thus even as he encouraged them to adopt English manners, Eliot emphasized the distance between Natives and English colonists, a distance only partially mitigated through conversion. And this distance allowed New England Algonquians to experience Christianity specifically as a community of Native Americans, even though Eliot modeled the terms of that community on English cultural systems.

Eliot envisioned a world for his converts in which order, rules, and systems replaced what he saw as randomness, incoherence, and aimlessness. He explains: "That which I first aymed at was to declare & deliver unto them the Law of God, to civilize them . . . to convince, bridle, restrain, and civilize them, and also to humble them" (*Clear Sun-shine* 17). He goes into more detail later, enumerating the steps to proper Christian living: "The order of proceeding with them, is first to gather them together from their scattered course of life, to cohabitation and civill order and Government, and then to form them (the Lord having fitted them) into visible Church-state" (*Strength* 7). The spatial reorganization of the Algonquians was central to their transformation; gathering them from their "scattered course of life" and bounding them within permanent, unchanging settlements was the means through which Eliot saw the possibility of "civill order," the first step in a Christian commonwealth. The reasons for civilizing them had a practical basis for Eliot. He tells his converts when they ask why they cannot join into their own church yet: "They were not so capable to be betrusted with that Treasure of Christ, lest they should scandalize the same, and make it of none effect, because if any should through temptation fall under Censure, he could easily run away (as some have done) and would be tempted so to do, unless he were fixed in an Habitation, and had some means of livelihood to lose, and leave behind him" (*Tears* 1). By settling them in English-style houses and providing them with substantial material possessions, Eliot made the possibility of abandoning all that they had accumulated less appealing for his converts. And at the same time he could turn his converts into a people whose values and choices mirrored his own, thus making them more understandable to himself.

For Eliot, an orderly, cohesive community was necessary for true conversion. James Holstun emphasizes the disciplinary, regulating elements in what he terms Eliot's Christian "Utopia." He points out that Eliot not only restructures the converts' relationship to land through a "gridded, enclosed, and rationalized New England landscape" (132), but that Eliot also restructures the converts' relationship to time through the enforcement of a Sabbath day. "The praying town's Sabbath is an enclosure of time which, like its enclosure of space, draws borders for and helps to define new collectivities and new individualities" (138). And not only were their lives to be restructured through the discipline of work and study, but their very language was to be transformed through a system, or "grammar," as it was conceived by Eliot in *The Indian Grammar Begun: Or, an Essay to bring the Indian Language into Rules, For the Help of such as desire to Learne the same, for the furtherance of the Gospel among them*. Eliot emphasized literacy as the core of true conversion. For him, reading provided access to a religion based in unchanging truths, and "men were brought to the truth by reason and, in reaching the truth, logic, metaphysics and history played their part" (Kellaway 7). *The Indian Grammar* was Eliot's attempt to bring order and reason to the lives of his converts by providing them access to reading and writing.

Eliot's own position as he attempted to bridge the gap between two languages, groups, and cultural systems remained somewhat tenuous, however. His *Grammar*'s full title suggests that it is only through his efforts that the Massachusett language can gain any sort of coherence or order. It is, after all, Eliot who has begun this Indian Grammar, and it is Eliot who is attempting to "bring the Indian Language into Rules." The audacious title is undermined, however, as soon as the grammar is begun. "Grammar," Eliot explains, "is the Art or Rule of speaking." He continues: "there be two parts of Grammar: 1) The Art of making words. 2) The Art of ordering words for speech. The Art of making words, is 1) By various articulate sounds 2) By regular composing of them" (1). Eliot develops his argument by erasing the difference between spoken and written language. In doing so, he acknowledges that the Massachusett language already contains its own rules, since it functions effectively as a spoken language. Ultimately, then, Eliot fluctuates between envisioning his project as the description of an already existing language and the creation of a new one. His work with the *Grammar* underlines the instability of his position; though he is central to the project of imposing order on the Massachusett language, that order demands his acknowledgment of a preexisting order within the Massachusett language.

By using the English alphabet to create a written language out of Massachusett, Eliot tries to render the language "coherent" based on an English standard. But Eliot writes in a letter to a patron, "There be corners & anomalities full of difficulty to be reduced under any stated rule" (quoted in Kellaway 137). English systems cannot fully contain Native language, and so Eliot must devise new letters to reflect sounds that do not have counterparts in English. He ends up with a total of twenty-seven characters for the Massachusett language. Well aware of his temerity in revising the English alphabet, Eliot writes defensively: "I have been thus far bold with the *Alpha-bet,* because it is the first time of *writing this Language;* and it is better to settle our *Foundation* right at first, then to have it to *mend afterwards*" (*Indian Grammar* 3). Invoking his foundational status in the creation of a written language out of Massachusett celebrates his importance, but Eliot ultimately reveals his own powerlessness in the face of already established systems and rules in the English and Massachusett languages that do not coincide as he would like them to. Bounded by the systems and rules of Anglo-American missionary culture, Native expression cannot be entirely contained by structures that don't suit it. The fact of Native expression alters those structures, even as it is maintained within them.

Eliot was thus in the disconcerting position of attempting to represent Algonquian language through the systems and structures familiar to Anglo-Americans just as he came to terms with differences that could not be accounted for within those structures. And in the same way that he was caught between English and Massachusett linguistic systems, he found his loyalties to his fellow missionaries and to the Natives he is converting constantly in flux. In his account of an early missionary foray to the Native inhabitants of New England, he emphasizes missionary group cohesion even as an opening prayer in English excludes the Natives. Eliot writes, "Wee began in an unknown tongue to them, partly to let them know that this dutie in hand was serious and sacred . . . partly also in regard of ourselves, that wee might agree together in the same request and heart sorrowes for them even in that place where God was never wont to be called upon (*Day-Breaking* 2). The distinction between "wee" and "them" is firmly established not only by the act of praying in English, but also by the unity of thought and action of the missionaries. That English community cohesion is extended in his *Indian Grammar* when he explains, "I . . . use the same Characters which are of most common use in our English Books" (1). The "our" in this case establishes a community of English readers, excluding for the moment Native readers. The community invoked by "our" shifts later on the same page, though, when Eliot aligns himself with the Natives, writing: "Our Alpha-bet is the same with the English" (1). In this case "our" is clearly readers and writers of Massachusett to whom the English are set in opposition. The missionary's loyalties become blurred as he at once aligns himself with the English and with the Algonquians whose language he has come to see as his own.[7]

Such fluctuations of missionary power and position are revealed in other circumstances as well. The confusion between control and acquiescence carries over into missionary language about prayer and the position of the missionary as the bearer of God's word. There is also a troubling blurring of the line between the missionary and God. Eliot even becomes confused about which are his own cultural assumptions and which are the "will of God." As he explains to his converts the basis for praying towns, Eliot erases the difference between the need to first be civilized and the ability to be trusted with "the sacred Ordinances of Jesus Christ." "I declared unto them how necessary it was, that they should first be Civilized, by being brought from their scattered and wild course of life, unto civil Cohabitation and Government, before they could, according to the will of God revealed in the Scriptures, be fit to be betrusted with the sacred Ordinances of Jesus Christ, in Church-Communion" (*Late and Further* 1–2). Eliot's sense of the importance of "civility" in the Christianizing of Natives transfers itself into the "will of God." And as this passage reveals, Eliot's position as Christianity's harbinger leads to a slippage between the "will of

God" and the "word of John Eliot." Thus Eliot at one point concludes, after he has established a particular set of rules by which his converts are to proceed, "when they understood the mind of God in this matter, they were desirous to set upon the work" (*Late and Further* 2). The will of God, the mind of God, and the intentions of the missionary have all merged as John Eliot establishes the conditions of the praying towns.

The rhetorical slippage between the English missionary figure and the God he represents becomes apparent as Natives struggled to come to terms simultaneously with English civil customs and with religious doctrine. The cultural changes that Puritan Church membership demanded were daunting even to the most sincere. In their public confessions, which Eliot translated and published for the New England Company, many of the converts expressed the challenges they faced on their circuitous path to conversion. These narratives were the public oral confessions of Algonquian converts written down by John Eliot, and they are clearly an acknowledgment of the importance of Christian—and therefore by extension Anglo-American— values and beliefs. Even as the narratives convey Eliot's particular sense of what a Native Christian should be, however, we can also get a sense for the ways in which they express Algonquian needs and desires that fall outside the parameters set by Eliot. As fervently as they express a commitment to Christianity, the narratives also mark the struggle to integrate, through transculturation, that Christianity into Algonquian life. Eliot thus provides a means for Native self-expression even as he attempts to control every aspect of that expression. Mediated as they are by Eliot, the narratives are nonetheless an early form of Native Christian self-expression, and that expression is not as bounded by Eliot's principles as he would wish.

Many Algonquians express the difficulty of the first important step demanded of them by Puritan missionaries: accepting that their own ways and perceptions were deeply flawed or sinful. As Bowden and Ronda have pointed out, the Puritan belief in "the depravity of human nature and the need of divine grace for regeneration" were unfamiliar concepts to New England Algonquians, who generally believed in the human ability to interact harmoniously with the natural world. The ideas of original sin and of eternal damnation had to be impressed upon Native converts before they could properly understand the Puritan notion of God's grace and Christ's salvation. For a people undergoing what must have felt like cultural annihilation from disease and the encroachments of Euro-Americans,

Puritanism offered an explanatory system for their rapid decline by placing the blame for these disasters on the Natives themselves. Accepting Christianity involved an acceptance of the idea that each individual is innately corrupt and utterly dependent for salvation on a god who was intimately linked with the English colonists. Waban, an early convert, explains: "Before I heard of God, and before the English came into this Country, many evil things did my heart work, many thoughts I had in my heart; I wished for riches, I wished to be a witch, I wished to be a Sachem; and many such other evils were in my heart" (Eliot, *Tears* 7). And Robin Speene says, "I remember my panwaning . . . my lust, my gaming, and all my sins; I knoe them by the Commandments of God" (30). Anthony, another convert, explains his confusion between sin and customary daily life: "Before I prayed to God I alwaies committed sin, but I do not know all my sins, I know but a little of the sins I have committed, therefore I thought I could not pray to God" (42). And Ponampam rather bitterly complains: "When you always came to us . . . I found that al my doings were sins against God . . . I saw that in every thing I did, I sinned: & when I saw these sins against God, I was weary of my self, & angry with my self in my heart" (20–21). Their usual way of life has become the very thing these Natives must struggle against.

Cotton Mather, ever interested in matters of Puritan conversion, emphasizes Natives' preconversion baseness when he writes directly to Native converts in *An Epistle to the Christian Indians* (1706): "While you were in your Ignorance, you were *wretched, and miserable, and poor, and blind, and naked . . . ye were, foolish, disobedient, deceived, serving diverse Lusts and Pleasures, living in malice, and envy, hateful and hating one another.* You lived in Darkness, and madness, while you lived; yea, you were *Dead while you lived;* and when you Died, your Spirits went into *utter Darkness* and the *Place of Torment*" (2). The shame that Algonquians voiced in their own pre-conversion state is confirmed and even encouraged as Mather heaps scorn upon them. But for Mather, not only must the Natives come to despise their lives before conversion, they must also show gratitude to the English for revealing this to them. He writes, "God in his providence hath stirred up the charity of the *English,* to bring you the knowledge of Him" (2). He argues that the Natives owe a great debt to the English: "It was great compassion in the English, not only to offer you many comforts of this life, but also to show you the *Way that leads to Everlasting Life.*" He continues, "You have cause to be thankful unto the Charitable English . . . the English have been your great Friends; you must be for them, as for your Fathers, and your Brothers" (3). Mather contrasts the "foolish," "wretched," and "hateful" Natives with the compassionate, "Charitable," and friendly English who have brought the Natives to salvation, and by doing so confirms the distance between them.

The vast gulf alleged by Mather and Eliot between the preconversion lives of Natives and genuine Christian behavior was not easily crossed by the Algonquians attempting conversion. As described by many Algonquians in their conversion narratives, the shift in perception between accepting their previous lives and acknowledging them as sinful and depraved was a painful and wrenching process. Nishohkou admits in his account, "when I was grown up, I loved lust, and delighted in it, I knew it not to be a sin, but an excellent delight" (Eliot, *A further Account* 38). Many found themselves longing for their old familiar ways. John Speene admits that "my heart run away into the country, after our old ways, and I did almost cast off praying to God" (*Tears* 28); in his second confession he adds, "And I did indeed go into the Country" (29). And in a fascinating passage, Anthony acknowledges that his desire for the old ways predates even his birth: "I confess, that in my mothers belly I was defiled in sin: my father and mother prayed to many gods, and I heard them when they did so; and I did so, too, because my parents did so: and in my childhood, (afore I could act sin) I did delight in it, as dancing and Pawwuag: and when they did so, they prayed to many gods, as Beasts, Birds, Earth, Sea, Trees, etc. After I was born, I did all such things" (*A Further Account* 9–10). What makes this passage remarkable is the active and sentient existence this convert attributes to himself before his emergence from the womb. David Brumble argues that such startling descriptions of life before birth signal a particularly Native world view that is distinct from our own Western perspective (1). Anthony also reveals the wrenching generational as well as cultural crises that conversion could involve. As literally a part of his mother's body, he acted and believed certain things with her. But as a convert, he must hate them and everything attached to them as sinful. But Anthony reconceptualizes the missionaries' stock phrase "from the mother's womb" to make it coherent to himself. Through such reconceptualizations, Christian Indians open a space for themselves even within what seems to be an utterly abject position.

Some Algonquians articulate their initial movement toward Christianity as coming less from an engagement with deep theological truths than from a longing for community. For them, Christianity paradoxically confirmed their identity as part of a Native community even as it attempted to eliminate traditional Algonquian practices. John Speene says, "When I first prayed to God, I did not pray for my soul but only I did as my friends did, because I loved them" (*Tears* 28). Owussumag complains, "When some of my neighbors began to pray, I went away into the Country, but I could find no place where I was beloved" (*Tears* 44). He continues, "Last year, I sought to go away afar off, but I could think of no place, but I should be in danger to be killed" (*Tears* 44). The solution, for him, was to stay at his home and resign himself to Christianity. And Anthony reasoned that praying with his converted brothers was surely not worse than any other way to show his love for them: "I thought, if any should kill my brothers, I would kill him: if any Warrs were, I would go with my brothers: and then that, if my brother make Warr, I would go with him, to kill men. Now he prayes, shall not I go with my brother? And my brothers love me, and they both pray to God, why should not I? (*A Further Account* 10). Anthony notes that such prayer "was not for love of God, or fear of God, but because I loved my brothers" (10–11). But if such reasons could pull converts towards Christianity, they could just as easily push them away. Anthony bitterly explains, "But then my kindred dyed: then my heart said, Sure it's a vain thing to pray to God; for I prayed, yet my friends dye: therefore I will run wilde, and did cast off praying" (12). Community, then, sometimes comes before Christianity in importance.

For many, choosing or not choosing Christianity is presented initially as quite a pragmatic decision. Monequassun, for example, acknowledges that he "prayed not for the love of God, but for the love of the place I lived in." "Because I loved to dwell at that place, I would not leave the place, and therefor I thought I will pray to God, because I would still stay at that place, therefore" (*Tears* 12). And Monotunkquanit says simply, "I went to *Cohannit,* not for praying, but to gather clams" (*A Further Account* 65). Nishohkou admits that his aims were generally sexual: "All I did was with respect to lust and women." He further admits, "If I cut my hair, it was with respect to lust, to please women; if I had long hair, it was with respect to lust. . . . When the Minister came to teach us, hee taught, and I came to meeting, but I came to look upon women, I understood not what he taught; sometimes I came, and understood nothing at all, only I look't on women" (4). Magus's hesitation was largely political: "When any bid me pray to God, I said I cannot, and none of our Rulers beleeve or pray to God" (*Tears* 36). These narratives, all approvingly transcribed by Eliot, are by Algonquians who eventually shifted from these perspectives to what they characterize as more "genuine" conversions. They remain a poignant reminder of the wrenching decision whether to convert or to "run wilde."

Much has been written about the extent to which Native converts were able to sustain a sense of their own culture in the praying towns. Neal Salisbury and Francis Jennings see the efforts of missionaries as integral to the colonial mission of waging "cultural warfare" (Salisbury, "Red" 54), and transculturation by Natives, they argue, was almost nonexistent. James Axtell, however, points out that many Natives, when faced with the cultural extermination that rapidly expanding colonial settlements seemed to offer them, chose conversion. "Rather than achieving a nativistic revitalization at the hands of a charismatic prophet, they used the religion of Christ to the same end. Even though it entailed wholesale cultural changes from the life they had known before contact, it preserved their ethnic identity as particular Indian groups on familiar pieces of land that carried their inner history" ("Some Thoughts" 51). And Harold Van Lonkhuyzen argues that in praying towns "contact with Europeans did not drastically alter traditional Indian goals; it simply made their realization through traditional means more difficult and finally impossible" (427). In judging such assessments, it is important to understand that the praying towns included many residents who did not fit Eliot's strict requirements for Puritan church membership. Even the narratives of those who seem to have rejected the old ways do not always fit the model of proper Puritan identity, as Anthony's anxieties over his prebirth activities indicate. In fact, despite missionary insistence on the absolute distinction between Christian and non-Christian, through transculturation by Native converts Christianity took a variety of forms. And as we have seen, contact with Algonquians affected Anglo-American missionaries such as John Eliot as well, disturbing their neatly defined world view. In the words of James Clifford,

> Stories of cultural contact and change have been structured by a pervasive dichotomy: absorption by the other *or* resistance to the other. A fear of lost identity, a Puritan taboo on mixing beliefs and bodies, hangs over the process. Yet what if identity is conceived not as a boundary to be maintained

> but as a nexus of relations and transactions actively engaging a subject? The
> story or stories of interaction must then be more complex, less linear and
> teleological. (344)

Participating in two cultural systems simultaneously, Algonquian Christians were caught up in a convoluted web of loyalties and values. One anguished convert said, "Because wee pray to God, other *Indians* abroad in the countrey hate us and oppose us, the English on the other side suspect us, and feare us to be still such as doe not pray at all" (*Clear Sun-Shine* 34). Even facing such suspicion and hostility, however, Christian Indians maintained close personal ties both to other Algonquians and to English colonists.

By the time of King Philip's War, the allegiance of the praying Indians became a crucial issue. Converts found themselves forced to choose between Algonquian family and community ties and a colonial social system that held out the religious promise of everlasting salvation to a lucky few. Decisions about allegiance were particularly complicated for converts who had lived with the English from a very early age, and whose loyalties were probably unclear even to themselves. The social and cultural positions of Algonquian converts and the missionaries who worked among them were tenuous even before the war broke out; that conflict would test the limits of their complex network of relationships.

## King Philip's War

King Philip's War, which Francis Jennings has called "the Second Puritan Conquest" (*Invasion* 298), had roots in the economics of exchange between the English and Algonquians. Lasting little more than a year, this war was materially and emotionally devastating to both sides, as at different points each faced the possibility of cultural annihilation. During 1675–76, English colonists and an alliance of Algonquian peoples under the leadership of Metacom, or "King Philip," fought a brutal war for survival; this war cost the English 2,500 lives and more than half their settlements in New England and the Algonquians approximately five thousand lives and the end of legal or cultural dominance in the area (Salisbury, *Sovereignty* 1). Eliot's converts straddled the two cultural systems, and they came to figure prominently in the conflict; as they chose sides, they inevitably stirred hostility on both sides.

Jill Lepore has pointed out that the English were quick to write extended historical narratives of the events of King Philip's War. "Even if the runs averaged only a moderate five hundred copies per printing," she tells us, "a minimum of fifteen thousand copies of printed accounts about King Philip's War would have descended on the very small Anglo-American book market between 1675 and 1682" (*Name* 52). These works focused on demonizing Natives and, conversely, martyring the Puritans. For the early Anglo-American chroniclers, centering the war on Christianity made it a spiritual rather than economic event, in the process masking its material basis and turning it into a battle of the righteous against the unbelievers.

Indeed, though modern historians generally agree that King Philip's War had roots in the unsettled political and economic relations among different colonies and their Native allies,[8] Puritans preferred to see the war as an apocalyptic battle of good against evil. Increase Mather, in *A Brief History of the War with the Indians in New England,* expresses the Puritan position: "That the Heathen People amongst whom we live, and whose land the Lord God of our Fathers hath given to us for a rightful Possession, have at sundry times been Plotting mischievous devices against that part of the *English Israel,* which is seated in these goings down of the Sun, no man that is an Inhabitant of any considerable standing, can be ignorant" (1). Land comes from God, not from Indians, although Mather tacitly acknowledges Native right to the land by referring to it as the land of "the Heathen People amongst whom we live." But it is now Puritan by "rightful possession," he says, thus denying the validity of Native claims. Both Francis Jennings and William Cronon argue that much tension between colonists and Natives attached to concepts of land ownership, or traditional beliefs about the kinds of authority each culture understood as ownership.[9] Mather's gesture toward land rights—its simultaneous erasure and acknowledgment—touches the problem at the base of King Philip's War, since Puritans insisted on the justice of their claims to land while making it impossible for Natives to retain their own claims. The Christian references that frame this passage further point to the assumptions that set up the War; if the English are the new Israel, and the Lord God has given them land, then the "Heathen People" to whom they stand in contrast are necessarily the enemy. Interpreting the Natives within a Christian narrative, Mather ignores the economic and social tensions between Natives and Puritans that initiated the war. He also ignores the Christian Indian entirely.

Initially, English narratives focused on the terrifying possibility that the Algonquian forces of King Philip, perceived as demonic, might actually win. Algonquians were seen as insidious creatures, ready to corrupt or destroy honest Puritans at every turn. One writer noted that "the *Indians* lie lurking and sculking in hideous woody swamps, and thence set on travellers or men at their labours" (*Brief and True* 5). This image of a dispersed and hidden people stands in stark contrast to that of bounded and clearly visible English-style towns. One narrative frantically proclaims, "The Rod of God's Anger is still upon us; for the *Pocanaket* Sachem *Metacomet, alias Philip,* still lives! . . . Yea he lives, and by his subtility proves a more forcible and perilous Enemy to us then ever we could have Imagined" (*A farther Brief* 3). Philip's "subtility" is the source of his power, and of Puritan vulnerability as well, this passage suggests. Indeed, certain narratives went so far as to credit Philip with an almost supernatural craftiness:

> Great is the Policy, and Wisdome the Natives do Act withal; for they compass the out-sides, and weakest Towns in the Country; and gather the People, and drive them in heaps, like Fishes before a Net and make them fly before them to the strongest Towns for Refuge; and say, they will drive them down to *Boston,* and to two or three more of their strongest Towns, where they, for want, shall starve, and famish one another, and at present (if the Lord shew not mercy) they seem as if they would destroy, and roul up the rest of our Nation, as a burdensome, and menstruous Cloth, and cast it out of their Land. (Wharton 7)

The terror that Philip induces is at once about annihilation and humiliation. The image of the Puritan nation as a "menstruous Cloth," from Isa. 30:22, is expanded here into a vision of Puritans as feminized blood and waste discarded by the all-powerful Native figure, integrating gender politics into racial horror.

The tales that circulated about Indian barbarity went into excruciating detail about the "exquisite Torments and most inhumane barbarities" of the Natives. Indeed, these accounts take a voyeuristic perspective as they attempt to "satisfie the inquisitive, who . . . would willingly hear of all the extremities that have happened to the suffering Christians" (*News From New-England* 1). One narrator argues that the Indians' "outrages are so many and different" that they "will not be brought into a fluent Narration." The reader, argues the narrator, must "accept them plainly and dyurnully according to the time, place, and manner as they were committed, which is the only way to avoid omissions" (1). And in fact many of the English chronicles of the war do read like lists of Native depravity rather than coherent narrative accounts. As these writers detailed the depravity, they confirmed that the war was a clearly defined battle of good against evil.

Whatever the physical destruction Algonquians inflicted upon the Puritans, it was their open contempt for Christianity that most offended the war chroniclers. By positioning the Indians as hostile to Christianity, contemporary accounts confirm the war's sacred cause, and thus the humiliation that the Puritans felt over the surprising strength of their enemy is rewritten as a reaction against sacrilege. When the writer of a series of tracts on King Philip's War, probably Nathaniel Saltonstall, reported that Philip's men asked a Puritan to grind a hatchet on Sunday, he signaled Philip's insensitivity to Puritan religious practice; the Indians' confrontational response to the Puritan's refusal, which was that "They knew not who his God was, and that they would do it for all him, or his God either" (*Present State* 4), made the anti-Christian position of the Natives even clearer. This shocking rejection of the Christian God is repeated in several accounts. Thomas Wheeler reports of the mockery Indians heaped on the Puritans in a particular battle: "The next day . . . they continued *shooting & shouting,* & proceeded in their *former wickedness blaspheming the Name of the Lord,* and *reproaching us his Afflicted Servants,* scoffing at our *prayers* as they were sending in their *shot* upon all quarters of the house And many of them went to the Towns *meeting house* . . . who mocked saying, *Come and Pray, & sing Psalms,* & in Contempt made an hideous noise *somewhat resembling singing*" (Wheeler 7). The combination of blasphemy and open violence makes this moment particularly scandalous.

Soldiers on the battlefield were not immune from the religious taunts of the Algonquians. The author of another narrative hotly exclaims, "Our Enemies proudly exhult over us and Blaspheme the name of our Blessed Lord; Saying, *Where is your O God?*" (*A farther Brief* 4). Edward Wharton, himself a Quaker, reports, "The *Indians,* I hear, insult very much, and tell the *English* Warriers God is against them, and for the *Indians;* and that the *English* shall (for their Unrighteousness) fall into their hands" (4). All these accounts emphasize the heathen or non-Christian nature of the Indians.

With the murder of John Sassamon, a Christian Indian, by Philip's men, religion assumed a central place in Puritan war rhetoric. Embedded within

English accounts are various narratives of the life and, more particularly (as Lepore emphasizes), the death of John Sassamon; indeed, almost every contemporary account traces the beginnings of the war to the killing of this man, who had connections both to John Eliot and his praying towns and to King Philip. Most people believed that Sassamon was killed for his Christian beliefs. Daniel Gookin states outright that "John Sasamand was the first Christian martyr of the Indians; for it is evident that he suffered death upon the account of his Christian profession, and fidelity to the English" ("Historical Account" 440). Nathaniel Saltonstall argues that King Philip's men acted out of hostility toward Sassamon's preaching: "They not liking his Discourse, immediately Murthered him after a most Barbarous manner" (*Present State* 3). And even when he adds Sassamon's betrayal of Philip to the English in a later version of the same events, Saltonstall still reads Sassamon's tragic demise at the hands of another Native as based on his Christianity. Increase Mather also accepts that Christianity is at the root of the Sassamon murder, arguing, "No doubt but one reason why the Indians murdered John Sausaman, was out of hatred against him for his Religion, for he was Christianized and baptiz'd, and was a Preacher amongst the Indians, being of very excellent parts, he translated some part of the Bible into the Indian language, and was wont to curb those Indians that knew not God, on the account of their debaucheries" (*Brief History* 2). Such versions emphasize Sassamon's sincerity as a convert and the trouble such devoutness brought him. Mather's version most closely links Sassamon with the English, since as a martyr he becomes the embodiment of the Puritan cause.[10]

Even though the English generally regarded Sassamon as a martyr, other Christian Indians were treated with suspicion. Indeed, it was only as a *dead* Indian that Sassamon acquired status among the English; those Christian Indians who were still alive were accorded none of the respect that Sassamon received. And as the war stretched on, they were enclosed, confined, and isolated, since they were not trusted by either side. Their fate at the hands of both their English and their Algonquian allies reveals their shifting political fortunes. For many of the English, the Christian Indians were only barely removed from other Indians in the war, and hostility toward them emerges throughout the narratives. Saltonstall, for example, tells of an incident in which the townspeople of Springfield were apparently betrayed by some nearby Christianized Indians. The reaction of the neighboring towns toward all Christian Indians is revealing: they "Rose without any Command or Leader, and slew all of them they could find, which was about thirty" (*Present State* 18). Saltonstall expresses his own rage at the Christian Indians and their position in the war, bitterly writing: "They that wear the name of *Praying Indians,* but rather (as Mr, *Hezekiah Ushur* termed *Prying-Indians*) they have made Preys of much *English* Blood" (*Present State* 19). The reference to Ushur's term recalls earlier characterizations of Natives as "sculking," or "snooping." And such qualities, the comment suggests, can only be used to the detriment of the English and the advantage of Philip's forces. Furthermore, Saltonstall's pun on pray-prey emphasizes the Indians' animal-like brutality as well as the threat that they pose to the English. This comment suggests that hostility toward Christian Indians had embedded itself in the consciousness of Puritan New Englanders.

In fact, both King Philip's forces and the English were uncertain about how the Christian Indians fit in. The primary problem for both the English and the traditional Algonquians was their unreadability, or their skill as dissemblers. Saltonstall explains that even when a Christian sagamore offered up his own son as well as sixty of his men to help the English in the war effort, his effort was not enough because the English "cannot know a Heathen from a Christian by his Visage, nor Apparel" (*Present State* 7). Lepore has convincingly argued that King Philip's War can be read as an attempt to delineate the boundaries of American identity by maintaining clearly marked subject positions, where Natives and Puritans remain clearly "tagged" as such. But Christian Indians threaten the validity of categories such as "enemy" and "friend."

William Hubbard emphasizes the potential changeability of an Algonquian Christian ally even as he praises him for saving an English soldier. He describes a trick this Indian resorts to in an attempt to save himself: "He used this policy, perceiving the Enemy had all blacked their faces, he also stooping down, pulled out some blacking out of a pouch he carried with him, discoloured his face therewith, and so making himself look as like *Hobamasko* as any of his Enemies: he ran amongst them a little while and was taken for one of themselves, as if he had been searching for the English, until he had an opportunity to escape away among the Bushes" (65). The reference to the Native spirit "Hobomasko" and his association with the Christian Indians, points to an anxiety over cultural mutation.

After all, if the Christian Indian can look just like a heathen, what is to stop him from simply turning into one? More important, how will the English know when such a transformation has taken place?

John Easton argues that Philip and his men distrust Christian Indians because of their political instability. He explains that these Natives "had a great Fear to have ani of ther Indians should be caled or forced to be Christian Indians" (10) (a view that undermines any personal agency in the decision to become Christian). Easton further points out that even in the view of Philip and his men, Christian Indians "wer in everi thing more mischeivous, only Disemblers, and then the English made them not subject to ther Kings, and by their lying to rong ther Kings" (Easton 10–11). Much like the anxieties expressed by the English, Easton here suggests that Philip's concerns revolve around the changeability and inconstancy of the Christian Indian.

The hostility that they faced from both sides during the war left the Christian Indians largely unprotected. One convert told John Eliot: "Oh, Sir . . . I am greatly distressed this day on every side; the English have taken away some of my estate, my corn, cattle, my plough, cart, chain, and other goods. The enemy Indians have also taken a part of what I had; and the wicked Indians mock and scoff at me, saying, 'Now what is become of your praying to God?' The English also censure me, and say I am a hypocrite" (Gookin, "Historical Account" 504).

As the war dragged on and seemed to go against them, the colonists' animosity toward the Christian Indians increased to a fevered pitch. In the winter of 1675, the colonists forced the Christian Indians to move to Deer Island, in Boston Harbor. Despite their stated loyalty to the British, these Natives were kept in what a modern historian has characterized as "concentration camps" (Bowden 132), with meager supplies of food and water. Even so, many of the contemporary narratives that mention this episode conclude that this arrangement "is much to a general Satisfaction" (Saltonstall, *Present State* 19). Even Benjamin Tompson rhymes, in his famous poem about King Philip's War:

> Be pleas'd to know there is an hopeful race,
> Who as you oft have been inform'd have grace.
> These are confin'd under Christian Wings,
> And hopes we have never to feel their stings.

A natural Prison wall'd with Sea and Isles,
From our Metropolis not many miles,
Contains their swarms. (13)

Tompson's characterization of Christian Indians as a "hopeful race" who have received God's grace sits alongside his less flattering description of such Indians as repulsively insectlike, in "swarms" and with "stings." These creatures must be kept in a "prison" which is close enough to be under constant surveillance yet far enough to afford the "Metropolis" a degree of security. Other narratives, arguing that the converts wanted this "protection," thereby deny the English betrayal of their allies. One states, "At the desire of the Honestest of them, all professing Indians are placed and provided for on certain Islands where they are out of Harms way; And by an Act of the General Court (which is our Parliament here) 'Tis Death for any of them to come off thence without License from the Magistrate" (*A farther Brief* 4). The suggestion that the Algonquians themselves have requested this treatment downplays the brutality of imposing a death sentence on a migratory people who are confined to a single township where food and shelter were at times in short supply.[11]

The English treatment of the Christian Indians appalled Daniel Gookin, superintendent of the Indians for the Massachusetts colony.[12] He condemned the colonists for turning their backs on those who had sacrificed everything to be like them and claimed that records of mass defections on the part of the praying Indians were grossly exaggerated. Most, he argued, were willing to suffer a great deal to remain loyal to their British allies. Gookin put himself in danger making these claims; at one point he even feared for his life for having stood up for the Indians. The animosity of the English toward Gookin ("Guggins") emerged most violently as this justice of the peace argued for the release of imprisoned Christian Indians. One writer claims, "the Commonality were so enraged against . . . Captain Guggins . . . that Captain Guggins said on the Bench, that he was afraid to go along the streets; the answer was made, you may thank yourself" (Saltonstall, *Present State* 13). When even the attempt to stand up for Christian Indians seemed a punishable crime, the Indians themselves were in serious danger. In following John Eliot's rules, Christian Algonquians marked themselves both physically and spiritually as distinct from their non-Christian cohorts. Yet English colonists treated such marks of solidarity with colonial society with disdain, emphasizing instead all that marked Native Christians as savage. Their ability to read and write made them valuable to both sides as translators and scribes, yet Christian Indians' liminal identity left them mistrusted by both.

## Mary Rowlandson and the Christian Indians of King Philip's War

In February 1676, at the height of King Philip's War, Mary Rowlandson was kidnapped from her home in Lancaster, Massachusetts, by Narragansetts and Nipmucks sympathetic to King Philip. An outlying English settlement, Lancaster was particularly vulnerable to Native attack, and before the town was fully prepared, King Philip's Algonquian allies struck, taking several prisoners including Mary Rowlandson and her children and burning the town.[13] Upon hearing news of the Lancaster assault, the community of Anglo-American Puritans pulled together to aid the Rowlandsons.[14] Because of the central role of Mary Rowlandson's narrative in the genesis of a colonial American identity, the role of Native converts as communicators and negotiators has been largely erased from the official mythology of colonial American experience. However, an alternative version of these events exists in the written record of Rowlandson's ransom. In the negotiations for her release, the governor and council of Massachusetts sent at least five messages to Metacomet (King Philip) by way of Christian Indians. Tom Nepanet and Peter Conway were given permission to leave Deer Island to risk their lives carrying messages for the English, while Peter Jethro and James Printer wrote the messages sent by King Philip's men. Although those Indians who sided with the English left no words of their own, the messages of Jethro and Printer, Christian Indians who sided with King Philip during the war, still exist. Those responses shed light on Christian Indians as crucial and often overlooked mediators in the process of intercultural negotiation.

With the encouragement of Daniel Gookin and the desperate pleading of Joseph Rowlandson, a letter was sent from Boston on April 3 by way of Christian Indian Tom Nepanet to open negotiations for the release of the captives. This letter, written by Governor Leverett in March 1676, states:

> For the Indian Sagamores and people that are in warre against us. Intelligence is come to us that you have some English, especially weomen and childreon, In Captivity among you.
> We have therefore sent the messenger offering to redeem them, either for

payment in goods or wampom, or by exchange of prisoners. Wee desire
your answer by this our messenger what price you demand for every man
woman and child, or if you will exchange for Indians if you have any among
you that can write your Answer to this our message, wee desire it in writing;
and to that end have sent paper pen and incke by the messenger. If you lett
our messenger have free accesse to you and freedome of a safe returne; wee
are willing to doe the like by any messenger of yours Provided he come
unarmed, and Carry a white flagg upon a staffe vissible to be seene; which
wee take as a flagge of truce; and is used by civilized nations in tyme of
warre when any messengers are sent in a way of treaty, which we have done
by our messenger. In testimony whereof I have set to my hand and seal.[15]
(68:193 MA)

In this opening letter we see an attempt to control the terms of the negotiation. Such negotiations, the letter suggests, should preferably take place in
writing, and for that purpose the colony sends along pen, paper, and ink.
They should also follow the terms of "civilized nations" which use the
white flag of truce.

The reply sent in April sharply restructures the rules. Although it does
make use of the pen, ink, and paper that the colonists have sent along, the
letter demands that Native negotiating terms be acknowledged and followed as well. Signed by several Indians, it is written by Peter Jethro. An
intriguing mix of bravado and information, the letter reads:

To Governor and Council in Boston, and people that are in war with us:

We nou give answer by this one man, but if you like my answer sent one
more man besides this one Tom Napanet, and send with all true heart and
with al your mind by two men; because you know and we know that your
heart great sorrowful with crying for your lost many many hundred men
and all your house and all your land and women child and cattle as all your
thing that you have lost and on your backside stand.

Signed by Sam Sachem; Kutquen and Quassohit, Sagamous; Peter Jethro
Scribe[16]

The letter continues with these addenda:

Mr. Rowlandson, you wife and all your child is well but one dye. Your sister
is well and her three child. John Kittell, your wife and all your child is well,
and all them prisoners taken at Nashaway is all well.

Mr. Rowlandson, se your loving sister his hand **C** Hanah. and old Kettel
wif his hand. +

Brother Rowlandson, prey send thre pound of tobacco for me.

This writing by your enemies—Samuel Ushattuhgun and Gunrashit, two Indian Sagamores.[17]

The letter is infused with language that rebuts the English attempt to control the terms of the negotiations. The initial request for another messenger, which may have been a delaying tactic, is also a formal request for more respect. Furthermore, the letter stresses that the release of the captives is contingent not only on the sincerity and forthrightness of the colonists ("send with all true heart and with all your mind by two men") but also on the determination of the Algonquians to negotiate on their own terms. The letter also emphasizes the position of weakness from which the colonists speak: "you know and we know that your heart great sorrowful with crying for your lost many many hundred men and all your house and all your land and women child and cattle as all your thing that you have lost." The physical and emotional losses of the English, this letter implies, are far greater than those of the Natives, which are unmentioned. Furthermore, the letter strongly emphasizes the degraded position of the colonists ("on your backside stand"); they are vulnerable, and have been defeated and humiliated by the superior Algonquian forces. But the tone of this letter is ambiguous. Is this a gloating, self-satisfied reminder of Native military superiority? If this is the letter referred to in *A True Account,* the English certainly read it that way: "An Indian Messenger, sent to his countrymen about the Redemption of Captives, returned with a very insolent Letter, that as yet they had no need to accept of Ransom for our Captives" (2).

The letter certainly does celebrate Algonquian strength. Those involved proudly and fearlessly acknowledge themselves by signing or leaving their mark; they want to be recognized as participants in this action. And they inscribe not only their names but their positions as sachems or sagamores in traditional Narragansett and Nipmuck social structures. Though colonial observers were quick to relate sachems to European monarchs, the Native Americans who signed this document proudly maintained their own titles and, by implication, political structures.[18] And at least for "Sagamore Sam" or "Sam Sachem" the title was hard won. According to Russell Bourne, several years before the war began, Shoshanin, or Sagamore Sam, was considered by many to be the rightful claimant to the sachemship of Nashaway, but the Massachusetts Bay General Court instead supported

Matthew, a converted Indian and a nephew of Nashawhonan, the recently deceased sachem. Thus, suggests Bourne, the attack on Lancaster, the English community adjoining the Nashaway Indians, had its roots in a very localized political struggle in which the English interfered in the traditional Native power structure. By signing his name and claiming his sachemship, "Sagamore Sam" was actively snubbing the English, who at least in his view had tried to take that position away from him.[19]

Further details emphasize Algonquian control over the terms of the negotiations, which they insist will take place along traditional lines. New England's Algonquian communities were run by consensus, with sachems functioning as spokesmen rather than as rulers (Bragdon, *Native People* 145–46; Simmons, *Spirit* 12–13). The number of signatories to this letter emphasizes this idea of consensus rather than an individual decision-making process. Clearly, there is agreement among the Algonquian allies on the proper course of action; the request for more than a single colonial representative may be a request for an assurance of English consensus as well. Furthermore, the sachems use an Indian style of oratory—formal, uninterrupted speech which includes repetition for emphasis and distinctive rhetorical flourishes (Bragdon, *Native People* 173–74). The repetition of the word "all" (it occurs five times in the body of the letter) and such turns of phrase as "true heart" and "great sorrowful with crying" also are part of this style.

The additions at the bottom of the letter mimic the idea of uninterrupted speech; the sachems say what they need to, and then others add what they have to say after the main speakers are finished. The expectation of gift-giving, central to Algonquian economic structures of reciprocity, is clearly present in the second part of the letter ("Brother Rowlandson, prey send thre pound of tobacco for me"). This letter, suffused with traditional speech patterns, confidently conveys in as many ways as possible the superiority of the Native alliance and the tenuous position of the English in this situation. The position of Peter Jethro, as scribe, is subsumed within the letter's expression of unity, strength, and Native pride.

The second ransom letter, though, is dramatically different. This letter was written by James Printer, John Eliot's Native assistant who had returned to his people to fight on King Philip's side. According to Margaret Szasz, James Printer was one of John Eliot's earliest and most crucial disciples along with Job Nesuton, a Massachusett who had become Eliot's chief interpreter and translator by 1650. These Native converts worked to-gether to help publish the 1663 Indian Bible, often considered John Eliot's crowning achievement, as well as other works. Originally from the Nip-muck tribe, James Printer may have learned to read and write as a young boy by being bound out to an English family.[20] By 1659, with the approval of John Eliot, he was apprenticed to Samuel Green, one of the earliest established printers in the colonies. Printer's and Nesuton's central roles in the publication of the Indian Bible have been neglected (credit has been given only to John Eliot) (Szasz *Indian Education* 113–20; Amory 41–42; Lepore, *Name* 34); it is clear, though, that Nesuton did most of the translat-ing, and Printer probably helped to smooth out the translation and set the type.[21] By the outbreak of King Philip's war, James Printer had spent over fifteen years as a printer and had positioned himself within colonial society as a highly skilled, literate tradesman. It came as a particular blow to Eliot and Green when he chose to ally himself with King Philip in the war.[22] Lepore indicates that Printer was taken captive by the Nipmucks (*Name* 136). But other historians suggest a very different relationship. As he was the son of the Nipmuck sachem Naoas, family loyalty may well have played into his decision. It is possible that he succeeded his father as one of the leaders of the Nipmuck tribe (Amory 41; Drake 114), and as most of the Nipmuck allied themselves with Philip, he may have felt the decision was not his to make.[23] His letter reads:

> For the Governor and the Council at Boston
>
> The Indians Tom Nepenomp and Peter Tatatiqunca hath brought us letter from you about the English captives, especially Mrs. Rolanson. The answer is, I am sorrow that I have don much wrong to you and yet I say the falte is lay upon you, for when we began to quarel at first with Plimouth men I did not think that you should have so much trouble as now is: there-fore I am willing to hear your desire about the Captives. Therefore we desire you to sent Mr. Rolanson and goodman Kettel: (for their wives) and these Indians Tom and Peter to redeeme their wives, they shall come and goe very safely: Whereupon we ask Mrs Rolanson, how much your husband willing to give for you she gave an answer 20 pounds in goodes: but John Kittels wife could not tel. And the rest captives may be spoken of hereafter.[24] (2:282 MA)

In this letter, James Printer is at the fore, with "I" generally replacing the unified "we." Caught between his allegiances to his Native kin and his commitment to those whose habits and world view he has come to understand and accept, Printer words his letter delicately. Gone are the proud references to Native political structures and traditions; instead, the tone is contrite and obsequious. The imperative is completely absent from this letter; instead, the word "desire" replaces a sense of obligation with a sense of solicitousness. Printer apologizes and then asks the colonists what they want ("I am willing to hear your desire about the Captives"). Even the ransom request is conciliatory; Rowlandson herself determines her worth, not her captors.

Another bit of writing has been attributed to James Printer that puts this ransom note in an interesting light. A note that was left after a February 21 attack on Medfield, only eleven days after the Lancaster attack and well before the ransom negotiations, shows a dramatically different perspective on the war.[25] It reads: "Know by this paper, that the Indians that thou hast provoked to wrath and anger, will war this twenty one years if you will; there are many Indians yet, we come three hundred at this time. You must consider the Indians lost nothing but their life; you must lose your fair houses and cattle" (Gookin, "Historical Account" 494). If we accept that this was penned by James Printer, we see a very different side of this man. The note predated both ransom notes, and was written at the height of Philip's wartime success. Printer's use of the plural "we" indicates his sense of unity with Philip's Algonquian alliance, as opposed to the distance he places between himself and this alliance in the later ransom note. Other clues indicate a more personal hostility. The note's language is suggestive: twenty-one is generally the age at which an indentured servant was released, or that concluded an apprenticeship such as the one James Printer had abandoned by joining the war on Philip's side (Axtell, *School* 118). The reference to English cattle and houses presages the first ransom note in that it emphasizes the losses of the English as against the comparative freedom of the Indians. Here, as in the first ransom note, there is a sharp, mocking rebuttal to English claims of superiority based on their material possessions. The reference to cattle and houses also explicitly touches on the aspects of English life that Christian Indians such as James Printer were supposed to embrace—settled, permanent homes and farms that committed them to a particular kind of community. Furthermore, the self-hatred that Eliot and other missionaries insisted was the first step in conversion here becomes the source of Algonquian power: if Native lives are insignificant, then Philip's losses in the war truly are meaningless, while the presumably superior English must sustain enormous loss. The language of abjection thus becomes a revolutionary weapon that James Printer can wield against the English. It is specifically as a Christian Indian who has absorbed Eliot's lessons that James Printer structures his liberation, which is simultaneously personal and spoken on behalf of his fellow warriors.

As the second ransom note indicates, however, James Printer's liberation is short-lived. The contrite tone of this letter suggests that he not only saw that Philip's forces were no longer fairing well in this war, but that Printer himself had come to regret his earlier defiant position against the English.[26] Indeed, the note is divided between a personal apology ("I am sorrow that I have don much wrong to you") and a message from the rest of the group ("we desire," "we ask"). But we should read the tone here with caution. After all, the deference is limited. Even if the Natives themselves do not decide Mary Rowlandson's worth, neither does the colonial government in Boston. Furthermore, the letter suggests that the husbands of these captives must venture into hostile territory to get their wives, shifting the danger from Native go-betweens to the colonists. And finally, the message negotiates the release of only two captives ("the rest captives may be spoken of hereafter"). The letter masterfully deploys the language of humility to maintain a significant amount of control over the situation.

But it is sharply rejected by the colonial government in Boston, both as a personal statement and as a message on behalf of the group. Not even addressing James Printer directly, the reply reads:

> To the Indian Sachims about Wachusets.—Wee received your letter by Tom & Peter, which doth not answer ours to you, neither is subscribed by the sachems; nor hath it any date, which wee know your scribe James Printer, doth well understand should be, wee have sent the sd Tom & Peter againe to you expecting you will speedily by them give us a plaine & direct answer to our Last Letter, and if you have any thing more to propound to us, wee desire to have it from you under your hands, by these our messengers, and you shall have a speedy answer. Dated Boston, 28 April, 1676. (30:201a MA)

More and more confident of their increasing wartime successes, the English reassert their control over the negotiations. And these negotiations over captives, this response suggests, leave no room for statements of regret or personal doubt. Demanding adherence to "anglicized" and "civilized" conventions such as an appended date and signatures, the English remind Printer of his obligations as a negotiator. What the colonists desire, they claim rather disingenuously, is a "plaine and direct answer to our last letter." As Printer negotiates a space for himself in the colonial system, he is rebuffed for straying beyond specific English boundaries.

Just as James Printer's role reveals unexpected dimensions to Rowlandson's captivity and release, the role of the aforementioned Sam Sachem also points to the variety of captivities obscured by the popularity of Rowlandson's account. The man known to the English as Sam Sachem of Nashaway, signatory of the first ransom note, found himself in an awkward position shortly after Rowlandson's release: in a letter of July 1676, he (among others) pleads that the English show mercy to Native captives. He addresses the letter not only to the English but also to Waban, a Christian Indian leader at Natick, and also to "all the chief men our Brethren, Praying to God," and the letter itself has several Christian references. For Sam Sachem, then, the Christian Indians were part of the colonial order, not part of the Native world. The isolation of the Christian Indians on Deer Island thus affected not only their relations with the English but their connections to other Natives as well. Not Christianized himself, Sam Sachem sees Christianity and Christian Indians as a potential avenue of negotiation. His letter states:

> We beseech you all to help us; my Wife she is but one, but there be more Prisoners, which we pray you keep well: *Muttamuck* his Wife, we entreat you for her, and not onely that man, but it is the Request of two Sachems, *Sam* Sachem of *Weshakum,* and the *Pakashoag* Sachem. And then that further you will consider about the making Peace: We have spoken to the People of *Nashobak* . . . that we would agree with you, and make a Covenant of Peace with you: We have been destroyed by your souldiers, but still we Remember it now, to sit still; do you consider it again; we do earnestly entreat you, that it may be so, by the Jesus Christ, O! let it be so! *Amen. Amen.* (*A True Account* 6)

This letter is "corrected" by the anonymous author of the tract it is reprinted in, who explains, "the Reader must bear with their Barbarisms, and excuse the Omission of some Expressions in them, that can hardly admit of good English" (*A True Account* 6); even so, the reference to "sitting still" suggests the earlier foolhardy crowing about the situation of the colonists who "on their backside stand." Here it is the Algonquians who must with humility sit and wait upon the desires of the now victorious colonists. And the use of the Christian "Amen, Amen" to close the letter suggests that Sam Sachem is willing to communicate with the English on their terms; it is their religion that he offers up to them, even as he had earlier rejected the right of the English to dictate the terms of negotiation. The chastened tone of this letter shows the dramatic rise and fall of individuals in the conflict as alliances were made and broken among various Indian groups and the various colonies. Finding himself in the unpleasant position that Joseph Rowlandson once occupied as the helpless husband of a captive, Sam Sachem reaches out to his former enemies. This reversal of fortunes is brought home even more forcefully in Sam Sachem's next letter, also published in *A True Account,* in which he writes to the English:

> My Lord, Mr. *Leveret* at Boston, Mr. *Waban,* Mr. *Eliott,* Mr. *Gooken,* and Coucil, hear ye. I went to Connecticott about the [English] Captives, that I might bring them into your hands, and when we were almost there, the *English* had destroyed those *Indians;* when I heard it, I return'd back again; then when I came home, we were also destroyed; after we were destroyed, then *Philip* and *Quanipun* went away into their own Countrey again; and I know they were much afraid, because of our offer to joyn with the *English.* (6)

With Sam Sachem now working on behalf of the English, the letter records his growing terror as his world collapses around him; the word "destroyed" appears three times in a single sentence. Desperate to show his allegiance to the English, Sam Sachem attempts to release English captives from another Native group, even though a few months earlier he gloatingly refused the request of the colonists for the release of Rowlandson and the other captives from Lancaster. His attempt fails, however; the English had already rescued their captives and destroyed Sam Sachem's allies in the process. The letter is thus apparently an attempt to prove his good faith, even if his actions have failed. Once a captor himself, Sam Sachem throws himself on the mercy of the English to save his wife from captivity. Thus he comes full circle: from captor to captive through his wife, Sam Sachem is eventually closed out of the war entirely.

A few months after the Rowlandson captivity and ransom, Richard Hutchinson gleefully announced in the title of a tract: *The Warr in New-England Visibly Ended. King Philip the barbarous Indian now Beheaded, and most of his Bloudy Adherents submitted to Mercy, the Rest fled far up into the Countrey, which hath given the Inhabitants Encouragement to prepare for their*

*Settlement.* King Philip was shot dead in a swamp, then beheaded and quartered (Church 451) in the traditional European style of punishment for enemies of the state. Despite his attempted alliance with his former enemies, Sam Sachem was hanged by the English in Boston (Hubbard 75–76, 110). James Printer returned to Boston after the war, resuming his position at Samuel Green's press.[27] His return, like his letter, was a complicated gesture. We do know that he brought several women and children from his tribe with him to Boston. Was he carving out a space for his people in the amnesty extended by the colonial government to Indians like himself? Was his return a calculated attempt at self-preservation, or was it a genuine appreciation of English culture—a culture in which he had, after all, spent most of his life?

In what Lepore calls "one of the most sublime ironies of King Philip's War" (*Name* 126), upon his return to Boston James Printer typeset one of the defining documents of the conflict in 1682— *The Soveraignty and Goodness of God, Together, with the Faithfulness of His Promises Displayed; Being a Narrative of the Captivity and Restauration of Mrs. Mary Rowlandson* (Derounian 245). Rowlandson's account of the events of her captivity has become in recent years one of the most written about, most anthologized narratives of early American literature, generating countless articles, class discussions, and conference presentations. For most modern readers it is Mary Rowlandson who shapes our understanding of captivity in King Philip's war, not the Algonquians who also felt its consequences.

But Rowlandson was not the only English person to tell the story of the Lancaster incident. Other chroniclers told it, and for most of them Joseph Rowlandson is the central figure and Mary a sad footnote to his suffering. The Puritan chroniclers emphasize that Joseph Rowlandson's suffering results from the loss of his possessions and family, both of which structure his identity in the community. He cannot reestablish himself in that community until he has re-collected all he can salvage from the disaster. The indifference to all suffering other than that of the patriarch is evident as Increase Mather writes:

> Mr. *Rowlandson* (the faithful Pastor of the Church there) had his House, Goods, Books, all burned; his Wife, and all his Children led away Captive before the Enemy. Himself (as God would have it) was not at home, whence his own person was delivered, which otherwise (without a Miracle) would have been endangered. . . .
> As this good Man returned home . . . he saw his Lancaster in flames, and

> his own house burnt down, not having heard of it till his eyes beheld it, and knew not what was become of the Wife of his bosom, and the Children of his Bowels. (*Brief* 22)

The distinction between material and emotional loss is erased in this passage; and it is Joseph Rowlandson's wrenching discovery of the loss of "*his* House, Goods, Books," "*his* Wife and all *his* Children," and even "*his* Lancaster" that is so devastating. The repetition of the word "his" structures the entire passage, making ownership and entitlement the primary relationship to all that is gone.

The emphasis in almost every contemporary version of these events is on the suffering of *Mr.* Rowlandson; captivity, for the Puritan writers, is a tragedy to those who are left behind, not to those who are captured. And both the Algonquian captors and the Englishmen who are left behind agree that the central dilemma for the English in King Philip's War is the loss of those material possessions that signal their personal status and their cultural positions as civilized, the women and children being living emblems of such material wealth. Writing from her perspective as a captive, Rowlandson disrupts that vision of the war. She undermines the expectations of those around her by positioning herself as an active agent of her own fate, thereby complicating her status as a mere object of exchange. Even as she undermines her status as object by writing her own narrative, however, Rowlandson participates in the financial exchange between men by assigning a monetary value to herself for her ransom. Paradoxically, then, it is by acknowledging her object status most starkly that she takes control of her own fate by negotiating a "deal" for herself.

Other ironies abound in her narrative. Characterizing herself as a lone Christian among savages, Rowlandson uses the Bible both to sustain herself in her misery and to give greater meaning to her suffering. To imagine herself as a Christian martyr struggling alone in the wilderness, though, Rowlandson must downplay those figures who might challenge her status as the only Christian—praying Indians. And indeed, despite their central role in her release from captivity, in her account the Christian Indians do not fare well. Whatever sacrifices such Indians made for the English cause, for Rowlandson they were never quite Christian enough. Even as they adopted the trappings of Anglo-American culture, she viewed them with suspicion and distrust as interlopers or frauds. Daniel Gookin points out that only through the intervention of two Christian Indians was Rowlandson ransomed,[28] but Rowlandson downplays the role of praying Indians and instead focuses on some of the outrages they committed against her family. Her daughter, she tells us, was taken on that fateful day "by a praying Indian, and afterward sold for a gun" (6). For Rowlandson this is not surprising; for her a praying Indian can trade in a helpless Christian child for a tool of death and violence without any remorse. In fact, her descriptions of praying Indians consistently emphasize their unscrupulousness and amorality. She tells us that one praying Indian "who when he had done all the mischief that he could, betrayed his own father into the Englishes hands thereby to purchase his own life" (23). Another, she tells us, was "so wicked and cruel, as to wear a string about his neck, strung with Christian' fingers." She sums up her feelings when she tells of a group of acculturated Indians: "My heart skipt within me, thinking they had been *English-men* at the first sight of them: for they were dressed in *English* apparel, with Hats, white Neckcloths, and Sashes about their wa[i]sts, and Ribbons upon their shoulders: but when they came near, there was a vast difference between the lovely Faces of *Christians* and the foul looks of those *Heathens:* which much damped my spirit" (20). For Rowlandson, Indians are a weak replacement for her ideal—the English Man whose Christianity is visible not only through his outer trappings such as sashes and neckcloths, but also in his "lovely face." Try as they might to adopt English fashions, Christian Indians could never erase their own "foul looks." Much as Eliot's converts struggled with varying degrees of surface and essential change, Rowlandson finds herself unable to reconcile the two. Indeed, as the above passage suggests, "Christianity" for Rowlandson is a racial as well as a religious category. Her hostility against Christian Indians is like that of many New Englanders during missionary efforts to convert Natives. In their minds Natives were not to "pass" for Christians.

At one point in her narrative Rowlandson bitterly mentions a Christian Indian who was so hypocritical that he apparently felt no compunction at brandishing a sword at her, threatening her with death, and then walking freely around Boston, masquerading as a "friend-Indian" after her release—a possible reference to James Printer himself (15). But Christian Indians were there at the moment of her captivity and made possible her ransom, and a Christian Indian typeset the pages through which Rowlandson disseminated her narrative. Even as she tries to write them out of the picture, Christian Indians are central to Rowlandson's story—and to the story of an emerging American identity. The anxiety they provoked in Anglo-Americans and other Natives does not disappear after the war but reemerges throughout the colonial period and beyond.

THE documents at the center of this chapter—the conversion narratives of John Eliot's praying Indians, Mary Rowlandson's captivity narrative, and the letters from her captors—would seem at a glance to have little in common; the conversion narratives are spiritual records, Rowlandson's account is a crafted literary work that shapes the trauma of captivity into an ideological form coherent to a Puritan readership, and the letters are hasty messages written with the express purpose of furthering a complex wartime negotiation. Each has its own political perspective. Nonetheless, these documents all point to the role of print culture in defining the emerging identities of colonial New England. Peter Hulme argues that those who attempted to cross cultures, whether they were White or Native, were in a particularly vulnerable position. "They became, as it were, cultural half-breeds inhabiting that dangerous no-man's-land between identifiable cultural positions, and therefore seen as inherently suspicious and potentially dangerous translators who might quite literally be traducers, crossing cultural boundaries only to double-cross their king and country" (142). The loyalties of the Christian Indians remained suspect to almost everyone, in large part because the very concept of a Christianized "savage" was unreadable. Owing loyalty both to King Philip and to the English king, Christian Indians in committing to one inevitably betrayed the other. Those such as Peter Jethro and James Printer faced hostility and distrust from all sides. For Rowlandson and others like her whose attitudes were molded by the war, Natives could dress like the English and even act like the English, but they could never truly be English, or Christian. And from the perspective of the Native communities, praying Indians betrayed their heritage, abandoning a people in spiritual crisis to side with the enemy. Praying Indians marked their separation from their tribes by seeming to reject traditional ways and by learning to read and write. Even when such figures returned to their people, they seem to have remained somewhat isolated. Caught in the middle of two cultures, these people served as intermediaries who had the power to write but who could no longer speak for their people.

Faced with this situation, Christian Indians forged new identities. There was a range of possible positions from which these people spoke—

after all, both Peter Jethro and James Printer were Christian Indians, but the tone of the letters they wrote is dramatically different. In fact, a large part of the anxiety these figures produced centered precisely on this range of subject positions, which suggested a disconcerting lack of fixity, or a remarkably fluid identity. As figures who challenged the very basis of English and Indian identity, Christian Indians provoked intense debate about the mutability of the human spirit.[29]

The narratives of the Christian Indians are a testament to their struggle to find a place for themselves in a colonial system that often seemed to exclude them. As they joined Eliot's praying towns, they came to terms with a set of expectations that to modern readers seem overwhelmingly about self-hatred and cultural annihilation. And when, on occasion, they returned to their indigenous communities, they embraced the traditional practices of their compatriots. In both circumstances, they adapted situations to what they saw as their own advantage, whether that advantage was spiritual, cultural, or personal. And in doing so they became something else—something that was not simply what those around them wanted to see. Christian Indians were often at the center of evolving relations between Indians and Anglo-Americans, recasting debates about ethnicity, community, and the possibility of spiritual and cultural conversion.

# CHAPTER TWO

# "THINGS THAT DO ACCOMPANY SALVATION"

*Indian Converts,* Transculturation, and Reculturation

✝

I shall, as the occasion offers, translate and insert some *such passages* written by them in their own Language, as I think will be subservient to the End herein aimed at. And however *inaccurate* such Writings may be, yet I shall chuse to keep as much as may be to the *very Words* of the *Indians* themselves, that the *Simplicity* of their Intentions may, by their own simple Expressions, the better appear.

—Experience Mayhew, *Indian Converts*

FIFTY years after King Philip's War had ended on the mainland, Experience Mayhew, a missionary on Martha's Vineyard, published *Indian Converts* (1727), an account documenting the conversion of the island's Wampanoag population. Mayhew addressed the tract to the Society for the Propagation of the Gospel (SPG) in England. Seeking to reassure his SPG benefactors that his missionary work had not been in vain, Mayhew catalogued in a series of short biographical sketches the Wampanoag men, women, and children who had converted since the missionaries' arrival on Martha's Vineyard in the 1640s. Though *Indian Converts* is written primarily in Mayhew's words, he intersperses fragments of Native writings throughout. By including the words of Native Americans (most written in Massachusett but translated by Mayhew for his readers), Mayhew makes his text a dialogue between the missionary voice and the voices of Native converts. The tensions inherent in the text between various subject positions and the power structures that inform them are deeply embedded in the history of Martha's Vineyard, both in terms of the Mayhew family's position and the complex and rapidly changing situation of the Native population, who spoke roughly the same language and shared the same culture as the Algonquian peoples of Eliot's praying towns and of King Philip's forces yet remained largely isolated from events on the mainland. Mayhew's missionary voice and the voices of Wampanoag converts coexist uneasily in these narratives; their interplay suggests some of the intricacies of cultural exchange in an eighteenth-century New England community.[1]

While Native American converts determined the extent of their participation in Anglo-American cultural practices through transculturation, Anglo-American missionaries such as Mayhew rendered the acts and traditions of Native peoples intelligible to themselves through what I call "reculturation." They accomplished this by appropriating and reinscribing the acts and traditions of Native Americans as already part of the dominant colonial culture, and therefore never really culturally "other." Or to use Stephen Greenblatt's metaphor of linguistic appropriation, "Whatever the natives may have actually thought and said [is] altered out of recognition by being cast in European diction and syntax" (571). John Eliot quite literally created a written language out of Massachusett following the practices of the Latinate languages, thus rendering the language more familiar to his English sensibilities. For Mayhew the process of reculturation was less overt, but his cultural assumptions led him to shape Native conversion narratives as he saw fit to render them comprehensible to an English audience. In the process, he attempted—not always successfully—to erase signs of cultural difference between his own understanding of conversion and that of the Wampanoags.[2]

The life of Tobit Potter, as recounted in *Indian Converts,* exemplifies the economic, social, and cultural complexities involved in Mayhew's representation of Wampanoag conversions. Mayhew reports that Tobit Potter was born in 1709 in Christian-Town, or Okahame, as it was known to the Wampanoags of Martha's Vineyard. His mother, Elizabeth Uhquat, was a pious woman with what Mayhew characterizes as a "wicked" past (194); Tobit was one of her two children born out of wedlock. Her moral lapses, Mayhew tells us in his biographical account of her, were in great measure attributable to the poor treatment she received at the hands of her English master on the mainland, who did not teach her to read or to understand any of the principles of religion (194). Despite her own experience, however, Elizabeth determined that the best course of action for her son would be to place him in the home of Edward and Mary Milton, an English family on the island. According to Mayhew the Miltons taught Tobit well, and he became an exemplary Christian under their tutelage. As he became more involved in his faith, certain questions that he posed indicated the depth of his concern. For instance, Mayhew tells us, he became anxious at one point over the issue of whether ministers prayed for everyone, or if as an Indian he was left out. He was most reassured by the scripture that stated, "God is no Respecter of Persons; but in every Nation, he that feareth him and worketh Righteousness, is accepted with him" (258). He was also comforted by the assurances of his minister, who quoted the Bible, saying, "If my Father and Mother forsake me, the Lord will take me up" (259). A familial divinity was particularly appealing to him, he said, since "he thought he had no body to take care of him" (259). Mayhew cites Tobit's interest in the spiritual comfort provided by the scriptures as a remarkable sign of his precociousness, and he is pleased by the several instances in which the child turned to sacred texts for emotional support rather than to the individuals around him.

After several years, according to Mayhew's account, Tobit was sent to live with another family, but he became unwell and was returned to his mother to die. His long experience as a servant in the homes of English families, however, put him in an odd position. "He not being able to speak *Indian* any thing well, and none of the *Indians* with him at the time of his Sickness, excepting his Mother, being able fully to understand what he said in *English*" (260), Mayhew tells us, he found himself isolated even as he was surrounded by Native people in his mother's home. Mayhew reports sadly, "His pious Mother sent for me to come and pray with him a little before he died; but he was become speechless before I could get to him; and so I could have no discourse with him" (260–61). Unable to make himself understood by those around him, and physically unable to speak by the time the missionary arrived, Tobit died without the spiritual guidance his long experience with the English had taught him to expect.

Tobit left no writing of his own, and because his mother was illiterate she could not record his final words and thoughts. Mayhew bases his biographical account on the words of the child's Indian mother as told to his White mistress, who then repeated them to him. Sometimes at two or three removes from the events he records, Mayhew's accounts must be

treated with a certain amount of caution. His role in translating and ex-
cerpting the written and spoken narratives of Wampanoag converts is a
crucial one, and his position of authority as both a missionary to the Wampanoags and a powerful social and political figure in English circles carries
its own series of social, political, and economic assumptions. These assumptions become especially visible as Mayhew narrates the lives of Native
women converts, whose private, domestic existences were in many ways
inaccessible to him. Through these accounts and the accounts of individuals such as Tobit Potter, which are the core of *Indian Converts,* we can see
the ways in which acts of reculturation and transculturation are mediated
through constantly shifting relations of dominance and subordination.

## Martha's Vineyard and the Mayhews

As the author of *Indian Converts,* Experience Mayhew continued in a long
family tradition of speaking for the Wampanoag population on Martha's
Vineyard. The island had a patriarchal political and social structure, with
the Mayhews as benign, well-intentioned rulers who perceived the needs
and desires of the Wampanoag population as inseparable from their own.
In addition to their enormous influence over the island's social and political affairs, the Mayhews influenced religious affairs as well.

Historians have generally characterized the missionary work of the
Mayhew family as far less rigid and controlling than John Eliot's work on
the mainland. Eliot's praying towns, structured around Old Testament law
and English practice, focused on the eradication of Native culture, while
the Mayhews focused instead on introducing Natives in their own environment to principles of Christianity in a more piecemeal fashion. Thomas
Mayhew Jr., the eldest child and only son of the governor of Martha's Vineyard, was the first missionary on the island, beginning his work with the
Wampanoags around 1643. He learned the Wampanoag language and in
1652 established the first school on the island.[3] His work was recognized in
several missionary tracts published by the Society for the Propagation of
the Gospel, and he was considered at least as important a missionary as the
eminent John Eliot. In 1657, Mayhew planned a brief trip to England to
arrange his financial affairs and to garner support for his missionary work
with the Wampanoag population. But his ship disappeared on the way to
England and nobody on board was ever found.[4]

After his death, his father, Thomas Mayhew Sr., who was already governor of the island, took over his son's missionary work. Also proficient in the Massachusett dialect of Martha's Vineyard, the senior Mayhew acquired the respect of the Native population by imposing as little as possible on the Wampanoag political structure already in place.[5] When he died at the age of eighty-nine in 1681, his grandson, John Mayhew, youngest son of Thomas Mayhew Jr., took over the ministry.[6] John's mission lasted until his death in 1689, and his eldest son, Experience, began preaching to the Indians in March 1693.[7] He was only twenty-one at the time, and his career as missionary and advocate for the Wampanoags of Martha's Vineyard spanned over sixty-five years. Of all the Mayhews, Experience was most comfortable with the Indian language as well as the customs of the people.[8]

The Mayhew family's religious and political control of Martha's Vineyard affairs was unusual in its longevity. Other individuals came and went, but generation after generation of Mayhews held powerful positions in every legal, political, and social structure on the island. Clearly, the Mayhews came to see themselves as central to the fate of Martha's Vineyard and its inhabitants and able to best represent the island's interests.[9] The repercussions of this confidence become particularly evident in texts such as *Indian Converts* that emerged from the encounter between the missionary Mayhews and the Wampanoag population of the island.[10]

By the time Mayhew wrote *Indian Converts* in the early eighteenth century, the Wampanoags had shared the island with Anglo-American settlers for almost one hundred years. Unlike the more strained relations on the mainland, generally the two populations on Martha's Vineyard lived side by side with relative ease, according to historians. Francis Jennings acknowledges Indian independence and the peaceful coexistence between settlers and Indians (232). James P. Ronda approvingly cites the "permissive environment" and lack of rigid legal codes enforcing cultural change, both of which allowed a specifically Native form of Christianity to flourish on the Island ("Generations" 370–71). Indeed, one sign of the amicable relations between colonists and Natives on Martha's Vineyard was the way in which the two groups weathered King Philip's war as observers rather than participants, even though the Wampanoags were culturally and linguistically close to the Wampanoag King Philip. The uncoercive style of the Mayhews' missionary efforts as well as the initially enormous population differential between the few Anglo-American settlers and the Wampanoag communities, these historians claim, allowed for Native cultures to survive and adapt in their own ways.

Claims about the relatively benign nature of colonialism on the island do little, however, to account for the rapidly declining economic power of the Wampanoags; most lived in poverty, and the dynamics between colonists and Natives were increasingly marked by unequal power relations. In 1645, an epidemic substantially reduced the Wampanoag population while leaving the English relatively untouched. As the English population increased, land exchanges between Natives and the English diminished Wampanoag holdings.[11] Native Americans had initially entered the colonial economy as landholders and as skilled providers of fish, feathers, and grains (Bragdon, "Native Economy" 31), but by the early eighteenth century the Wampanoags had incorporated English agricultural and social practices that made them far more dependent on English goods. In the process, they had accumulated debts that weakened their economy. As this occurred, Wampanoag labor became more valuable than the previous products of that labor and master-servant relationships between colonists and Natives replaced more equal relations of exchange. Furthermore, the early development of the whaling industry in the eighteenth century meant that Wampanoag men were away from their families for months at a time, which necessarily involved renegotiating traditional domestic patterns. For example, Joseph Uhquat, the stepfather of Tobit Potter, was away on a whaling voyage when the sick child returned to his mother's home to die; thus Tobit's mother Elizabeth was left alone to grieve and pick up the pieces of her fractured and dispersed family.[12]

By the early eighteenth century, then, the Wampanoags' economic strength on Martha's Vineyard was rapidly dwindling as they became more heavily invested in the process of transculturation, a process that accompanied and was most clearly embodied in religious conversion.[13] By the time of Experience Mayhew's account, Natives had accepted significant numbers of Anglo-American practices. Experience Mayhew cites approvingly some of the ways in which the Wampanoags adopted English manners, a step which he saw as integral to true conversion to Christianity: "In respect of their Apparel, they are generally Cloathed as the *English* are, & they by degrees learn the *English* way of Husbandry: several of them have good Teams of Oxen, with which they Plough and Cart, for themselves &

Neighbours, as the *English* do. Many of them have also *Horses, Cows, Sheep & Swine.* They have also among them some that have learned Trades" (appendix to Cotton Mather, *India Christiana* 94). Kathleen Bragdon's studies of probate records and linguistic acculturation also indicate the acceptance among Natives of livestock, husbandry tools, and such household items as cooking pots, as well as tools of other trades.

Bragdon suggests, however, that important divisions were maintained between Natives and the English. She explains, "Consistent use of the term 'Indian Planter' [while terms for English planters were "yeoman," "husbandmen," "gentleman," and so forth] suggests that although Anglo-Americans expected cultural conformity from the Indians, they still insisted on some measure of distinction between themselves and their Indian neighbors" ("Probate Records" 140). Indeed, the child Tobit's anxiety about whether the prayers of the White minister also included him as an Indian may well have had roots in such distinctions. And the Wampanoags sustained such distinctions as well. For example, Bragdon notes that Natives maintained linguistic distinctions; English terms for currency, land measurement, introduced cultivated plants, and domesticated animals entered the Massachusett language relatively unchanged. She suggests that this "may . . . reflect a deliberate separation of the two languages by native speakers" and furthermore that "Massachusett was clearly the language of the home" ("Linguistic Acculturation" 130). This separation had tragic consequences for Tobit, who had forgotten his Native language and was therefore shut out from an important source of comfort and community in the Wampanoag home in which he died. Even as Native acceptance of Anglo-American practices and beliefs would seem to suggest the eradication of the differences between Natives and the English, certain social, economic, and linguistic distinctions were nevertheless maintained.

The most significant single shift in cultural practice for the Wampanoag was the adoption of a written language. This shift reveals the ways in which cultural appropriations involved intricate adaptations rather than wholesale rejection of traditional patterns. The Anglo-American Protestant emphasis on literacy as a prerequisite for true Christianity linked religion to cultural change.[14] For the Wampanoags the acquisition of literacy must have seemed daunting, since it was so intimately linked with the abandonment of traditional spirituality. But for Mayhew it was a promising sign of what he saw as the eventual transformation of Natives into a civilized people, and his text is filled with moments that seem to confirm this process. The narratives by the Wampanoags themselves, however, reveal a more complex process that involves a gradual and highly selective acceptance of various elements of English culture as they fit into traditional Wampanoag structures of meaning. To understand how these competing narratives coexisted we must come to terms with the cultural influences informing each perspective.

The Native acquisition of literacy highlighted the social and economic inequality of Native-English relations. The practice of binding Wampanoag children out as indentured servants to English families was a common way for parents to help their children acquire literacy skills when schools were not available. English families would teach Wampanoag children the rudiments of reading and writing along with other English cultural practices such as household management or the acquisition of a particular trade. This system solidified the unequal relations of Wampanoags and Anglo-Americans by strengthening the links between power, literacy, and Englishness. The case of Tobit Potter shows some of the unfortunate consequences of attempts by Indian parents to provide their children with Anglo-American skills—the alienation of the child from a family system that maintains its Native roots and that child's acceptance of his inferiority in an English economic structure.

Even so, Wampanoag uses of literacy were extraordinarily varied and often independent of English dominance. The first school for Native pupils on Martha's Vineyard opened in 1652; its pupils were taught to read and write to enable them to read the Bible. Though the first teachers were English, Native teachers rapidly assumed leadership, and by the time that the New Testament was translated into Massachusett in 1661, some Wampanoags were able to read and write in their own language.[15] As literacy was integrated into Wampanoag culture, it took on multiple uses besides spiritual fulfillment. For example, Kathleen Bragdon and Ives Goddard have noted several land deeds that had no legal value but were kept by Wampanoags in the Massachusett language as personal records of exchanges occurring outside of English control. Written records, they suggest, supplemented traditional verbal agreements, and as such they often bore the marks of oral exchanges. Even those records which involved specific legal requirements (depositions, wills, and deeds) often were adapted to Wampanoag cultural practices; for example, rather than limiting

witnesses to the required two, such documents had as many as twelve witnesses, in recognition of the traditional Wampanoag emphasis on consen-
sual decision making. Wampanoags thus appropriated the tools of the
dominant culture for their own cultural practices.

Because the Wampanoags were literate primarily in Massachusett, their
ability to enter English colonial discourse—and thereby define themselves
to a larger audience—was limited. In this situation Experience Mayhew,
literate both in English and Massachusett and an important figure in colonial English circles, served as judge and translator for the Wampanoag population. His name appears as official translator on many of the land deeds
registered for Martha's Vineyard.[16] And just as he translated Wampanoag
land deeds, he simultaneously translated their religious conversion narratives in his role as missionary. And so, at least in the eyes of the colonial
power structure, Mayhew was the means through which the Wampanoags
became legally, economically, and spiritually accountable.

## Indian Converts

Positioned precariously at the furthest chronological edge of Puritanism
but before the Great Awakening, Mayhew's 1727 narrative is an odd mix-
ture of moving personal testimonial and conventional rhetoric. Borrowing
from multiple sources to create his text, Mayhew expands the generic conventions of the missionary tract. An important model for Mayhew was, of
course, Eliot's own seventeenth-century tracts, loosely defined conglomer-
ations of historical narrative, missionary letters, and miscellaneous information about "the progress of the gospel" among Native groups. Such documents functioned to enlighten the English public about the actions of
missionaries in the colonies, with the related intention of soliciting interested benefactors. They also served as beacons of moral enlightenment for
the English, who could be inspired both by the sacrifices of missionaries
who ventured into the wilderness and by the gratitude and joy of the converts who through much hardship and struggle could participate in what
English citizens could take for granted—Christian communities. Fragmentary, informal, and sometimes philosophical, the Eliot tracts were not
only a generic model for Mayhew[17] but also contained much of the information on early conversions on Martha's Vineyard that Mayhew included
in *Indian Converts.*

Experience Mayhew's account shares many of the qualities of the Eliot

tracts, but unlike those tracts, which were not formally structured, Mayhew's text is made up of a series of individual biographies. His choice of
the biographical format is unusual. Though earlier spiritual biographies
exist, they were often attached to specific collections of preachers' writings,
funeral sermons, and so forth, and were rarely published separately (Watkins 24–25). Biography in the seventeenth and eighteenth centuries had as
its primary purpose recording the lives of remarkable men, whose names
would already have been familiar to contemporary readers for their public
deeds.[18] Though these lives had a rich religious component, they were not
primarily records of religious faith, but were meant to serve as models for
how to live well.

In Autobiography or first-person narrative, on the other hand, was a con-
fessional form whose primary purpose was to mark the workings of grace
on the life of the individual. The narratives in *Indian Converts* can be understood as autobiographies in the sense that they are conversion narratives
in the tradition of the Puritan confession, given with the purpose of
publicly voicing one's intention to become a church member. Edmund
Morgan emphasizes the particularity of the American Puritan conversion
narrative. To apply for membership in a Puritan church, he writes, "appli-
cants . . . are required to make a declaration of their experience of the work
of grace. . . . they must describe how they became convinced that they had
received saving faith, and then must stand cross-examination about the
experience" (*Visible* 62). Patricia Caldwell notes that such narratives generally contained a typical sequence of Puritan theological conditions for conversion: "sin, preparation, and assurance; conviction, compunction, and
submission; fear, sorrow, and faith" (2). Thus, for example, Mayhew's bio-
graphical/autobiographical account of Tobit Potter's life is far more concerned with the workings of grace on his life than with the particulars of
his lived experience. We are told which verses from the Bible provided
comfort for him, but nothing about the daily chores that characterized his
life with the Milton family.

In many ways the Mayhew narratives follow the highly conventionalized form of the Puritan conversion narrative. And what is perhaps most
remarkable about them is their very unremarkableness. Predating the enthusiasm and multiplicity of the Great Awakening, when the form shifts
to a more emotional, personalized narrative, the Mayhew accounts are
closer to the seventeenth-century variety in which the centrality of God

overshadows the personal. As Laurel Ulrich stresses in her study of the lives of women in northern New England, the purpose is not to record individual personality but rather to transcend it. (Ulrich notes ruefully, "It is difficult for us to approach a world in which neither innovation nor individuality was celebrated, in which the rich particulars of daily life were willfully reduced to formulaic abstraction" [3].) Such narratives also function to obscure the specific social and economic dynamics shaping the lives of those being celebrated. To come to terms with these abstractions, Ulrich emphasizes, we must look carefully at the assumptions that underlie them, and attempt to understand the extended meanings of stock phrases and formulaic language.

Patricia Caldwell also cautions against giving in to the ideas of stereotype and stultifying adherence to convention; in her analysis of spiritual conversion narratives she sees instead a complex form with multiple literary and religious manifestations (39–41). Daniel Shea agrees, noting that "spiritual autobiographies, of whatever origin, do not reduce to the credal assertions of the writer, but are instead a form of argument in which the narrator's attempt to assemble and fashion evidence out of his experience may easily falter or yield an unexpected conclusion" (ix). Though much of the narrative content follows conventional structures, then, a close examination of how these structures work together, as well as what is said and what is left unsaid, can open such texts to rich interpretive analysis.

If we are willing to see the autobiographical component of these narratives as accounts written by Natives, even heavily mediated as these are by Mayhew, the narratives become autoethnographies, through which colonized people actively engage with the language of the colonizer as a means of establishing a place for themselves in the colonial order. The Wampanoag writers of Mayhew's text engage with the structure and form of the conversion narrative as a means of expressing their identities specifically as Native converts. Thus the narratives reveal much about the cultural position of Christian Indians in the evolving society of Martha's Vineyard.

That Mayhew speaks for the Native converts reflects his sense of authority over their lives yet he is petitioning for them to be admitted into the community of "visible saints" who are the core of the New England church. The converts have already formed their own churches on Martha's Vineyard, and many of those Mayhew describes have important positions in those churches as ministers and deacons.[19] That Mayhew brings these

"Puritan Indians" to the attention of an English audience indicates his desire to assure them a position in the larger Christian community. This inclusiveness is an important shift in colonial practice and belief; previous generations of Mayhews, open though they were to Native conversions, refused to accept the possibility of integrated churches. As William Simmons points out, Native churches were conceived of by the English as necessarily "subordinate . . . and geographically separate" ("Conversion" 214). Experience Mayhew, however, cites instances of Native ministers preaching to English congregations, and he stresses the impact of his converts' spirituality not only on other Natives but on the English as well. On many levels, then, Mayhew's passionate attempt to validate Wampanoag churches in the eyes of the English Christian community is a remarkable gesture toward inclusiveness.

His "open-mindedness" is tempered, however, by the main criteria for entry into his list of converts: the individual in question must be already dead. This condition had important implications for the living, the main one being that acceptance of the conversion of these Indian saints did not necessitate any change in the day-to-day interactions, with their attendant power differential, between Natives and English colonists. Just as Sassamon's martyrdom a generation earlier had no clear effect on the way Native Christians were treated in King Philip's War, so Mayhew's admiring narratives of Wampanoag conversion had no clear impact on the Natives' social and political position on the island. Native inclusion was an abstraction; practically speaking, Indian churches remained segregated and in the eyes of many were inferior to English churches. In fact, the only practical positive effect of the acceptance of already dead Wampanoag converts as members of a greater spiritual community would have been vastly increased English respect and admiration for Mayhew and his family of missionaries, who were together able to engineer such conversions.

More significantly, however, Mayhew's gesture toward inclusion involves a troubling transfer of representational control. As he brings Natives to the attention of the larger public, he appropriates their ability to speak for themselves. Mayhew modifies and frames their narratives to fit his own and his audience's understanding. Thus even though he has before him conversion narratives written independently by Native Americans, he tells his English audience: "The Indians, of whom I am to speak . . . must be considered as a People in a great measure destitute of those advantages of

Literature, which the English and many other Nations enjoy. They have at present no scholars among them . . . nothing may at present be expected of them, that will look polite or accurate: nor can there be much published from any writings of their own, which would be to my present purpose, and entertaining to English readers" (xxiii). Mayhew wrests the writing of the Wampanoags from its original context: "I shall . . . translate and insert some such passages written by them in their own language, as I think will be subservient to the End herein aimed at" (xxiii). Dependent though he is on the Wampanoags for the authority to speak as a missionary, ultimately his position within dominant structures of power allows him to define them on his own terms.[20] This representational shift puts the Bible verse on Mayhew's title page in a new light. Citing Acts 15.8–9—"Giving them the Holy Ghost, even as he did unto us: and put no Difference between us and them, purifying their Hearts by Faith"—Mayhew assures himself that the "Faith" with which he writes his narrative erases the "Difference" between himself and the converts about whom he writes. And the fact that these converts are already dead assures Mayhew that they can no longer act in ways that are unintelligible to him; he can speak for them and as them, textually structuring their lives to suit his own purposes.[21]

## Reculturation and Transculturation

To make his subjects suitable for an English audience, Mayhew fills his text with moments of reculturation, when he reads traditional Wampanoag values as Christian values. He consistently praises Natives for the sincerity of their conversions, citing qualities such as generosity, hospitality, and charity, all values held by the Wampanoags long before the arrival of the English. He tells us of Yonohhumuh, a magistrate who "was observed to be a Person of remarkable Charity" (89) and who was so generous that he gave away the corn he had grown if there were people who had none. He also mentions William Lay, a minister, Samuel Coomes, a magistrate, Annampanu, grandson of a sachem, and David Paul, a lay leader of the community, as being remarkable for their charity to those less fortunate than themselves. But though such traditional Wampanoag values were easily seen as Christian virtues, they may have meant radically different things to Mayhew and the converts themselves. Most of the Natives who held positions of authority as ministers and magistrates in their communities came from families whose prestige was established long before the coming of the

English. As figures of some importance, these people had a traditional set of obligations to their community—one of which was to ensure that nobody went hungry. As Bragdon puts it, "generosity and sharing were obligatory in Native social relationships (*Native People* 131).[22] Thus Mayhew's carefully noted mark of true "Christianity" in the form of charity and hospitality was a traditional Wampanoag value that intersected well with Christian ideals but was in no way limited to Native Converts.

For Mayhew, alliances between traditionally powerful families and the newly forming group of Christian converts are a clear signal that the best of Wampanoag society is ready and willing to embrace the morally and culturally superior forces of Anglo-American control. He comments on the number of sachems as well as their advisors—the chief councilmen ("Ahtoskouaog") and counselors ("Ohtoskow")—and members of their families who are linked to Anglo-American power structures such as the church and judicial system set up in Wampanoag communities. He points out which marriages forged alliances between the daughters of sachems and noblemen and the rapidly expanding group of "godly men" who formed a new power base. For Mayhew, the generally high status of converts indicates that the moral superiority of Christianity has become apparent to the Wampanoag elite. And though conversion was undoubtedly sincere for many Wampanoags, it may also have had pragmatic roots in the sense that traditionally powerful families were able to maintain their control within their own community by becoming central to the newer forms of power emerging—the Christian churches and the secular structures of community control.

Mayhew also records distinctions in the marks of true conversion that are based on gender. Such gendered distinctions hint at some of the other gaps in his narrative, as we recognize that at times he not only sees what he wants to see, but also is limited in his access to the social and cultural roles of Wampanoag women. Though some men are remarkable for charity and generosity, for Mayhew these virtues seem to be particularly relevant to pious women; nearly every biography of a Wampanoag woman convert mentions her charity and generosity to the poor. And the ways in which women and men manifest these virtues are quite different; men give commodities such as grain, meat, and milk, whereas women give time, comfort, and the results of their labor such as clothing, prepared meals, and housewares. For example, Dinah Ahhunnut was "ready on all

Occasions to visit and help" her neighbors with acts of "Kindness and Charity" (138). And Old Sarah, or Assannooshque, was perfectly compassionate in her charity, according to Mayhew, which "she manifested by feeding them when they were hungry, visiting them when they were sick; and in every other way wherein she was able to help and relieve them" (142–43). Mayhew points out that she was aptly named, as "the Character of this woman exactly answereth the Signification of her *Indian* Name, which properly signifyeth a *Woman that is a Giver of Victuals,* tho the Name was, as I suppose, given her while she was an Infant, and not after she appeared to be such a one" (143). Katherine, or Wuttonaehtunnooh, although poor herself, "used to make Baskets, or something else that she could dispose of to the *English,* or some of the best Livers among the *Indians;* having sold the same for something the Sick most needed, she would visit them, and carry those good things to them" (170). And Hannah Tiler's charity was so all-inclusive that she would knit a pair of stockings for the mentally handicapped daughter of a poor English neighbor, "the doing of which she freely gave her, and would not by any means be hindered from doing so as long as she lived" (192–93).

Mayhew also approvingly notes the neatness and cleanliness with which certain women maintain their households and their families' clothing. He praises Abiah Paaonit, wife of the minister Elisha Paaonit, for the "great Care" she took of her husband; he notes approvingly her habit of "keeping his Apparel in whole and in good order, his Linen clean and neat," and he says that she "carried her self in all respects towards him as a Minister's Wife should do" (158). The Indianness of this family and even of their church is obscured as Abiah becomes the generic model of a minister's wife, and the qualities that make her such become signals of her inherently English Christianity. And in a moment that simultaneously marks difference even as it erases it, Mayhew also praises Sarah, wife of Japheth Hannit, for keeping her wigwam neat and clean, just as a Puritan goodwife would. He explains, "The matts, or platted Straw, Flags and Rushes with which it was covered, being wrought by her own Hands; and those of them that appeared within side the House, were neatley embroidered with the inner Barks of Walnut-Trees artificially softened, and dyed of several Colours for that end. . . . The house thus built was kept neat and clean, all things in it being in their proper Places" (167). Even as he describes a traditional Algonquian home that would have been utterly foreign to most of his English readers,[23] he undermines its particularity by positioning it among the best English homes.

One of the things that made women such as Sarah Hannit, Abiah Paaonit, and their converted peers so remarkable, according to Mayhew, was their adherence to the strict family hierarchies that accompanied the divisions of labor. Indeed, Wampanoag Christians maintained strict divisions of labor according to gender, just as Puritan families did. Men worked at trades or as farmers, doing work that generally took them away from the house, while women maintained and regulated the inside of the home.[24] On occasion women helped their husbands outside, as did Mary Coshomon at harvest time (181). According to Mayhew, the male head of the household said prayers and taught morals to the family; his wife deferred to him and instructed her children through example; and the children listened to their parents and obeyed them always. There was one notable lapse in the neat parallel to English hierarchies, however. As Daniel Gookin had noticed several years before, "the men and women are very loving and indulgent to their children" (149). Mayhew explains to his English audience that "it has been a Custom amongst our *Indians* to teach their Children Forms of Prayers, and sometimes to call them to make use of them in their Presence; and hence, I suppose, it hath come to pass, that young People among the *Indians* have thought it no Presumption to call upon God for his Mercy, when their Parents have been by, and heard them" (176). Though this rather shocking challenge to parental authority held potential pitfalls for Mayhew, he notes that it was ultimately the parents who authorized their children's disruption of the English norm in which parents always led prayers and children always listened respectfully—a fact that only barely mitigates the boldness of the children involved.[25]

As he cites many examples of humility throughout his narrative, the children's lack of this virtue is of great concern to Mayhew. Specifically, humility toward the English was always a sign of a good Christian; Mayhew tells us of William Lay, or Panunnut, that "he always appeared to have a very cordial affection for the *English* . . . and was ready to take Advice of them on all Occasions" (27). Humility was particularly important in wives' behavior around their husbands, even in the most horrific circumstances. When faced with her perennially drunk husband who could not provide for the family, Hannah Sissetom was "constantly yielding Obedience to his just Commands, and not vexing and provoking of him by any hard Words, but used in a very dutiful manner to advise and intreat him" (185). Mayhew also approves of humility toward God and his servants, or ministers. He tells us of Joash Panu, himself a minister, that he was "humbly sensible of his Insufficiency for the great Work to which he was called" (65). Mayhew also cites Mary Coshomon, who said "she look'd on the Officers of the Church of Christ, as Dressers of the Trees planted in God's Vineyard; and that she greatly needed to be under such Cultivations, by Instructions, Admonitions, and Reproofs, as Members of Churches might expect to enjoy" (180). And Wuttununohkomkooh, one of the most pious women according to Mayhew, "was a lowly Woman, low in Stature, and withal of a most lowly Mind; and so exactly answered the Notation of her Name, which signifieth *a humble, or lowly Woman.* She discovered nothing of Pride in her Deportment, unless it were in honouring her self by a very regular conversation" (137).

The connection between humility and power, however, was quite different in traditional Wampanoag society and Christian society. For the Natives, humility had an extensive and complex role in maintaining relations of power. Bragdon notes that "people demanded a share of the bounty that was available, and were confident that, in exchange for deferential behavior, or by virtue of their status as 'petitioners,' their requests would be granted" (*Native People* 133–34). The assumption of this inferior role carried with it the certainty that the person or persons in authority were obligated to extend whatever help they could. And in a society that fostered sharing and acts of generosity as a basis for social exchange, the greatest crime was reneging on the obligations that emerged from such patterns of reciprocity.[26] In a paradoxical way, then, strength came out of the expression of humility or deference in a way that was not necessarily part of the social fabric of Anglo-American expressions of Christianity.

Gender relations may well have been affected by this Native structure of reciprocity and humility, and Mayhew's approving comments on women's inferior position may have had more to do with his own assumptions than with the lived experience of Native women. Certainly in light of the social function of humility, the actions of certain wives toward their husbands take on a more nuanced meaning. Wives are to be passive in the face of their husbands' abuse and sinfulness, as is clear from the above example of Hannah Sissetom, and also from the example of Hannah Tiler, who would not involve civil authorities even after her neighbors encouraged her to because of her husband's drunken rages. It is only through their patience and humility that women effect change in their households; we hear from Mayhew that eventually Hannah Tiler "did so far overcome [her husband's] Evil by her Goodness, that he carried himself more kindly to her than formerly he had done" (191). Men are reformed only through the good influence of their wives, never through the wives' "talking too angrily to [their] husband[s]" (190). And situations improve even more when men hand over control to their spouses. We see, for example, that William Tuphaus wavered between wasting his money by spending it on excessive drink and being "too sparing" (96). Eventually his wife convinced him of the error of his ways, and he left "the management of what he had in the House to her" (97). After this, "they lived comfortably, and served God chearfully" (97). Thus hierarchies are multilayered and paradoxical—strength comes out of the seemingly powerless position that wives accept in ways that Mayhew does not seem to fully recognize.

This relationship between power and humility also holds with children. For example, Eleazar Ohhumuh "did divers times go to the Places where his Father was drinking, and with such Earnestness, and so many Tears, intreat him to leave his drinking Company and go home to his own House" (225). The father "was not able to withstand the Importunity of his afflicted Child" (225), and after his child's early death "he totally quitted his immoderate Use of strong Drink" (227) and became a morally upstanding person. It is specifically through the lack of force or strength that women and children are able to affect change, and the paradoxical role of humility in Native traditions with its attendant obligations may well have played a part in these domestic struggles.

This question of the social role of humility in intersecting cultural traditions points to some of the larger complications of transculturation and reculturation. If conversions tended to occur along kinship lines and by maintaining an already present series of social relationships, the enormous shift in world view that was assumed by the English to have taken place in the conversion to Christianity may well have been rather a simple, straightforward maintenance of the status quo. As an English man with strong social and cultural investments in the saving power of Christianity, Mayhew can have had only a limited sense of the ways in which Native men and women adapted Christianity into their culture.

The shifting naming practices of Natives further shows the complexity of this situation. For men, a shift in naming styles occurred which took approximately two or three generations. The first generation of Native converts had one Indian name, which may have changed throughout a person's lifetime, but which fully represented the individual. Some examples of such names are Hiacoomes, Janawannit, Mittark, and Wunnanauhkomun. The next generation had two names simultaneously, an English name and an Indian name; Mayhew tries to provide both for his readers. Thus we read about Paul, or Mashquattuhkooit, and William Lay, or Panunnut, and David, or Wuttinomanomin. Mayhew explains the third and last step as follows: Japheth Hannit's name comes from his Father's, which is Pamchannit; "which name being contracted into Hannit only, by leaving out the first two syllables of it, became afterward the sirname of his son *Japheth* and others of his Offspring: a thing very common among our *Indians*" (44). What Mayhew does not specify is that more often than not the first names of these Indians are English names such as Stephen, Elisha, Isaac, Abel, and James. Thus men developed a system of naming that incorporated both English and Indian names.

Women's naming practices differed from men's. After the first generation, they seem to have maintained an Indian name and an English name simultaneously, one for their home and community, and the other for their interactions with the English. Thus they did not move to the third point in which both English and Indian names converge, but rather they maintained separate identifying markers. Hannah Ahhunnut, according to Mayhew, is "commonly called by the *Indians Pahkehtan*" (140). Similarly, "Old Sarah" is known by the Indians as Assannooshque. Hannah Nohnosoo is also called Nattootumau, and Katherine is also called Wuttontaehtunnooh. By maintaining distinct identities for their interactions with the English and for their Wampanoag communities, rather than eventually merging the two as Wampanoag men seem to have done, women may well have been central to maintaining traditional Wampanoag practices within a private, domestic world. The gendering of this world suggests some of the textual problems implicit in having Mayhew, an Englishman and to a certain extent an outsider, explaining a reality to which he may not have had complete access. The patterns of conversion that Mayhew sets up are contingent on his understanding of Wampanoag lives, and his limited access to the private world of both male and female converts no doubt had a profound affect on his understanding.

Another way Mayhew's limited access to the domestic landscape and his role as transcriber complicate the situation is seen in his description of the cultural position of sachem/magistrate and shaman/priest. According to Mayhew's description, the organization of Indian social and political power remained relatively intact, and the power of the magistrate replaced that of the sachem relatively unproblematically. He tells us, for example, that the praying Indians on the east end of the Island "earnestly desire[d] that Christian Civil Government might be set up over them . . . which being done according to their Desire . . . *Tawanquatuck* became a Christian Magistrate among the People, over whom he had before ruled as an *Indian Sachim*" (82). Similarly, Yonohhumuh, who was a chief councilman for the local sachem Mittark, simply became a Peantamaenin or "praying man," and as such was able to do his work as an advisor more effectively, according to Mayhew (89).

The minister seems to replace the powwow in the same unproblematic manner. Mayhew explains the position of the powwows: "these *Pawwaws* [were never] able to do the *Christian Indians* any Hurt, tho others were frequently hurt and killed by them." (7) His point is that the powwows don't practice deception, or have false magic; instead, they have wrong magic. Daniel Gookin explains this further:

> There are among [the Indians] certain men and women, whom they call powows. These are partly wizards and witches, holding familiarity with Satan, that evil one; and partly are physicians, and make use, at least in show, of herbs and roots, for curing the sick and diseased. These are sent for by the sick and wounded; and by their diabolical spells, mutterings, exorcisms, they seem to do wonders. They use extraordinary strange motions of their bodies, insomuch that they will sweat untill they foam; and thus continue for some hours together, stroking and hovering over the sick. Sometimes broken bones have been set, wounds healed, sick recovered; but together therewith they sometimes use external applications of herbs, roots, splintering and binding up the wounds. (154)

Through the process of reculturation as it is practiced by both Mayhew and Gookin, the authority of the powwow is interpreted according to a Christian world view; if the power does not come from God, it must come from Satan.[27] The solution for missionaries is to replace the power of evil spirits with the force of the Christian God.

Through Native acts of transculturation, however, Christianity replaces

powwowing without doing away with the Algonquian belief structure that
sustained it. This structure is based on the principle that disease is sent as
a sign that all is not in harmony in the spiritual world, and that only by
communicating effectively with the other world can the problems of this
one be resolved. Thus Japheth's farewell address includes the admonition
to his people that "you do also trouble the common People by your Sins,
by bringing on them various Sicknesses and pestilential Diseases, and all
other divine Chastisements" (53). By acting sinfully, the people bring down
disease, and it is only by truly believing in God—the most powerful figure
in the spirit world—that disease can be eliminated.[28] At least initially,
then, the authority of priests is based on their authority as shamans. They
acquire power through the people's understanding that they can communicate with the spirit world and act as guides in righting the balance of the
world.

But eventually a split between the functions of the powwow as spiritual
guide and as healer opens up, allowing for a gap that causes problems for
both the Native community and English missionaries. The role of the sha-
man as healer is never fully occupied by ministers; instead, the power to
heal, based as it was on dream visions in traditional Algonquian societies,
seems to be appropriated by a different segment of Wampanoag society. A
traditional source of power and inspiration for powwows or shamans
among the Wampanoag, dreams held a sacred place in Native cosmology.
As Native converts insisted on the role of dreams in their experience of
Christianity, they tapped into a source of tension both in their own society
and in Puritan theology.

Hannah Nohnosoo, or Nattootumau, is a healer and midwife who uses
her deep faith in God to guide her in her medical practices. Mayhew describes her admiringly as someone who, in the forty years of her membership in the Indian Church, "constantly behav's herself as became a good
Christian, so as to adorn the Doctrine of God her Saviour in all things"
(164). He also tells us that "having very considerable skill in some of the
Distempers to which human Bodies are subject, and in the Nature of those
Herbs and Plants which were proper remedies against them, she often did
good by her Medecines among her Neighbors" (165). This skill is something that Nattootumau attributes entirely to God—it is only through
him that she has any power to heal. Her insistence on the supernatural
origin of her healing power opens up an intriguing possibility: were Native

women taking over the religious curing function of the powwow? In Wampanoag society powwows could be women, although we don't hear of many.[29] Though Nattootumau does her healing in the name of God, as any Puritan would, she does it in ways that seem remarkably similar to the ways in which powwows relied on the spirit world to affect their cures; when asked to help a person, Nattootumau is heard to reply, "I do not know but I may, if it please God to bless Means for that end, otherwise I can do nothing" (165).[30] By associating healing abilities with prayer and communion with God, and by speaking of herself as a mere vessel for God's work, Nattootumau manifests traditional Native beliefs about healing through direct access to the powers of the spirit world.

Nattootumau is not an isolated example—the biographies of Hannah Ahhunnut (141) and Abiah Paaonit (159), among others, refer specifically to these women's power to communicate with God to help those who were ill or women who were giving birth. Furthermore, a significant number of Mayhew's accounts of Wampanoag women include dreams or visions in which God or his angels appear (only one man, Wuttinomanomin, was associated with apparitions). For example, at Abigail Kesoehtaut's death, a voice was heard rising above the house, repeating over and over, "wunnantinnea kanaanut," which Mayhew translates as "there is favour now extended in Canaan" (147). Similarly, the night of Ammapoo's death, her daughter saw "a Light which seemed to her brighter than that of Noonday" and "two bright shining Persons, standing in white Raiment at her Mother's Bed-side" who disappeared immediately. Abiah Paaonit saw a vision late one night that was "as it were a Window open in the Heavens, and a Stream of glorious Light issuing out from thence, and lighting upon her" (160). The connection between Wampanoag women's apparent power to access the spirit world and their healing abilities may have seemed unremarkable to missionaries who had little access to the private, domestic, female sphere of Wampanoag society. But as the role of the powwow fractured, did it go "underground" the way women's naming practices did?

Even though Puritans back in England spoke about their dreams, in New England "a deep suspicion of 'revelations and dreames' is firmly established in Puritan psychological theory" (Caldwell 16). One of Mayhew's missionary predecessors wrote in 1648, "I attribute little to dreams, yet God may speak to such by them rather then to those who have a more sure Word to direct and warn them" (Eliot tracts, *Clear Sun-shine* 10). This

tentative acceptance of the dreams of Native converts suggests that some
Puritan divines felt that dreams could be appropriate for those who did
not have access to God through the Bible or through regular church atten-
dance. Seventy-five years later, such a possibility must have seemed too
threatening to those who had experienced the social upheaval that figures
such as Anne Hutchinson or the Quakers elicited by suggesting their
dreams had the same authority as the Bible. Indeed, the Puritans' violent
reaction against the Quaker emphasis on dreams and visions marks their
hostility toward the notion of divine inspiration. Furthermore, the exile by
Puritan ministers of Anne Hutchinson—another midwife—because of
her claim to direct access to the "voice" of God points to their anxiety
surrounding a supposedly direct access to God, unmediated by the clergy.
Certainly Mayhew was well aware of the Puritan suspicion of the role of
dreams. Why, then, is Nattootumau a Puritan saint but Hutchinson a sinner? For Mayhew, at least, the answer to this question is unclear. Unable
to accept the explanation of an earlier generation of missionaries, but unwilling to abandon the possibility that his converts had some sort of experience of God's divinity, Mayhew clearly doesn't know what to make of the
dreams and visions of these women. Of the voices chanting at Abigail Kesoehtaut's death, Mayhew asks anxiously: "Query. *Whether the Person that
dreamed the Dream now related, ought to take any other notice of it, than she
should of any common Dream; or what she should think concerning it?* A Solution of this Problem would gratify both the Person that had the Dream,
and him that has related it" (148). Like Eliot before him, Mayhew is caught
between his optimistic view that Native Christianity is what Anglo-
Americans make it and his suspicion that Native Christians bring with
them a different set of rules that influence their religion. Just as Eliot in
shaping a written Massachusett language was forced to bend to a preexisting structure even as he insisted on the originality of his own structure,
here Mayhew is confronted with unavoidable difference even as he
struggles to explain it away. And it is in the gap between missionary expectations and Indian reality that Native Christianity names itself, not as a
strictly indigenous system nor as a creation of empire but rather as a mix
of the two.

Thus Mayhew's power to define Native Christianity seems particularly
circumscribed. He is filled with doubt about his ability to properly interpret evidence. Of Abiah Paaonit's vision, for example, he says, "What no-

tice ought to have been taken of this Phaenomenon I shall not undertake to declare, but shall leave to the Judgement of the Judicious" (160). But he stresses that whatever the feelings of others, "the Woman herself who saw this Light, was somewhat affected at what she had seen, and divers times spake of it as some little Glimpse of the Glory of the Heavenly World which God had been pleased to favour her withal" (160). His discomfort is evident in his attempts to distance himself from these accounts. Such moments of his uncertainty about his own ability to properly interpret evidence reveal the limits of his power to control the nature of the narrative he is writing; much as he wants to define the experiences of Natives in terms that he is comfortable with, ultimately he is left with the details that they impart to him. And those details can at times bring him to question his own assumptions about faith and religious practice.

## Autoethnographies

Interspersed liberally throughout Mayhew's narrative are the words of the Wampanoag converts themselves, which Mayhew assures his audience he has replicated exactly. Sometimes written, sometimes spoken, they constitute an important record of Native conversion. These words, however, must be regarded with caution. One problem is the arbitrariness of Mayhew's choices about who to include. He tells us briefly, for example, of a man about whom he has little information and whom he therefore could not include among the "Good Men." This man, Simon Netawash, apparently left a record of himself, but Mayhew claims, "I have heard that there was a Paper written of his dying Speeches; but it not coming into my Hand, I cannot here insert it" (133). Thus we have only an idiosyncratic sampling of those converts with whom Mayhew came into direct contact. Furthermore, there is the problem of the time difference between when the words were spoken and when Mayhew wrote them down. In some cases, it seems, there is quite a lapse of time between the two. Moreover, occasionally words are recorded that are several removes from the person who spoke them, as in the case of Tobit Potter's words, which are repeated by his mother to Mary Milton, his mistress, who repeats them to Experience Mayhew, who then writes them down. Perhaps most important, though, is the problem of linguistic accuracy. The words we read have been translated by Mayhew from Massachusett to English, so we are necessarily getting an already mediated version of what was said. Mayhew himself is the first to admit that his translations do not always capture meanings perfectly; he tells us, for example, that the words of Abigail Kesoehtaut's dream "may be thus rendered in *English,* tho they are much more emphatical in *Indian*" (147).

Despite these problems, the fragmentary Wampanoag voices in Mayhew's text offer a significant opportunity to look at the words—however mediated—of Native American converts. Through these autoethnographies, Natives struggle to reconcile the experience of Nativeness with the concept of salvation.

True to the form of the Puritan personal narrative, we see in these texts countless examples of humility and self-loathing. Jerusha Ompan, Mary Manhut, and Rachel Wompanummoo, for example, are all deeply concerned about their sinful lives, and pray that Jesus Christ will forgive them their various transgressions. Though such moments do resemble standard Christian expressions of humility and devotion, that humility, as we have seen, is also part of the system of Wampanoag reciprocation, in which the supplicant ensures the favor of the benefactor by setting off a series of cultural obligations.

Though in many ways these narratives fit the patterns established by Anglo-Americans, they are remarkable for the intensity of the community ethic that imbues them, especially in regard to the idea of unity as a nation. Jonathan Amos's prayer for his people begins, "We *Indians* are poor miserable Creatures, and our Faith is exceedingly weak" (40). Jedidah Hannit, a seventeen-year-old girl, dreams "that there was a very dark and dismal time shortly coming on the *Indian* Nation" (232). Her identity as a member of her Native community is so powerful that her thoughts and dreams center on her people rather than her own fate. Indeed, her sense of belonging is strong enough to override her own desire to avoid suffering; she prays to die before this terrible time, but as she is dying (she tells her family after surviving) she hears her brother-in-law call her, telling her that "her Father and Mother and other Friends would be exceedingly troubled, if she went away so suddenly and left them" (233).

Useful here is Arnold Krupat's notion of the Native American sense of identity as defined by its relation to the community rather than by a Western sense of individualism.[31] In these texts individuals insist on remembrance; the Wampanoags in Mayhew's narrative struggle to to leave some record of their own existence as presences within a larger community. Spending his last energies reaching out to his people, Japheth, for example, writes "an affectionate Address" to his congregation only a few days before his death "with his feeble and dying Hand" (53). Elizabeth Pattompan asks her father to write down her words "for the Benefit of her relations" (240); when he puts this off, Mayhew tells us, the child appears to her father in a dream to remind him to write down her words. In several other instances a relative of the dying person writes down his or her words to preserve something of that person, and those words are almost without exception directed outward, to the community at large.

As in the conversion narratives recorded by John Eliot years before, for many of these converts Christianity provides the means for the reassembly of a greater, more permanent Native community. Jerusha Ohquanhut tells her friends, "If you are sorry for my leaving of you, seek for me with Jesus Christ, and there you shall find me, and with him we shall see one another for ever" (246). Japheth makes the same point: "Before we knew God, when any Man dy'd, we said the Man is *dead;* neither thought we any thing further, but said he is *dead,* and mourned for him, and buried him: but now it is far otherwise; for now this good Man being dead, we have Hope towards God concerning him" (47). The child Job Tuphaus says, "*I love my Relations . . . but I am willing to leave them all and go to God . . . tho I go a little before my Friends and Relations, they must quickly follow after me*" (243). Mary Coshomon worries that if she does not draw closer to God in this life "she should be excluded from his Presence in the World to come, and not be admitted into the Company of such as would be then happy in the Enjoyment of him, but only *see then afar off, she her self being shut out from among them*" (179). As these Natives struggle to overcome loneliness and impermanence, they commit themselves to God, through whom, they believe, the Native community will be reassembled in a better place. The loss of community or the increasing fragmentation of the meaning of "Nativeness" on Martha's Vineyard is countered in these narratives by the consistent attempt to imagine a permanent, unified community that is distinct from that of the English. The frequent pleas for remembrance reflect a heartfelt desire to reconfigure the Native community as essentially Christian—and therefore everlasting. As economic power disintegrates, Christianity and literacy become means by which a Wampanoag identity can maintain itself within colonial society.

THROUGH *Indian Converts* we come to know about the lives of various members of the Wampanoag community. And although he does not include any particular section about his own life, Mayhew becomes a significant presence through his textual asides about himself. He tells us that William Lay, or Panunnut, spoke to him after Mayhew's father's death, and "earnestly desired me, who was then but a Youth, to study the *Indian* Tongue, and become a Preacher to them, as my Father and Grandfather had been before me" (27). He adds revealingly, "and truly his Importunity was none of the least of the Motives which influenced me to engage in that Work" (27). He tells us as he is writing about Abigail Manhut that "it is so long since this Maid died, that I cannot distinctly remember anything concerning her" (220), then breaks off to report, "But while I was writing this Account of her, my aged Mother came in and told me, that she lived and laboured some time in my Father's House, carrying herself very well while she was there; and that my Father esteemed her a very pious Person" (220). We also get glimpses of Mayhew's missionary work. He tells us that as Jacob Sockakonnit was dying, Mayhew visited him and became concerned with the state of his soul. He then tells us, ruefully, "I intended to have again visited him, but he dy'd sooner than I thought he would have done; so I missed the Opportunity" (119). Similarly, he visits with Elizabeth Uhquat on her deathbed, but "not speaking with her before I went to *Boston* in *June,* she died before my Return; which, when I understood, I repented the Delay" (196). He did have several edifying conversations with Deborah Sissetom before she died, and when she asked him to pray for her, he complied. He then reports, "Having done as she desired, she expressed much Thankfulness to me for the Pains I had taken for her Good, and so I took my leave of her" (274). We have here a remarkable record of the intimacy of the interactions between this Anglo-American minister and the Wampanoag Christians of Martha's Vineyard. And the range of relationships available to the individuals involved complicates what at first glance seems a rather stark power differential.

Occasionally Mayhew asks us to accept his judgments without corroborating details. For example, he tells us that Jerusha Ompan was greatly disturbed by a certain problem, but he continues, "What her Trial in particular was, I think not convenient to relate, only will say it was what was no fault in her" (177). By shielding Jerusha Ompan from the curiosity of his readers, Mayhew aligns himself with her on a very personal level. Clearly he is immersed in the daily life of Wampanoag communities across Martha's Vineyard and feels passionately about representing them in ways that he sees as beneficial to them. As strong an advocate as he is, however, he has still appropriated their voices. The Wampanoags write for their families, children, and friends, but Mayhew has given their words to a different audience to be judged on different terms. He explains, "[Some Indians] having preserved in *Writing* some Memorial of their pious children, written immediately after their Death, put the same into my Hands while I was about this work" (xii). His purpose is less to memorialize children, though, than to advocate for wider recognition of the power of the Christian community on Martha's Vineyard. To attain this goal, Mayhew structures his narrative in ways that misrepresent the Native community. His constant reassurances to his British audience that Natives are, after all, "naturally" Christian and ultimately not substantially different from the English eliminate markers of cultural integrity and any sense of Native community as different from colonial community. As part of the family of true believers, Native families and communities are textually fragmented through the division of the biographies into categories such "Religious Women," "Pious Children," "Good Men," and "Godly Ministers." Through this process, Mayhew emphasizes that Native Americans cannot be accepted into the Christian community as culturally other but rather as individuals petitioning to become members of an extended English family on English terms.

But Mayhew's project is not without internal tensions. The disruptions of Native families so crucial to the project of accepting converts individually start to break down as Mayhew reconstitutes those families through his own textual asides and explanations. For example, Rachel Amos "was the Wife of Deacon *Jonathan Amos,* mentions *Chapter I. Example 15.* and was a Daughter of that good *Miohqsoo* mentioned in *Chap. I*" (152). And Abigail Ahhunnut, who had three husbands, was once married to Deacon David (example twelve from the first chapter); "the last of her three Husbands was that *Job Ahhunnut,* whose third wife she was; of which three, that *Hannah* mentioned in our Third example was the second, and one now living the fifth, tho he be yet not sixty Years old" (163). The children become even more intricately connected to converts Mayhew has carefully separated from one another in his text; for example, Bethia Tuphaus "was a Daughter of that *William* and *Bethia Tuphaus* above-mentioned, and a Sister of the Youth last spoken of" (230). And Sarah Coomes "had for her Great Grandfather, on the Father's side, the memorable *Hiacoomes,* frequently before-mentioned; and for her Grandfather, that good *Samuel Coomes* mentioned in *Chap. II. Example 7.* On the Mother's side she was a Granddaughter to that good Deacon, *Jonathan Amos,* mentioned *Chap. I. Example 15*" (263). Clear kinship patterns emerge, and despite the categories that deemphasize family in favor of individual conversion, family connections become more important as the narrative continues.[32] Furthermore, despite Mayhew's acts of reculturation, he is also drawn in certain instances to what makes Natives distinct—their attraction to song and the singing of hymns (105), their "indulgent" attitude towards their children (176), and even their tendency to avoid staying in bed when they are sick (160). Even as Mayhew argues for their overall similarity to the English, he marks differences that undermine his argument. As Mayhew "translates" the words and acts of the converts, his own understanding of religious experience is itself transformed as he makes room for a Native experience of conversion.

Reading these artifacts of transculturation involves a process of double translation in that the words of Native converts are intimately connected to the words of Experience Mayhew. Mayhew's determination to mediate between Native converts and an English audience, thereby defining the Native converts' position in the larger Christian community, affects Natives' ability to be heard outside their own community. Yet Mayhew's authority as a missionary is contingent on the Natives' own redefinition of the conversion experience. So although Mayhew and the Wampanoag converts of Martha's Vineyard have seemingly different uses for Christianity, their mutual interdependence subverts the possibility of a single, coherent narrative by or about either of them. Elizabeth Cook-Lynn recently asserted that "how the Indian narrative is told, how it is nourished, who tells it, who nourishes it, and the consequences of its telling are among the most fascinating—and, at the same time, chilling—stories of our time" (57). The dynamics between Mayhew's missionary voice and the voices of Native converts simultaneously obscure and highlight different elements of that story.

# CHAPTER THREE

# CAPTIVITY AND
# CHRISTIANITY

## Stockbridge, New Stockbridge, and
## the Place of History

✝

After I had seen these things (which it is impossible to describe) I took an opportunity to inform them how improper such a method of worship was: how sinful and displeasing to the great God. Upon which they told me they knew no harm in it—they made their application to the great God, and to no other. I inform'd them that God was not to be worship'd in such a manner; and when I had instructed them as well as I could, they resolv'd never to do so any more, and those of them who had been best taught were much troubled, that they had taken so wrong a step.

> —Letter from Timothy Woodbridge to Stephen Williams,
> describing a powwow, 1735

A white person in charge of publication or dissemination can make an Indian text into something very much like a confession by remaining silent about his or her involvement in the material, when in fact the Indian who spoke or wrote it meant it to be an argument, a meditation, part of a dialogue, or a protest.

> —Laura Murray "'Pray Sir, Consider a Little' . . ."

TWENTY-SIX years after Experience Mayhew wrote *Indian Converts,* Samuel Hopkins wrote *Historical Memoirs, Relating to the Housatunnuk Indians* (1753). Hopkins compiled this loosely structured narrative to commemorate the work of his friend and colleague, John Sergeant, missionary to the Stockbridge Indians in western Massachusetts, four years after his early death. As its subtitle informs us, the book was to give "an Account of the Methods used and the Pains taken, for the Propagation of the Gospel among that HEATHEN TRIBE, and the Success thereof, under the Ministry of the late Reverend Mr. JOHN SERGEANT." The opposition of the two capitalized terms—"Heathen Tribe" and "John Sergeant"—establishes the assumption of the text, which is that Sergeant, as a representative of civilization, was to restructure "Heathen" life through the "Propagation of the Gospel." The source for much of the book's information is John Sergeant's diaries, even though, Hopkins laments, they became over time rather sparse. For Sergeant, Stockbridge was an embattled home, and his writings rhetorically structure his tenure there as a captivity. He thus ensured that Natives and Anglo-Americans would see themselves in opposition, and furthermore that Anglo-Americans would have the moral and cultural upper hand. Filling out Sergeant's journals with letters, missionary society records, and personal recollections, Hopkins pulls together an account of the mission's first fifteen years that is imbued with Sergeant's sense of place, and the book stands as the Stockbridge community's most complete early history.[1]

Mahican writings from the Stockbridge settlement's first thirty years are extremely sparse. The earliest Native writings are in land transfers and court cases, where little more than a signature or mark was required to indicate a Native presence. Such items as written confessions and professions of faith, standard in New England churches, were not preserved by the first few ministers of Stockbridge. But in the early 1790s, several years after the removal of the Mahicans from their lands along the Housatonic River, Hendrick Aupaumut, a Native leader of New Stockbridge in upstate New York, wrote several documents that provide an important counterpoint to Hopkins's *Memoirs*. Though both wrote for an Anglo-American audience, and both purported to show the beneficial effects of Christianity on the Mahican people, their respective documents suggest radically different versions of the history and meaning of the Stockbridge Indians' encounter with Christianity. As histories, both Hopkins's and Aupaumut's writings attempt to define interlocking notions of home, community, and personal identity. For both, the authority to write history is the authority to define community. Both versions of Stockbridge history have at their core the struggle over Christianity and its place in the community. *Historical Memoirs* positions Stockbridge comfortably within an Anglo-American

Christian tradition; Aupaumut's writing, on the other hand, attempts to integrate Anglo-American and Native American concepts of nationhood, community identity, and Christian theology. Aupaumut, in projecting a Christian identity back into Native history, wrests from Anglo-American missionaries the authority to define and control Christian meaning. For the process he fuses the contending elements of his identity as a Native, a Christian, and a diplomatic representative of the United States.

## History of Stockbridge

Founded as an experiment in cross-cultural exchange, the first settlement at Stockbridge was unusual in that it was conceived as an Anglo-American-style township comprising both Christianized Natives and a small number of White settlers. Daniel Mandell suggests that the arrangement seemed mutually beneficial, at least initially. Russell Handsman and Trudie Richmond point out that "Mahican peoples actually lived in the Berkshires for much more than ten centuries before colonial settlement began" (6); indeed, archeological sites and early colonial records point to Mahican settlements stretching the length of the Housatonic River.[2] Clan relationships established systems of trade and an extended community that provided links within and between Mahican peoples, who lived along both the Hudson and Housatonic Rivers (8–9).[3] By the eighteenth century, trade and family alliances also connected the Housatonic Mahicans to several other Indian nations to which they lived in close proximity—the Housatunnuks, the Wappingers, and the Wyachtonoks (Brasser 33). Well before the founding of the Stockbridge township, the Natives along the Housatonic River consisted of many small family clusters dominated by the Mahicans but influenced by a variety of Native traditions. These Indians had already had extensive dealings with the Dutch, and though relations had generally been amicable, by the early eighteenth century much of their territory had already been traded away to them.[4] When the English came upon the scene, the Housatonic River Indians, including the Mahicans, wanted mutually agreed-upon boundaries to be firmly set. They also wanted a stable, harmonious community and the material assistance a missionary community would provide (Mandell 18–19). From the Native perspective, the settlement at Stockbridge was a way to ensure a permanent community that would continue long-standing Native practices and alliances.

From the English perspective, Stockbridge would provide a range of

benefits besides the gratification of knowing that the local Native population had available to them the word of God. The Massachusetts colony
wanted a stable, settled township, influence with other tribes in the area,
and most especially a buffer against French and Indian strikes from Canada
(Mandell 18).[5] Such attacks had had a devastating impact on New England
both psychologically and economically, as one of the most famous captivity
narratives of the eighteenth century, John Williams's *Redeemed Captive*,
made clear.[6] Williams's son, who had been a captive with his father as a
small child, strongly advocated establishing Stockbridge as an outpost to
protect New England. Stockbridge, then, was for the English an unstable
extension of their New England home, which was to be shared with Natives who would presumably adapt themselves to English practices as
time passed.

The mission at Stockbridge started in 1734 when the young John Sergeant traveled with the local Natives along the Housatonic as they went
on their seasonal rounds, attempting to convert them to Christianity. Sergeant and his colleague Timothy Woodbridge, hired as a teacher for the
settlement, traveled with their "congregation," teaching and preaching
among them, and eventually gained the respect of Umpachenee and Konkapot, two Native leaders.[7] Sergeant was ordained at a formal ceremony in
1735, which his Mahican congregation attended.[8] When the township was
formally established in 1739, Sergeant's ministry reached out to both Natives and White settlers. Initially, the White population of Stockbridge was
strictly limited to four families, who were allotted specific lands upon
which to live and farm; they were to serve as proper Christian models as
the Natives eased themselves into the new modes of living the settlement
offered them.[9] Despite its overwhelming Native presence, Stockbridge was
seen by the English as their community, which was to participate in their
historical traditions. This English claim to the history of Stockbridge was
tenuous at best, since Native settlement in the area was long-standing, but
in 1739 Stockbridge was named by the English after a town in the county
of Hampshire, England, purportedly "from the general resemblance of the
scenery in the two places."[10] The name of the town was one clear signal
that however tenuous the connections might be, its history was to be that
of an English community.

By the 1740s, relations between Mahicans and Anglo-American settlers
had deteriorated significantly. Growing English families demanding their

own homesteads and shady land deals benefiting them greatly diminished Native land holdings in Stockbridge and caused resentment among the Natives. At the same time, Anglo-American settlers resented an increasing tax burden that was not shared by the Mahicans.[11] Even as the Mahicans in Stockbridge were joined by other groups such as David Brainerd's Kaunaumeek congregation and converts from the local Moravians, a high mortality rate from disease and a low birthrate combined to keep the Native population of Stockbridge relatively constant while the English population expanded by leaps and bounds.[12] In 1744 the town voted to separate into Indian and English portions (Mandell 33, 24), and separate constables for Whites and Indians were elected beginning in 1747. The town map thus finally marked a reality that had been developing for years: distinct populations with divergent needs and desires. Mandell points out that "though the Indians formed a majority of the populace until well past 1758, the colonists gained a clear political supremacy in 1746" (24). The French and Indian War of 1754 proved disastrous for Stockbridge Indians both in terms of casualties and economics (Brasser 36), and in 1765 the general court granted Indians permission to sell their land to pay off debts. The result was dramatic; in 1766 land sales from Indians to Whites increased almost 500 percent (Mandell 43). And just as the town gradually shifted into the hands of White settlers, so the church was transformed from a mission station to an Anglo-American community church that no longer focused on its original Native members. Although records indicate that Natives were active in the Stockbridge church through the 1780's,[13] after Sergeant's death in 1749 statistics on church membership show a clear shift in priorities from Native conversion to tending the Anglo-American Christian community. According to Charles Webster, Sergeant admitted to Church membership "50 or 60 Indians and 12–15 English persons during his ministry" (6). Though his successor Jonathan Edwards left an unclear legacy, Stephen West, who followed Edwards, admitted 504 people to church membership, among whom only twenty-two were Indians (6).[14] In fact, in 1773 West officially abdicated his role as minister to the Mahicans, giving this position to John Sergeant Jr., son of the original missionary (and the only churchman since his father to learn the Native language of his congregation).[15] After fighting alongside the colonists again in the American Revolution, the Indians returned to find their land settled by squatters; they almost immediately accepted an offer from the Oneida in upstate New

York to settle there (Mandell 29), abandoning to Anglo-Americans what had once been promised to them as their own town.

As if clearing the slate and starting again without the presence of Anglo-Americans, the Indians settled in New Stockbridge in the midst of existing Native settlements. Stockbridge had been founded on six miles square, which the Massachusetts legislature had officially given to the Housatonic Indians in 1735 (Field 240); in 1784 New Stockbridge was founded on six square miles in upstate New York, given to the Stockbridge Indians by the Oneida tribe. Established on land within the Oneida reservation, New Stockbridge was adjacent to yet another Native Christian group called the Brotherton Indians, whose stated purpose was to establish a community of Native Christians away from the encroachments of White settlers. But the settlement in New York was to prove no more successful than that in Massachusetts. The Native population became divided over a series of issues, one being the choice of minister for the community, and another being the role of agriculture in the settlement.[16] In 1818 seventy-five Stockbridge Indians left for Indiana, accompanied by some of the Brotherton Indians; in 1822–23 the rest followed. In 1832 the group moved to Wisconsin, and in 1839 they sold some of their land there to allow traditionalists to move to Kansas. Many didn't survive the trip, and those who did were enveloped by the Kansas Native population. In 1856 the Wisconsin group moved again, eventually settling in Green Bay where their descendants still live today.

## John Sergeant's Captivity Narrative

Hopkins's *Historical Memoirs* reveals much of John Sergeant's struggle with missionary life and Native Americans and his contending impulses toward wealth and status as opposed to poverty and sacrifice as he begins his work while still at Yale and eventually settles into marriage and family life. Sergeant's fragmentary journals trace an evolving relationship between Anglo-American settlers and Native converts in the community, as his almost complete dependence on the good will of his Native converts gives way to his increased stature in the community and his alliance with the powerful Williams clan.

Sergeant's narrative of his life and work involves a complex engagement with the language of captivity, which circulates around the Stockbridge mission and gives Sergeant a means through which to give coherence to his life and his place in the community. By selectively appropriating the language of the captivity narrative—which in this period had become immensely popular—Sergeant structures the relationship between Native Christians and Anglo-Americans that he sees emerging at Stockbridge as an oppositional one. At the same time, through his rather unusual decision to reconfigure himself as a captive rather than as a missionary, he reveals his anxieties about his own powerful position in the community.

Sergeant's use of the captivity trope gives widely recognizable meaning to his personal suffering. Several critics have suggested that through Puritan captivity narratives, such Biblical precedents as the Babylonian captivity, Job's sufferings, and the parable of the prodigal son were adapted to a particularly American experience (Slotkin 101–3). In fact, Slotkin suggests, "By the late 1740's the captivities had become so much a part of the New England way of thinking that they provided a symbolic vocabulary" readily available to the general public (96–97). For Sergeant, captivity provided a way to represent place and to connect the history of Stockbridge to an extensive (and comfortingly familiar) Western tradition. In a journal entry from September 1734 Sergeant uses the language of captivity to give his sacrifice the character of Protestant martyrdom: "I was sensible I must not only lose a great many agreeable amusements of life, especially in leaving my business at College, which was the most agreeable to me that could be, but also to expose myself to many fatigues and hardships, and I know not to what dangers, among a barbarous people" (Hopkins 20). The notion of sacrifice and suffering implies a moral superiority over those who are the agents of his suffering, and suffering itself brings him the assurance of God's love in a way that can never be felt in the comforts and pleasure of college life. This moment in the text suggests a strong connection between the missionary experience and the trauma of captivity: both the missionary and the captive struggle in isolation to maintain their moral and spiritual superiority over the strangely seductive Natives who surround them, and both sacrifice bodily comfort for a greater spiritual good.

Captivity and its connection to missionizing are central to Stockbridge's existence. The community had been conceived by its Anglo-American founders as a buffer against the captive-taking by the French and their Native allies, and the Housatonic Mahicans' conversion to Protestantism made this buffer possible. More specifically, the negotiations that preceded the founding of Stockbridge were conducted by Stephen Williams, who

had himself been a captive several years before with his father, Puritan minister John Williams, in New France.[17] In a letter published in Boston, Stephen Williams evokes his own captivity as a central cause of his interest in
the founding of Stockbridge, explaining, "[Stockbridge] has cost me, with
the other Ministers, some hundreds of Miles travel." He continues, "I have
been solicitous for the Welfare of the poor Heathen, ever since I was a
Prisoner with them, and have with Concern observed the little prospect
there has been of bringing any of them to receive the Protestant Religion,
by our Missionaries at the Forts, where the Indians make but short stays,
and are either drunk or busy about their Trade, all the while they tarry"
("A Letter" vii). This moment when Williams inverts his own captivity is
compelling. As with the journey he endured as a boy, he has traveled hundreds of miles because of the Natives. Unlike the forced march of his childhood, however, as an adult his journey takes place of his own free will. In
this case, Williams can afford to have pity on all Indians, which he characterizes as "poor Heathen[s]" who are either too drunk or too busy to "receive the Protestant Religion" that would be the source of their redemption. If as a child his life depended on the Natives who controlled his fate
completely, as an adult Williams has redefined Natives as poor and weak
figures deserving only pity from powerful, active men like himself. Williams has inverted the earlier relationship between himself and his captors;
as an adult he is solicitous of their welfare as he "redeems" them from their
ignorance. Williams's captivity as a child is thus rhetorically redefined
through his paternalistic actions as a minister willing to save the "heathens"
from their own religious captivity.

Though Williams can redefine his own captivity, he cannot erase his
younger sister's marriage to a Mohawk, a relationship the entire Williams
family characterizes as a continuation of her childhood captivity. This relationship haunts the early years of the Stockbridge mission, and even as late
as 1741 Sergeant writes a letter to Williams which highlights the reality of
captivity in the daily existence of the community. He begins, "I congratulate you on the second visit of your Captive sister, by whom I write this. I
pray it may be the pleasure of the most High to restore her now to you."[18]
He continues, "When I was at Newark Mr. John Richards enquired of me
after his captive Sister, and desired me to use what endeavours I could that
she might be persuaded to make a visit to New England, or at least to

Albany, that he might have opportunity to see her" (July 24, 1741 STL).[19] As Eunice Williams stands before him, a grown woman who has thoroughly adopted Mohawk cultural traditions, Sergeant writes a letter about her for her to carry to her brother, in which he seeks further information about another captive. This letter locates Stockbridge as an intermediate place from the perspective of New England—somewhere between the "savagery" of New France and its Mohawk population and the settled New England Puritan center. Both as a lived experience for the founders of Stockbridge and as a rhetorical tool in the battle to save souls throughout New England, the language of captivity surrounds Sergeant and finds its way into his own writings as he explores his own history and the history of Stockbridge.

For example, captivity is eroticized and inverted in Sergeant's letters to and about the women he loves. Before Sergeant married Abigail Williams in 1739, he had an extended but ultimately futile two-year courtship with Hannah Edwards, a sister of Jonathan Edwards. In his letters to her he evokes his own potential captivity at the hands of Native Americans, setting them beside his captivating love for her. He confides to Hannah, "I am more than ever I was before convinced of the mighty power of Love. One would have tho't, the wildness of this country, the Savage manners of the people, that inhabit it . . . would have banishd from my breast the soft & tender passion, the tempting pains & pleasing anxieties of love. But so it has happened, ever since I saw you last, a certain uneasiness (which I suppose is what they call love, has attended me which I neither can, nor am willing to get rid of" (July 28, 1735 BL). In this version of captivity he is invulnerable to the "Savage manners of the people" but overcome by love. Through Sergeant's juxtaposition of love and savagery, Stockbridge is again distanced from the New England center. But Sergeant rewrites the fear of savagery by placing his own danger not in the hands of Indians, but in the hands of his lover. Whether captivity occurs through his lover or through Indians, however, Sergeant defines himself as the victim rather than the aggressor. As such, he sees himself as the helpless captive whose purity and moral superiority are constantly embattled. A playful letter the following year makes the relationship between sexual and racial captivity more explicit. Sergeant writes to an unidentified friend in a letter dated March 1, 1736:

> Our Indians are this week gone out to make sugar. Mr. Woodbridge & I
> design to go out to them next day after tomorrow: & live with them, till
> they return if we can hold it out. Perhaps we shall be so taken with them
> and their way of living, that we shall take each of us a wife from amongst, &
> sadly disappoint all other fair ones that may have any expectations from us
> and indeed I am almost of opinion this will be our wisest course; lest if we
> don't disappoint them they will us.[20]

In this letter Sergeant explores the specter of "going Native." As in his
earlier letter, he elides love or sexual union and crossing cultures. Here
Sergeant plays on the multiple meanings of the word "taken"; he begins by
suggesting that he and Woodbridge will be "taken" by Indians, implying
both a physical captivity and an enchantment or fascination with them.
Then he suggests they will each "take . . . a wife," suggestive of both sexual
and sacramental union. His final comment also inverts the apparent source
of trouble, since any suggestion of danger comes primarily from disap-
pointed New England ladies rather than from the wilderness of Stockbridge.

As Sergeant imagines marriage with a Native wife, Anglo-American culture remains dominant. The ideological underpinnings of this rhetorical
strategy are clear: the missionary appropriation of all things Native is re-
inscribed as a relationship in which the woman/Indian willingly—even
lovingly—gives over her heart and soul as well as her wealth and property
to her husband/colonist. Eunice Williams, however, was the tragic inversion of the situation, since she had gone over to her husband's people and
was no longer a member of Puritan colonial society. While Eunice Williams had become a cultural symbol of loss and tragedy for the Anglo-
American community, for Sergeant, captivity and intermarriage are ideas
to be toyed with, not serious threats to his identity as a relatively privileged,
educated White male. His hypothetical position as a victim of captivity is
fluid; even as a victim he would retain the power to make choices and
direct his own life and the lives of others. Indeed, his comments suggest
that the chief pleasure of going Native would be to disappoint the "fair
ones" who threaten constantly to disappoint him. Thus even in his vic-
timhood he retains a great degree of control; what he gains from a perceived captivity is the moral authority over those who have victimized him.

Rather than consistently suggesting the kind of power relations that
characterize a captivity narrative, in which the central figure is the weak,

fragile victim, at times Sergeant's imagery points instead to the power of the missionary as the central figure whose goal is to radically alter the epistemology of his converts. We find out, for example, that the Indians decide to disrupt their own communities to move to a spot that would be more convenient for their missionary (Hopkins 23). And in a letter from Yale, where he is finishing his degree, Sergeant writes to his Indian converts, "When I had heard that you concluded, in your late general meeting, to embrace Christianity, it was more pleasing to me than cold water to a thirsty man in the heat of summer, or a plentiful meal to one almost starv'd with hunger, or good success to one who has hunted a good while in vain" (Hopkins 37). His imagery of hunting and eating is most revealing. If Sergeant is the consumer, then the Natives are objects to be consumed. These images point to Sergeant's power, and suggest his ability to dominate the Native population. In fact, throughout his letters and journals Sergeant vacillates between two ways of defining his situation as he explores the limits of his own power.

Like the writers of captivity narratives before him, Sergeant defines himself in opposition to the exotic habits of the Natives around him. He dismisses the "Notions, Customs, and Manners of their Nation" as "sundry childish and ridiculous things" (Hopkins 24). David Sewell points out the power dynamics of such comments: though the captive may have to endure moments of physical or emotional discomfort at the hands of Native Americans, he or she ultimately can claim "linguistic victory" over his or her captors by controlling the terms of the story: "The captive transforms a brute experience . . . into a narrative where the Indian is verbally created, described, and judged, always subject to his former prisoner's interpretation of events" (42–43). By ridiculing the traditions of the tribe he has come to live with, Sergeant maintains his own superiority and, perhaps more important, marks his continued alliance with Anglo-American culture. He may live with the Mahicans, his comments seem to suggest, but he is hardly one of them. The traditions by which they live remain to him utterly foreign. With such judgments, the language of captivity with which Sergeant is so comfortable seems to shift to the language of missionary control. He dismissively describes another situation he has been apprised of in which Natives unthinkingly adhere to tradition: "There is a large heap of stones, I suppose ten cart-loads . . . which the Indians have thrown together as they have pass'd by the place; for it us'd to be their custom, every time any one pass'd by, to throw a stone upon it. But what was the end of it they cannot tell; only they say their fathers us'd to do so, and they do it because it was the custom of their fathers" (Hopkins 24). For Sergeant, the Mahicans' obedience to "the custom of their fathers" is childish. To emphasize this point, he continues, "These things Ebenezer told me . . . which are such childish fables that I had not taken notice of them, had it not been that they believ'd them, as childish as they are; which shows us how easily men brought up in ignorance are impos'd upon, and should methinks excite us the more to pity them" (Hopkins 24–25). If the Mahicans are childish, Sergeant suggests, his own ability to see the foolishness of such beliefs makes him paternally responsible for their welfare.

Sergeant records his alienation from the Native community and his redemption from his rhetorical captivity not through his own return homeward, but rather through his transformation of Stockbridge into a place he can identify as his home. While maintaining for himself the position of the victimized figure, Sergeant creates a sense of fear and anxiety in the Stockbridge Indians that reaffirms his own sense of cultural superiority. Even before they have grasped much of Christianity, Sergeant emphasizes to his converts their cultural inadequacy and their personal responsibility for overcoming that inadequacy by becoming more Anglicized. In a letter to Stephen Williams in 1735, Sergeant paternalistically reports: "They said they were sorry and ashamed of their former vices; and were resolved to live in obedience to the laws of christianity for the future for they heartily approved of them: and could not be easy till they had profesed themselves Christians, and taken the obligations of xtianity upon them by baptism" (November 28, 1735 STL). Only through a complete sense of their own inadequacy can Natives be properly Christianized.

For Sergeant, the particular practices and beliefs of Congregationalist Protestantism that he transmits to his converts is central to his English identity and to his sense of what kind of place Stockbridge should be. When his friend and colleague Timothy Woodbridge sees the newly converted Natives conducting a powwow to their new Christian God, we can assume that Sergeant would have responded with the same horror. In their attempt to bring Christianity fully into their lives, the Natives follow their own traditions of worship, drawing Woodbridge unknowingly into a ceremony that is utterly foreign to him. He writes, "I asked them, if they were willing I should be present to see their Devotion? And, before they gave me an Answer, the oldest *Priest* lift up his Eyes towards Heaven, and spake very earnestly; after which they told me I might be there" (Hopkins 36). Immediately, then, Woodbridge's authority is undermined, since the priest seems to speak directly to God. And what follows horrifies Woodbridge even more. The Indians present "began rapping their Sticks, and singing" for about an hour, after which "the *Priest* rose up, and threw off all his Cloaths, except the Flap that cover'd his Nakedness: and then, naked, pass'd from one End of the *Wigwam* to the other, with his Eyes fast shut, seeming to be in the utmost Agony; used all the frightful Motions and distorted Gestures imaginable" (ibid.). Woodbridge acts quickly. "I inform'd them that God was not to be worship'd in such a manner." But some Natives protested, saying "they knew no harm in it—they made their application to the great God, and to no other" (ibid.). Woodbridge then reports, "When I had instructed them as well as I could, they resolv'd never to do so any more." Furthermore, and much to his satisfaction, "Those of them who had been best taught were much troubled, that they had taken so wrong a step" (ibid.). Both Sergeant and Woodbridge condemn the Natives for making Christianity unfamiliar to their English sensibilities. If Natives are to become properly Christian, they must reject the dramatic "customs of their fathers" and instead adopt the more sedate practices of their Anglo-American fathers—men like Sergeant who considered their culture "childish."

Not surprisingly, the task of turning Indians into Englishmen turns out to be a complicated one for Sergeant. He grouses in 1741, "You will easily perceive in the perusal of this *Journal* that the Indians are a very difficult people to deal with; whoever undertakes to have much to do with them had need to fortify himself with an obstinate patience. Opposition I always expected, but met with it in instances where I dreamed not of it, and least expected it" (98–99). And in a letter to a benefactor, he bitterly explains his lack of success by blaming the Natives. "The truth is," he says, "the Indians are perhaps as fickle and irresolute in their determinations as any people in the world; and when they seem to be wholly recovered from their vice, easily relapse into their foolish and wicked national habits" (138). Ironically, when Sergeant fails in his attempt to change Indian "national habits," he explains this through the changeableness of Indians. To him, only English practices have stability and weight, and the Indians' failure to adopt them confirms at once their inferiority and their otherness.

But though Natives are "fickle" and "difficult," the children of the Natives seem particularly bright and full of potential to Sergeant. Early in his ministry he writes to the commissioners of the Society for the Propagation of the Gospel that "if I do not judge amiss the Indian children excell the generality of ours in pregnancy of parts and good humour." He continues enthusiastically, "I am sure I could not have found an English school anywhere that would have pleas'd me so much" (31). It is through these children that Sergeant sees the possibility of Native redemption. He reports to Stephen Williams in 1742, "I have for some time had tho'ts and now almost come to a resolution to undertake it, if God spare my life, to set a free School for the Education of the Indian Children" (February 14 STL). This school, in his mind, would go even further than the local school set up by Timothy Woodbridge. As his vision for his school expands, he eventually publishes a plan for the education of Native children that calls for the total eradication of all that marks them as Native.[21] Through Sergeant's comments on education we see the rhetoric of captivity inverting itself in the starkest manner. His anxieties about losing his own culture surface most explicitly through his plan to transform Native children; if Sergeant once feared the possibility of "going Native," through his boarding school he proposes "to *root out* their vicious Habits, and to change their whole Way of Living" (*A Letter* 5). If he once felt himself the isolated victim of strange people with foreign customs, he proposes much the same isolation for Native children in his plan to separate children from their families and communities and place them in his boarding school to be supervised by two masters—"one to take the Oversight of them in their Hours of *Labour,* and the other in their Hours of *Study*" (4). His quest to redeem himself as a captive to the strangeness of this exotic culture involves the relentless policing of Native culture to keep it in line with English practice. In other words, the process of making Stockbridge his home involves erasing all marks of Nativeness from the Natives themselves.

Patrick Frazier, a historian of the Stockbridge Indians, has suggested that by the end of his life Sergeant "may have become somewhat discouraged by the erratic moral progress of his mission, or he may have become distracted by his own secular progress" (67). In fact, Sergeant's last will and testament includes no mention of Native Americans or even of his life as a missionary, but instead reads like the will of any reasonably prosperous young Englishman with a wife and family among whom to divide his estate. Sergeant spent his life working through ways in which Christianity could best be brought to the Native population of Stockbridge; his conclusion seems to have been that this could occur only through the obliteration of all that was Native.

## Native Voices of Dissent

As they accepted missionaries into their community, one generation of Mahicans witnessed overwhelming changes in most facets of their life— material culture, religion, subsistence activities, and political organization. Unfortunately for us, however, that generation of Natives was not alphabetically literate, and the only existing record of the mission at Stockbridge is written by Anglo-Americans such as Sergeant and Hopkins. Although biased, this record does provide important information about Native responses to Christianity and an increased settler presence in their territory, and through it we see the costs involved in the Mahican acceptance of Christianity. Though Sergeant imagined himself as a captive, others expressed their growing concerns differently. In particular, Umpachenee, a Native leader of the Housatunnuk Indians, developed his own ambivalent relationship to the evolving Stockbridge community. Sergeant's journal record of Umpachenee's battle with alcohol points to some of the tensions inherent in missionary records of Native actions. Sergeant constructs Umpachenee's drinking not only as a community crisis but also as a crisis point in the relationship between the missionary and his Native convert. His journal provides one interpretation of the unfolding events of Umpachenee's life, but it also shows Umpachenee himself, without ever picking up a pen, recording his own version of the history and meaning of the Stockbridge community.

Though Sergeant clearly admires Umpachenee, his flattering description of "the Lieutenant," as he is called, is not unqualified: "The Lieutenant is a clear-headed, smart man, of a deep reach, and pleasant humour, and is one of the best speakers we hear; is free in conversation and talks excellently well. He . . . shews great compassion towards the rest of the Indians and seems heartily to lament their miserable condition . . . *And tho' he is reckon'd somewhat haughty, yet always shews himself modest and teachable enough*" (Hopkins 46–47; italics added). From their initial encounter, then, Umpachenee's character contains puzzling contradictions that elude Sergeant's understanding.

From the start Umpachenee seems to have been suspicious of the claims of the English and reluctant to trust them, and throughout the record of Stockbridge there are signs of his continued resistance to English influence. Umpachenee does not go to Sergeant's ordination (Frazier 35), and although reasons for his absence remain unclear, it perhaps indicates his ambivalence toward rapidly expanding Christian influence. Sergeant does eventually baptize the Lieutenant and his family, but only after convincing himself that Umpachenee has become dramatically altered: "From this time he seems to have had a new heart given him" (Hopkins 46). Unlike Konkapot, another Native leader, Umpachenee in his natural state is hardly a suitable candidate for Christianity, but instead must undergo transformation.[22]

Though Sergeant is convinced that conversion has changed Umpachenee's heart, it does not seem to have lessened the Native leader's suspicions about the English. In a meeting on April 20, 1736, with several commissioners of the Massachusetts court, Umpachenee expresses his concerns for the material well-being of his people. He explains that he is himself Christian and happy of it, but "there were two or three things which appear'd dark in his eyes. He wonder'd they had been neglected so long, and desir's to know the true spring of the great favour so suddenly shown them" (59).[23] He continues: "If it was from love and good will towards them, he for his part accepted it with thankfulness; but possibly there might be some secret spring and moving cause he was not acquainted with, that might lessen their obligations to gratitude" (59). The first agreement between Massachusetts and the Mahicans had taken place in 1720, and for fourteen years the Natives were largely ignored. Umpachenee suspects that the town of Stockbridge was set up primarily as an excuse to steal the Natives' land. He is most concerned about the practical implications of Christianity for his people, and though he is "well satisfied with the truth of the Christian religion so far as he understood it" (59), he does not trust the motives of the English in bringing this religion to his people. Unable to separate English actions and beliefs, Umpachenee ultimately rejects their religion.

One of the most significant concerns of Natives such as Umpachenee was that through Christianity their liberty might be curtailed, and Dutch colonists manipulated this concern to aggravate the English usurpers. In December 1734 Sergeant finds that the audience for his lectures on Christianity has fallen off significantly with the arrival of Dutch traders. He reports bitterly that "these traders tell them that the religion we are about to teach them is not a good one; that we design in the end to serve ourselves by them, to make slaves of them and their children—and the like" (28).[24] The Indians were deeply troubled by this claim, which reinforced their suspicions about the English. Sergeant explains: "Upon these insinuations I understood some of the Indians were very much disgusted and affronted; that the Lieutenant was out of humour [and] that his brother especially was in a great passion" (28). Cautious about the potential outcome of the emerging relationship between themselves and the English, the Natives— and most especially Umpachenee—were very vulnerable to suggestions that their independence was at stake.

The Natives of Stockbridge saw a clear opposition between liberty and slavery, and with the example of the enslavement of African Americans always before them they were wary of any attempts by Anglo-Americans to curb their freedom. Thus when a Dutch tavernkeeper blamed Ephraim Williams, the major landholder in the area, for curbing the Natives' freedom to drink through various town mandates, Natives were deeply concerned—especially when this tavernkeeper spread rumors among the Indians that this was part of a larger plot by the English to destroy them. According to Sergeant, the tavernkeeper told the Indians that "Capt Williams desir'd to gain the Mastery over them all, & govern them as he pleased; that as their liberty in this matter was abridged by him, they might expect the same in other things by degrees, till they were entirely enslaved" (28). Any attempt to limit freedom was treated with alarm by Natives, but Anglo-American attempts to limit Native drinking were particularly problematic.

For missionaries the link between alcohol consumption and freedom was largely negative. In particular they were appalled by what they perceived as the Natives' lack of restraint. Such "liberty" suggested a freedom from responsibility, or what missionaries characterized as a dangerous lack of control. Thus eighteenth-century educator Eleazar Wheelock writes disdainfully of the "ungovernable appetites" of Native drinkers, which are "unbounded" and "admit [no] restraints" (*Continuation* 1771 23). Peter Mancall suggests in his study of Native American drinking patterns in early America that it was not the amount of alcohol that Indians consumed that disturbed Anglo-Americans but instead the resultant "chaos"; Mancall points out that Natives never drank nearly as much as Anglo-Americans.[25]

It was drinking to reach inebriation that was the problem; Anglo-American observers believed that losing one's reason from alcohol consumption was a sign of weakness.[26] Or as John Sergeant says scornfully of his converts, "Indians . . . are not much more fond of Drinking, than of their Liberty, by which they understand an unbounded Licence to do whatever their Inclinations lead them to without any restraint at all" (Hopkins 91).

Paradoxically, the language of missionary disapproval is about both liberty and captivity. Indeed, through alcohol, the opposition between liberty and captivity is shattered: Natives are "captivated" by alcohol, but the result is unbounded freedom. In 1721 Cotton Mather wrote about this problem: "But what has of all things the most Threatening Aspect upon them, is, The love of *Strong Drink,* which strangely Captivates the *Indians;* insomuch that *very few* are found Able wholly to resist and conquer the Temptation, when 'tis laid before them" (*India Christiana* 41). And the "Attestation by the United Ministers of Boston" for Experience Mayhew's 1727 *Indian Converts,* which may well have been written by Mather as well, repeats the image of captivity: "What has the worst Aspect of all upon them is, the Love of intoxicating Liquors, which marvellously captivates them, and bewitches them" (xvii). This paradoxical concern over "unbounded licence" and the captivating power of alcohol illuminates the missionary anxiety over Native drinking. The disruption, the disordering of the natural state of things, is the source of tension: missionaries, whether disruption is characterized as captivity or liberty, it is precisely the lack of control that is threatening. The figure of the drunken Indian works rhetorically and ideologically as a threatening and disruptive element that must constantly be repressed, or controlled, but nevertheless constantly emerges. Over and over in documents by and about Christian Indians we see the recurring figure of the drunken Indian. The struggle to eliminate Native drinking becomes the centerpiece of many missionary documents.[27]

Though missionaries saw excessive drinking as a cultural trait of Native Americans, it was also connected to Anglo-American culture in many ways. As Mancall points out, trade with Anglo-Americans is the primary relationship through which Natives acquire alcohol. And as a passage in Sergeant's journal suggests, for at least some Natives drinking is also connected to early industrial projects such as mills and dams, which were central to the missionary attempt to convert Natives through work. Sergeant reports the dream of an Indian stranger, Maumauntissekun, who has come into Stockbridge to explore the possibility of conversion after his strange vision:

> being sent by some of his companions, designing a drunken frolick, to get some rum for that purpose, when he had obtain'd it, in his return he drank so freely of it, as to get drunk, and lying down to sleep, night came upon him, which proved to be so dark that when he awaked, he was lost & could not find the way to his companions; but presently heard a noise like the Pumping of water, and saw a great number of Indians lying drunk and naked, and cold nasty water pumping on them, while they were not able to get out of the way, and were in great distress; and heard a voice, which said to him that he must take notice of & avoid Such wickedness, being admonished by such a sight of wretchedness. This vision (as he call'd it) or dream perhaps, continued for some time, with a strong light shining about him. Then he heard a noise like the blowing of a pair of bellows; which was followed with a violent blast of wind, which dispersed the Indians into the air. (1739 BL)

In Maumauntissekun's vision, pumping water, the noise of bellows, and a violent blast of wind, which lead to the dispersal and destruction of Natives, are linked to community projects through which Native communities were to be "civilized" and "anglicized."[28] As he connects the effects of excessive drinking to the effects of such projects, he sees his own demise and that of his friends. His own interpretation of his dream leads him to conclude that he and his friends are to stop drinking to avoid their own dispersal, but the dream seems to point as well to the dangers involved in the Christian message of the missionaries.

The connection between alcohol and Christianity is further emphasized in a 1796 petition ascribed to the Stockbridge Indians. The petition expresses ambivalence about alcohol, described simultaneously as "our enemy" and a "strong Hero." It is unambivalent, however, about the destruction alcohol has caused: "Our ancestors were conquered immediately after you came over this island by the strong Hero, who does still reign among Indian tribes with tyranny; who has robbed us of everything precious in our eyes. By the power of our enemy, our eyes have been blinded, our young men seems become willing slaves to this despotic hero" (Jones 270). The idea that the young men become slaves to drink echoes the language of captivity that missionaries use to describe Native alcohol consumption. But the petition says that it is the responsibility of the English to control it: "He is your own begotten son, and his name you call Rum. And the names of his officers are Brandy, Wine and Gin, and we know you have power to control him" (ibid.). Characterizing rum as the "own begotten son" of the English, the petition links alcohol with Christ. And the petition sharply reminds the English that they have an obligation to control the effects of this "hero," as it is through their influence that he "reigns among Indian tribes." The passage emphasizes English fallibility since *their* "begotten son"—not Christ but rum—is a "despotic tyrant" who has robbed the Indians "of everything precious in [their] eyes." Explicitly connecting the role of alcohol with the spread of religion, the petition emphasizes the similarities between the two as effects of English colonization.

This connection between alcohol and Christianity for Native Americans is elaborated in Sergeant's journal. Sergeant explains that though the Lieutenant has always drunk on occasion, he invariably humbles himself afterwards "with a due appearance of seriousness, gravity, and resolution of better obedience for time to come" (Hopkins 76). But in 1739 Umpachenee starts drinking with more intensity than ever before.[29] The timing and intensity of Umpachenee's drinking bouts during this period suggest that rather than being a mere sign of personal weakness, they signal his disapproval of Sergeant and his mission. Nancy Lurie suggests that drinking has long been a political tool of Indians seeking to establish their identity as distinct from mainstream culture. By appropriating the negative stereotype of the "drunken Indian," Natives can define themselves as a group with political goals distinct from Anglo-American goals. Clearly aware of Sergeant's antipathy toward his occasional drinking, Umpachenee may have been expressing disapproval of Sergeant by rebelling against his rules. In the journal there is a sense that Umpachenee is directly challenging both Sergeant and Williams, as both men were involved in efforts to limit Native drinking in Stockbridge. Sergeant fined Indians who brought rum into town, and Ephraim Williams attempted to close down local tavernkeepers who sold rum to the Indians (Frazier 50–51; Jones 65). Umpachenee's continued drinking in the face of such blatant attempts limit Native drinking constitute a defiance of the Anglo-American community's authority to make decisions about his actions. By engaging in the behaviors that mark him as inadequate in terms of Sergeant's missionary goals, Umpachenee openly calls those goals into question, in the process challenging the very meaning and history of Stockbridge.

If Umpachenee is openly challenging Sergeant and his larger purpose, the missionary's journal does not suggest that Sergeant's own actions provoked such a challenge. In several pages devoted almost entirely to Umpachenee and his drinking, Sergeant does give several clues about his own complicity in exacerbating the situation—accusatory sermons, veiled threats, and open contempt for Umpachenee's behavior—but nonetheless proclaims his surprise and sense of personal betrayal at Umpachenee's behavior. Sergeant's version leaves only the tantalizing suggestion that there is more going on than initially meets the eye. For example, August and September are almost entirely unrecorded in his journal, despite their importance in his own life and in the life of the community. On August 16, 1739, a date that is unmentioned in the diary, John Sergeant married Abigail Williams, an event that Electa Jones, a nineteenth-century historian of Stockbridge, writes "was particularly gratifying to his people. Ninety Indians attended the wedding, and demeaned themselves with great gravity and propriety" (65). Popular legend, however, reflects that Abigail scorned the Native population, preferring the wealth and status of her father to the missionary labor of her husband.[30] Sergeant's marriage into the wealthiest family in Stockbridge marks his rise in English society and his commitment to the further Anglicization of the whole community. The marriage is not included in his journal, however; there is only one entry for the entire month of August, which mentions Umpachenee's decision to absent himself from Communion because of a recent bout of drinking. This entry concludes on the ominous note: "This was the beginning of his defection from his Steadfastness, which he has since carried to a great & unhappy length; and I fear will not end short of total and absolute apostasy."

This drinking bout occurs eleven days before Sergeant's marriage to the daughter of Ephraim Williams. Williams and Umpachenee had already had run-ins over land, and the Williams family was a source of tension in the Native community.[31] The wedding of their closest ally to the daughter of their antagonist surely cannot have been a happy moment for the Natives of Stockbridge. But Sergeant's journal evades this issue by omitting the wedding from the mission's history. The next entry in Sergeant's journal, on September 5, says, "Set out upon a visit to my friends in New Jersey." Although he does not mention it, this trip is undoubtedly to introduce his new bride to his family and friends from his home in New Jersey. Sergeant erases the events of his own life, thereby masking his own possible culpability in launching Umpachenee's drinking bout, and by doing so presents Umpachenee's behavior as irrational and unpredictable. When Umpachenee directs his anger toward Sergeant and his new father-in-law, Sergeant expresses surprise at the connection Umpachenee makes between himself and Williams. Returning to Stockbridge with his wife on October 20, Sergeant writes that in his absence "the Lieutenant degenerated further; had repeated his excessive drinking once or twice." He adds without explanation that the Lieutenant "grew much prejudiced against Capt Williams & me." The next day he reports, "The Lieutenant Still increased in his wickedness giving himself up to drinking, talking against me, and Capt Williams, & in general against the English; and throwing stumbling blocks in the Indians way." Having omitted his marriage from the record, Sergeant makes Umpachenee's complaints seem irrational. A month later Sergeant tries to approach Umpachenee directly about the problem, taking "sundry opportunities to talk with him, to no effect." He explains, "Tho' he would not pretend to justify his conduct, yet said, he had no heart to reform, but would insist upon it, that cap't Williams and I were the occasions of his Apostasy."

From this point on connections emerge among Umpachenee's drinking, Sergeant, and the mission. Sergeant sees Umpachenee's excessive drinking as a challenge to the order and regulation of Christian living, so he responds specifically as a minister from his pulpit: "In my preaching I reflected with some severity on what had lately happened, & represented to my auditory the dreadful consequences of Apostasy from the Christian faith." The Lieutenant, however, is unmoved by this apparent threat: "The Lieutenant, who was in a temper to cavel at everything, found great fault with what I said." The next week Sergeant writes, "Preach'd on the Subject of Excommunication. The Lieutenant was not at meeting; but pretended some body, that heard me, told him, that I said, incorrigible Sinners must by an act of authority be banish'd out of the place. His disposition is to cavel at everything." By February 17 Sergeant has begun to think more aggressively about taking action against Umpachenee. Yet he hesitates, saying that "upon his desire to have a little more time to consider, I put off proceeding against him." By March 27, however, Sergeant has lost his patience entirely. He reports: "Attended the Publick fast. at this the Lieutenant cavell'd, as he has a disposition to find fault with everything & seems bent to do all the mischief he can." He continues, "As there appears no hope of his reformation, I suppose, we must be obliged to proceed against him with the utmost rigour of ecclesiastical Authority: which, what effect it will have, God knows." Sergeant defends himself from any implication of wrongdoing: "I have taken a great deal of pains with him in a private way to reform him; but as far as yet appears without any good effect," and he concludes bitterly, "I believe he will be finally lost . . . it is to be hoped, he will do less mischief under the character of a known & censured apostate, than of an hypocritical professour."

From the beginning of the section on drinking to the end, Sergeant has attempted to erase his own complicity in the situation. Shifting from defensive silence to wounded pride to anger against Umpachenee, Sergeant not only ignores his own role in Umpachenee's downfall but suggests that Umpachenee is the one who is threatening the well-being of his people. Sergeant reports: "Thro the Lieutenant's example (whose influence is very great among the Indians) drunkenness prevailed to an unusual degree." By February, Sergeant's tone has shifted to open irritation. He reports: "Preach'd as usual. The Lieutenant was all this week drunk; and gave the utmost disturbance to his own family and neighbours; as he is the most turbulent [illegible] in the world, when in Liquor; for his natural haughtiness then breaks forth without any restraint." By accusing Umpachenee of such personality flaws, Sergeant deflects Umpachenee's criticism and comforts himself. Eventually, Sergeant can no longer disguise his frustration with the perennially drunk Umpachenee, and works himself into a moral outrage over the Indian's "betrayal" of his people.

While alcohol has "captivated" Umpachenee, Sergeant is strangely captivated by the problem of Umpachenee's drinking. In page after page of his journal, Sergeant writes obsessively about Umpachenee's condition. Laura Murray points out that "a white person in charge of publication or dissemination can make an Indian text into something very much like a confession by remaining silent about his or her involvement in the material, when in fact the Indian who spoke or wrote it meant it to be an argument, a meditation, part of a dialogue, or a protest" (35). Though Umpachenee's drinking is not strictly speaking a text, Sergeant's detailed journal descriptions do attempt to reshape Umpachenee's actions into a properly "readable" narrative of a single Indian's tragic descent into religious and cultural apostasy. Despite his attempt to control the narrative of Umpachenee's downfall, however, Sergeant cannot fully avoid his own complicity in the situation. By returning to the problem time after time, Sergeant emphasizes the ways in which alcohol and Christianity are both part of the simultaneously "liberating" and "captivating" message of Anglo-America.

Eventually, Sergeant is able to write to his friend Stephen Williams:

> My success in the Grace of GOD has of late been more visible than ever since the first year or two of my being employed in this service. Sundry persons seem to have been very effectually wrought upon and become Obedient to the faith by a more than common realizing sense of Divine things, and an almost universal reformation of manners has prevailed. Many notorious drunkards seem entirely to have broke off from their beloved strong Drink, and of their own accord and some the most unlikely to human appearance have resolved to taste no more strong drink, among whom the Lieun is one and is again reconciled to our conversion, and we begin to conceive good hopes of him, tho we are not altogeather without fears. (February 14, 1742 STL)

Apparently Umpachenee's faith did return: Hopkins reports that Umpachenee "recover'd from his apostacy; confess'd his wickedness, was resolv'd to charity, and walk'd orderly to the day of his death, which was August 10, 1751" (171).[32] Was this return to Christianity an acknowledgment of Anglo-American control? Was it an attempt to integrate Christianity into a staunchly Native sense of the world? Or was it simply a personal change of heart based on individual factors no longer accessible to us? His reenclosure within the Christian fold—real or imagined by Hopkins and Sergeant—garners little of the notice his apostasy received. As a drunk he is fascinating; as a Christian he is worth only a single sentence. With only his transgression giving voice to his version of Stockbridge's history, Umpachenee's final actions remain unknowable to us; with his return to the fold, his life disappears from the writing of Stockbridge.

Nancy Lurie and others have pointed out that drinking as a form of protest is a dangerous game. She says, "The tragedy is that the Indian protest has been so prolonged that in some cases it becomes a way of life with disastrous consequences for the people concerned" (331). Indeed, if Umpachenee's drinking can be characterized as a gesture of protest, it seems to have been a futile one. Rather than bringing attention to a situation he objected to, Umpachenee's drinking was perceived as a personal weakness, and he became a burden not only to the minister who offended him so deeply but to his own family. But his struggle with alcohol, however personally devastating, does point to a community crisis whose existence is gestured toward but never fully grasped by Sergeant as he records its effects. As one modern observer points out, "Alcohol or alcoholism is *not* the problem. Neither is it *the* greatest problem facing native people today. Alcoholism is just a symptom of the fundamental problems facing native people" (Maracle 2). Umpachenee's drinking signaled a growing discontent with the situation in Stockbridge; to examine it without looking at the social and political circumstances surrounding it ultimately denies its larger significance.

## Stockbridge and New Stockbridge: Hendrick Aupaumut and the Place of Conversion

Umpachenee didn't have the literacy skills to record his view of the personal and cultural betrayal that Stockbridge represented, but Hendrick Aupaumut, one generation later, did, and the story he tells is at least as tormented and ambivalent as that protest Umpachenee waged through alcohol. As an emissary for the newly formed American government and as a Native Christian sachem of the uprooted Mahican people, Aupaumut explicitly connects the history of Stockbridge with the broader narrative of an emerging national identity. Aupaumut's position as a literate eighteenth-century Native sachem, soldier, and political figure was unusual, and his writings reveal his sense of the troubled history of Native-White relations in the early republic. The hoped-for community of Anglo-American and Native Christians in Massachusetts collapsed within his lifetime, but the issues underlying Stockbridge's rise and fall—the problems of difference and cohabitation; the interplay between racial, national, and cultural identities; the politics of land use, social control, and deception; and the meaning of Christianity as both a religion and a cultural system—became pressing national concerns as the American government pushed toward its Native neighbors in the west. Through his various writings Aupaumut makes available to us his version of these issues.

Aupaumut's account of his journey to the western tribes and his history of the Mahicans can be read as an autoethnography through which he explores his own position as a Christian Indian with conflicting loyalties. One is a travel journal written to his superiors within the American government and the other is a fragmentary history of his tribe written for unclear reasons, but each connects the idea of home with a sense of communal and personal identity that is specifically Mahican. The theme of placelessness at the center of both documents expresses the position of Christianized Natives who are peripheral in certain ways to both Native and Anglo-American cultural systems. Primarily about Aupaumut's search for community, both documents are records of movement and migration, and they are both suffused with a nostalgia for home. Twice named after places they had lived (Muhekkunnuk, Stockbridge), the Mahicans had no land that was their own. Instead, Aupaumut grounds Mahican identity in past customs and traditions, a past into which Aupaumut inscribes Christianity. By merging Christianity with Native tradition, Aupaumut attempts to erase the tensions between Native identity and Anglo-American cultural traditions associated with Christianity. But if this erasure resolves the conflict for Aupaumut, it does little to improve his relations with other Natives who viewed his commitment to Anglo-American culture with suspicion.

Aupaumut was born in 1757, eight years after Sergeant's death and five years after Jonathan Edwards's arrival in Stockbridge as Sergeant's replacement. Probably a student of the elderly Timothy Woodbridge or his son, both of whom taught at the Stockbridge mission school during Aupaumut's youth, Aupaumut gained an education that emphasized the importance of reading and writing as opposed to the oral traditions of his people.[33] The years of Aupaumut's youth were a time of enormous change for Stockbridge's Native population. Though Mahicans had an extensive history of settlement along the Housatonic River, contact with Dutch and British colonists had depleted their population substantially; as remnant tribes joined the settlement at Stockbridge, various Native traditions merged with those of the Mahicans, producing a syncretic identity for Stockbridge Indians. Furthermore, as English colonists moved into the area, they challenged Native oral traditions by creating their own versions of Stockbridge history and by threatening Native land claims through an emphasis on written treaties and deeds. A member of an important Mahican family, Aupaumut was well versed in the oral traditions of his people; as Woodbridge's student he was comfortable with written language as well. Just as countless New England Christian Indians had before him, Aupaumut learned to adapt to competing systems of knowledge.

Not only was the Native population undergoing dramatic alterations, but relations between Anglo-American settlers and Native Americans were changing significantly as well. As Aupaumut grew up in Stockbridge, he witnessed English settlers shift from grudging recognition of a Native presence to open contempt and hostility toward his people. During his lifetime the town was officially divided into an Indian and a White settlement; the church employed two ministers, one for the Indians and one for the Whites; and land was rapidly passing into the hands of Anglo-Americans. And although his own school may not have been directly affected, the years of Aupaumut's early childhood were filled with troubling developments in the education of Natives at Stockbridge. The elder Sergeant's scheme for an Indian boarding school had barely been put into place at his death; it was left to be carried out by others who rapidly squandered charity funds on projects that had little to do with providing any sort of education for Native pupils. Far from being at the center of the town, the Native population had become little more than a source of ready income for the less scrupulous members of the White community who benefited from illegally gotten Indian land and questionable expenditures of missionary funds.[34] Even so, Aupaumut maintained friendships with White settlers from Stockbridge even after his people had left for New York. In a 1791 letter to Timothy Edwards, who lived in Stockbridge,[35] Aupaumut reminds him to "give my love to all my friends" and signs it "from your true friend" (STL). Clearly, whatever the political tensions were in Stockbridge, friendships between individuals persisted.[36] Aupaumut's sense of home was integrally connected to Stockbridge, Massachusetts.

At eighteen Aupaumut enlisted on the side of the colonists in the American Revolution. It seems clear that he was deeply committed to the American cause; he distinguished himself as a soldier and came to the attention of several officers during the war.[37] Between 1791 and 1793, Aupaumut was enlisted as a diplomat to the tribes along the Ohio River whose neutrality was crucial to the well-being of the emerging American nation.[38] The western tribes included the Shawnee, Miami, Delaware, Ottawa, Chippewa, Mingo, Potawatomi, Wyandot, Kikapoo, Wea, and Piankashaw, all of which had joined into a pan-Indian confederation allied with the British[39] and thus posed a significant threat to the newly formed American government, which wanted to avoid such losses as frontier battles had already inflicted and above all to avoid a full-blown war. Aupaumut's role, then, was to soothe the growing antagonisms among the American government, the western alliance, and the British, and to introduce the western tribes to the more conciliatory policy the Americans had recently adopted. The political goals of this trip proved untenable for the U.S. government since the tribes remained suspicious of the new American policy. But Aupaumut's record of these missions, particularly the last one, remains an important element of the story of Stockbridge as well as the larger story of Christian Indian identity when read in conjunction with his Mahican history.

As autoethnographies, both Aupaumut's 1792–93 journal of his diplomatic mission and his Mahican history were written for the benefit of his Anglo-American colleagues, and both are at once intensely personal and part of the larger record of his people. For Aupaumut, the expedition to the western tribes is inseparable from the history of his own tribe, and his actions cannot be judged separately from the broader context of that affiliation. He explains at the outset of his journal: "Before I proceed in the business I am upon, I think it would be necessary to give a short sketch what friendship and connections, our forefathers, and we, have had with the western tribes" ("Short Narration" 76). Aupaumut's reliability, he suggests, is the same as the reliability of his forefathers, and an understanding of past relationships will necessarily illuminate current ones. He refers to himself as "the Muhheuconneew," letting his tribal affiliation represent him, and says, "When I come to reflect in the path of my ancestors, the friendship and connections they have had with these western tribes, and my own feelings towards them, I conclude that I could acquaint them my best knowledge with regard of the dispositions, desires, and the might of the United States" (ibid.). His record of his negotiations as a Mahican is simultaneously about his own feelings and about the history of his tribe, as is his gradual coming to terms with the United States' betrayal of the Indian people he encounters. Because of the disillusionment written into the journal, the narrative takes on a distinct character that separates it from typical government documents.

The message of peace from the U.S. government to the western tribes that is at the center of Aupaumut's journal exemplifies the conflict facing Aupaumut. Beginning with a reference to itself as "the fifteen sachems of the United States" (93), the American government rhetorically presents itself as an alternative to the pan-Indian confederacy of the west, manipulating Native terminology as a way of ensuring its own credibility. Most significantly, the United States uses Aupaumut to represent its connection to Native Americans. The message Aupaumut reads to the western Indians reminds them that Aupaumut is "your own col[o]r" (93), and so, by implication, a living emblem of the congruence of the two powers. Then follows a set of equivalencies: the Indian confederacy should not listen to "flying birds" (rumors) because the American government does not; the American government never speaks to other nations deceitfully, just as the Indian confederacy does not; the American government loves its "children, women, young men and old parents" (94), just as the Indian confederacy does. By connecting love of family to a lack of political deceit, the government presents its current message as an unchangeable, universally recognizable truth.

But a message transcribed by Aupaumut to the U.S. government from Big Cat, a Delaware sachem, dismisses the American claim to truth. Big Cat lays out several rumors about the message of "the great men of the U.S.":

> They speak good words to Muhheconnuk [a reference to Aupaumut], but they did not speak so well to the Five Nations, and they speak contrary to the Big knives [frontier settlers and soldiers], that the Big knives may prepare for war and fall upon the Indians unawares; and the Presidend of the U.S. did declare that he claim from the mouth of the Miamie river on Lake Erie to its head from thence to the head of the Wabash river, and down the same to the mouth of it, and that he will by no means restored to the Indians. (124–25)

The new government, Big Cat suggests, has made new promises, and even promises that contradict each other. But until its actions support its words, its message of peace will carry little weight. He tells the government, "If you will lengthen your patience, and manifest your power in withdrawing the Big knives from the forts which stand on our land—then repeat your Message of peace to us. Then we will rise immediately, and exert ourselves to promote peace" (125). As an intermediary between the U.S. government and the western tribes, Aupaumut puts the weight of his own extensive traditional alliances behind the message of the Americans. But even as he speaks for the United States, assuring the other tribes that their message is sincere, by the end of his account it becomes clear that he is himself somewhat suspicious of the message he is carrying. As a Christian soldier and diplomat for the United States he has embraced the structures of Anglo-American culture, but he is nonetheless wary of the practices of the new government, which have not always benefited his people. Indeed, big promises and assurances of eternal alliance preceded his own people's expulsion from Stockbridge. The biggest problem as evidenced in his journal, then, is his own position—as an educated, Christian Stockbridge Indian, what are his allegiances?

Aupaumut answers this question for other Natives by reaching into the past and the traditions of his people to situate himself in the present. He writes down his words to the Delaware: "Our good fathers have left good customs, and path to go by, so that in all occasions we are to put each other in remembrance of the ancient Customs of our fathers as well as the friendship" (99). He refers to himself and his audience as "the poor remnant of our ancestors" (ibid.), a nod to the displacement and fragmentation of once substantial Indian peoples with the implication that those ancestors lived better and wiser lives. And he makes a point in his journal of proving that his Native audience agrees with him. He reports the words of a Delaware chief, which largely echo his own: "Our good ancestors did hand down to us a rule or path where we may walk" (87). The formality of the exchange that Aupaumut records between himself and the western tribes is based on their mutual acknowledgment of the past relationships. And Aupaumut stresses both to his Anglo-American readers and to his Native hosts that all his actions are in keeping with those of his ancestors (91). Thus when an Indian asks Aupaumut whether he supports Indian confederation, he replies, "It is a happy thing that we should maintain a Union. But to us it is not a new thing. For our good Ancestors, (who used to have compassion to each other,) many, many years ago, have agreed to this. And we, who are of their desendance, should not hisitate, or, as it were, ask one another whether we should like it. But we must always remind each other how our ancestors did agree on this subject, that we may never forgo that" (101). Aupaumut at once denies the newness of what he is proposing and presents consensus and agreement as foregone conclusions. Aupaumut's alliances with the western Indians are foreordained, he claims, since the past holds the key to all current decisions. Aupaumut avoids the history of Anglo-American betrayal and usurpation that is so vivid to all involved and instead restructures the interaction as one between Natives. In the process, he ignores the implications of his own anomalous position as both a Native speaker and a writer working for Anglo-Americans by representing himself and his message as having participated in an extensive Native past.

Throughout his travels Aupaumut is careful to maintain obligations established by tradition, and he records these obligations and his fulfillment of them throughout the journal. "It was the business of our fathers to go around the towns of these nations to renew agreements between them, and tell them many things which they discover among the white people in the east" (77–78); thus the diplomatic visits are not only U.S. business but his own. Over and over, as he enters a new village, he passes along news just as his ancestors did.[40] Aupaumut also carefully records the exchange of wampum which marks the importance of each occasion. He suggests that without wampum as a physical manifestation of the reciprocity and exchange that are integral to treaty negotiations, communication would collapse. In fact, when the British demand to see him at their fort, he refuses to go since, he explains, "I have not seen any token or Message in strings of wampom, or writing, nor Tobaco . . . I am not to regard empty messages" (106). Language without ritual, both in its oral form and in its physical manifestation through wampum, is meaningless for Aupaumut.

And in fact Aupaumut scrupulously follows Native rituals and traditions of treaty negotiation that connect tribes to one another. Scholars have noted the ceremonious, ritualized language and actions, the careful, deliberate replies, and the extended time periods that mark the negotiation of Native treaties,[41] and all of these are evident in Aupaumut's record. For example, he writes down the ritual acts and formal language of Tautpuhqtheet, the Delaware chief who welcomes him:

> I now wipe off your tears from your eyes and face that you may see clear. And since there has been so much wind on the way that the dust and every evil things did fill your ears, I will now put my hand and take away the dust from your ears, that you may hear plain—and also the heavy burden on your mind I now remove, that you may feel easy, and that you may contemplate some objects without burden. . . . You have waded thro many miry places and briers on your journey. I now wash your legs and wipe them clean, and I pull all briers which stick on your legs and feet—and then I take the nicest weesqui, which contains the pure oil, and put the same on your legs and feet that you may feel easy. (87–88)

He also records his own response, which echoes the welcoming address:

> As I come to you, when I beheld your face, I saw your tears flowing down, for the reason of much difficulties and crosses. I now put my hand on your face and wipe off your tears, so that you may see things clear, and that to a great distance. . . . Since there is so much wind, and much dust flying about,

your ears are stop'd, you are almost deaf. But I now stretch my hand and take away all the dust from your ears, that you may now hear. And I also put my hand and clean your throat, and take away all heavy burdens which now hangs on your mind, and cast it away, that you may now understand what is good for your children, and that you may have comfort. (88)

Aupaumut is clearly aware of appropriate ceremonial customs, and he invokes them to reinforce the traditions he shares with the "western Indians" as well as to signify their importance to himself. The ceremonies through which the tribes communicate are Iroquois, particularly the "words of condolence" from the Iroquois Deganawidah epic. The adoption by the Mahicans of elements of Iroquois ceremonial practices points to the interconnections among the various groups, which Aupaumut stresses throughout his narrative. For example, he begins his journal by detailing the nature of intertribal relationships in familial terms. Thus, he explains, the Delawares are "grandfathers" to the Mahicans, the Wyandots are their "Uncles," and the Ottawas, Chipewas, and Potowotamis are their "grandchildren" (77). These interconnections are maintained through ritual, and through ritual, home is no longer merely a geographical site but rather it becomes a constantly shifting space made familiar through repetition of language and through certain physical manifestations. In other words, ritual makes home available to displaced peoples through language, or more specifically through shared history.

As a leader of the Mahican tribe, Aupaumut intends to improve the lot of his own people by renewing ancient ties with other Native groups. His trip allows him to follow up on other tribes' promises of land and quite literally to find a home for himself and his people. He does not disguise this intention in his journal, writing his response on behalf of the Mahican people to a Munsee chief: "We rejoice to find that you have such concern for us as a nation—that you have reached our hand, and lead us to a place where you thought we may set down" (84). Aupaumut's quest for home thus takes multiple forms; in one sense it is the search for a geographically suitable site, while in another it is a search for the connection and familiarity made available through properly performed ritual. Through ritual even distant lands become familiar, and the Munsee offer of land to the Mahicans gives the familiarity of ritual a physical reality.

In working for the U.S. government, Aupaumut also maintains and even expands the traditional Mahican role as a diplomatic envoy.[42] Alan

Taylor emphasizes the mutually beneficial relationship Aupaumut was trying to develop with the United States: "On behalf of the Americans, he
offered to exercise his people's tradition of influence among the western
Indians. . . . In return, Aupaumut meant to strengthen that tradition by
acquiring, and sharing with his western contacts, information about and
influence among the American national leaders" (443–44). In his narrative
Aupaumut reminds his Anglo-American readers of his position as a Mahican. "Since the British and Amaricans lay down their hatchets," he writes,
"then my nation was forgotten. We never have had invitation to set in
Council with the white people . . . but last winter was the first time I had
invitation from the great man of the United States to attend Council in
Philladelphia" ("Short Narration" 92). As Aupaumut grasps the opportunity to reposition himself and his people, he addresses his own and his
people's search for the familiarity of home in a variety of ways.

While representing himself in the journal as a Mahican working to improve the situation of his own people, Aupaumut also claims to be improv-
ing the situation of all Natives. Gregory Dowd suggests that the post–
Revolutionary War period was the peak of pan-Indian unity. The alliance
of accommodationist and more radical or "nativist" forces, Dowd writes,
"produced the most united, independent Indian resistance in North American history" (93). In particular, he emphasizes that this Indian unity drew
on "developing notions of Indian identity and separateness from white
people" (103). Aupaumut clearly participates in this moment of pan-Indian
unity, although his position is ambiguous, as his journal reveals. He tells a
Shawnee council that his work is for "the welfare of our own colar" (91).
For Aupaumut, however, accommodation to the Americans would in the
long run be the most effective means to secure the future of all Natives, a
stance that puts him at odds with many other Native groups. Such ambi-
guity makes Aupaumut a fascinating figure, and it forces us to confront
our own assumptions about what determines nationalism, loyalty, and
integrity.

Aupaumut makes clear to his Anglo-American readers that they must
have the best interests of all Natives in mind. But his journal goes even
further, suggesting that Whites must always remember that they remain
peripheral to Native alliances. Aupaumut says this indirectly by including
an allied sachem's response to the British who inquire into the purpose of
Aupaumut's mission: "How came you to ask us such questions? Did you

ever see me at Detroit or Niagra, in your councils, and there to ask you where such and such white man come from? or what is his business? . . . Do you not know that we are upon our own Business? and that we have longed to see these our friends, who now come to us, and for which we rejoice?" (103). Although this retort is directed at the British, Aupaumut's inclusion of it in his journal suggests that he and his allies see Native needs as distinct from those of both the British and the Anglo-Americans. As a record intended for Anglo-American readers, Aupaumut's journal discreetly leaves out the details of what is vaguely characterized in this exchange as "our own Business."

As committed as Aupaumut may be to a pan-Indian alliance, because he has involved himself with the diplomatic forays of the American government he puts himself in the uncomfortable position of challenging the basis of the current pan-Indian confederacy. His claims on the part of the U.S. government to represent a better alliance necessarily disrupt the racialized character of the western confederacy and potentially his commitment to pan-Indian unity, especially since Aupaumut's connection to the U.S. government necessitates withholding information from his Native allies. For the Natives with whom he is negotiating, the various twists and turns of British and then American policy leave them deeply suspicious. Aupaumut records the words of a Shawnee speaker, who remembers an old message from the British that directly contradicts current diplomatic agreements. The speaker reports bitterly, "I could show the wampom of this speech" (104–5). Though the British may have used traditionally Native structures of diplomacy, those structures did not carry the same meanings for them, and so they were able to abandon their policy with ease. The western Indians have no reason to believe that the Americans will be any better; Aupaumut explains that "in these days some these nations seemed much stupified by reason of a thousand stories" (105). As a representative of the Americans and keeping a journal for their benefit, Aupaumut distances himself from other Natives by attempting to convince them that they are wrong about the Americans.

But while he records his alienation from other Natives, Aupaumut also records his growing disillusionment with the U.S. government. He reports to his superiors that he protected the reputation of the new government despite the specific examples of Anglo-American brutality and injustice that the western tribes described to him. He tells the western tribes that "the United Sachems [the U.S. government] will not speak wrong. Whatever they promise to Indians they will perform" (127). But in his final assessment of the journey, he sharply rebukes his Anglo-American superiors for their dishonesty, pointing out the evasive ways he was forced to address the arguments of the western Indians: "In all my arguments with these Indians, I have as it were oblige to say nothing with regard of the conduct of Yorkers, how they cheat my fathers, how they taken our lands Unjustly, and how my fathers were groaning as it were to their graves, in loseing their lands for nothing, although they were faithful friends to the whites. . . . I say had I mention these things to the Indians, it would agravate their prejudices against all white people" (128). By embedding his protest in a journal written specifically for Anglo-American government officials, a text he knows they will have to read and acknowledge, Aupaumut directly confronts Americans with their own duplicity.

This challenge to the American government becomes insistently personal for Aupaumut. He stresses that he has staked his own reputation and that of his entire nation on the actions and words of the United States. He tells Timothy Pickering, to whom the journal is addressed, that he has worked relentlessly for peace during the last two years. "I have as it were sacrifice all my own affairs, and my family, for the sake of peace," he reports, and "this last time have gone from home better than Eleven months, and have gone thro a hazardous journeys, and have suffered with sickness and hunger, and have left my Counsellors with the nations who are for peace, to promote peace and forward every means of peace while I am absent" (131). His sacrifice is not only personal, however. He concludes his journal by repeating his words to the western nations, which stress the connection between the American government's integrity and Aupaumut's as a Mahican: "Let us now look back in the path of our forefathers, and see whether you can find one single instance wherein, or how my ancestors or myself have deceived you, or led you one step astray. I say let us Look narrowly, to see whether you can find one bone of yours lay on the ground, by means of my deceitfulness, and I now declare that you cannot found such instance" (129). The words he has directed to his Native listeners have another meaning to the government he represents; rather than serving simply as a signal of his own integrity, they become a warning that there is no room in this interchange for deception. As Aupaumut links the American government, the Mahican people, and himself, he stresses the importance of scrupulous honesty, even as he has already acknowledged his own complicity in the American government's deceptions. Aupaumut's words serve as a reminder of personal, tribal, and national repercussions of deception as he finds himself balancing between his obligations to the western Indians and those to the American government.

Aupaumut's liminal political and diplomatic position becomes even more tenuous as he discusses his Christianity. Even as he intends to help the western Indians as a brother and a friend, as a devout Christian he is going among the unconverted, and he fears for the state of his soul. Although he avoids any mention of his Christianity in the journal itself, a letter addressed to Timothy Edwards shortly before his journey shows the complexity of Aupaumut's position. He expresses his anxieties about apostatizing and returning to a "heathen" state in this letter, saying, "I now earnestly beg of your prayers for me & for my companions—that we might not join any Idols of Heathens whether temporal or Spiritual Idols—And further that I may be able to speak the things which may be for the good of those Nations" (June 5, 1791 STL). Even as he embraces traditional Native diplomacy and past relationships, Aupaumut associates the beliefs of the western Indians with idols or false Gods. He furthermore assumes that he has the best interests of such nations in mind, and that these interests involve eliminating such idols. He rhetorically distances the western Indians from Stockbridge and from himself by degrading their religious beliefs and by attempting to protect himself from them. As a Christian, he suggests, he is different from other Natives, and he sincerely wants to maintain that separation even as he presents himself as one of them. His rhetoric of Native unity thus conflicts with his sense of himself as a Christian, and as time goes on, much of his writing centers on reconciling this conflict.

In particular, Aupaumut attempts to reconcile his fragmented loyalties to the Mahican people, to other Natives, and to Anglo-Americans through his history. Around the time of his western journeys Aupaumut wrote a history of the Muhheakunnuk (Mahican) people that expresses a very particular Native identity.[43] By simultaneously assuming the superiority of Christianity and his own people's innately Christian past before the arrival of Whites, Aupaumut defines his tribe's Nativeness as not only different from—and in certain ways better than—that of other Indians, but also different from that of the Whites who have so consistently let him down.

The history presents a vision of community based on nostalgia for a purer Mahican past, in which Anglo-Americans are intruders and other tribes are insignificant. Aupaumut's fusion of Native history and Anglo-American religion through the appropriation of Christian language to establish his tribal history allows him to define Christianity as distinct from its Anglo-American roots.

Aupaumut's history seems to have passed almost immediately into the hands of White observers of his tribe; as with his journal, it is possible that he wrote the history at the request of an Anglo-American.[44] Thus it too may be a critique specifically directed at an Anglo-American audience. In his construction of a utopian tribal past as evidence for his own community's moral superiority, Aupaumut uses the language of tradition and continuity that is so central to his journal to challenge what he sees as the corrupting influence of Anglo-American culture. The history layers the past in such a way that the Mahicans' realization of home and community is doubly deferred. The history claims, "Our forefathers asserted, that their ancestors were emigrated from west by north of another country; they passed over the great waters, where this and the other country is nearly connected . . . and that they lived by the side of great water or sea" ("Extract" 100). The Muh-he-con-nuk are named after the body of water by which they lived, "great waters or sea, which are constantly in motion, either flowing or ebbing" (ibid.). The history thus opens with migration and movement. Famine disperses this first settlement, after which the tribe regroups around the Hudson River, which the people tell each other "is like Muhheakunnuk our nativity" (ibid.). Aupaumut's own band eventually settled along the Housatonic River in Massachusetts, not the Hudson, after which they moved to upstate New York. Aupaumut's history does not reach into his own lifetime; his loss of his home in Massachusetts is left out of the history of his tribe. But if home is deferred in the history, traditions and sense of community are lovingly described. Much as Christianity emphasizes covenanted community over geography, Aupaumut's history locates the glory of the Muhheakunnuk people in their traditions rather than in their connection to a particular piece of land.

He explains that in the time before the Anglo-Americans came, the Mahicans "were more civilized than Indians are now in the wilderness; as it was said that they lived in towns, and were very numerous" ("History," *First Annual Report* 100).[45] Thus Aupaumut establishes that Anglo-

Americans are not the foundation for Native improvement; in Native history the tribe's salvation is independent of Anglo-American influence. After the first settlement, however, "There arose a mighty famine which obliged them to disperse throughout the regions of the wilderness after sustenance, and at length lost their ways of former living, and apostatized" ("Extract" 100).[46]

But even after the "apostasy," according to the history, the Indians lived comfortably before the Anglo-Americans arrived. For example, there was abundant land and game, and the Natives had effective plowing and hunting techniques (99–100). Furthermore, the number and quality of warriors were high, and the Mahicans were respected in war as well as in peace by the western tribes (Jones 16). The governmental structure of the tribe provided stability and security (20–23), and the people had developed effective ways to manage communal life. Aupaumut even describes the process by which murder was avenged, concluding with the retort, "But such murders were seldom committed before White people brought many evil spirits across the great waters, to this island" ("History," *First Annual Report* 45). He emphasizes that before the arrival of the Anglo-Americans, "they seldom feel much want, and they were very well contented in their condition" (Jones 15). Thus he inverts the missionary message, which suggests that Anglo-Americans bring salvation, and emphasizes instead their corrupting influence. And if the Anglo-Americans are a corruption, it is the past of the Mahicans that holds within it the promise of a better future.

In particular, Aupaumut's fusion of the language of ancestral nostalgia and the language of Old Testament history powerfully reconfigures contemporary power relations. His history contains utopian elements that recall the language of Genesis and the Garden of Eden, while the ten rules received from the "one Supreme Being who dwells above" (Jones 18) and handed down from generation to generation according to the Mahican history recall Moses' ten commandments (Peyer, *Tutor'd Mind* 114). When read against the complaints in Aupaumut's diplomatic journal, these commandments, which differ from the Christian version at certain points, read as an implied critique of White people. For example, those that do carry over from the Bible are references to those acts Aupaumut explicitly objects to in the Anglo-American government—lying, stealing, murdering. He also uses the phrase "obey your Sachem" (Jones 20), an oblique reference to the "Big knives" who go against American diplomatic policy and are the source of much tension between the U.S. government and the western tribes.

Those commandments that do not have a specific counterpart in the Christian decalogue are certainly part of Christian theology, and thus Aupaumut deploys them as critiques of Americans as well as instructions by which to live. The first is that "you must love to all men, and be kind to all people" (Jones 18). This is followed by "If you see any in distress, you must try to help them" (ibid.). Aupaumut points out that "you must consider that some future time you will also stand in need of such help; but if you will not assist, or have compassion for the poor, you will displease the Good Spirit" (ibid.). This passage is striking when set beside several petitions signed by Aupaumut from the Mahicans to various states, reminding them of their debts:

> Bretheren; wise men; attend. You once was small, very small. I then was great at that time. I took you under my arm, and helped you. I am now become small, very small. You are become great, very great, you reach into the clouds. You are seen all over the world. I am not now as high as your ankles. I now look to you for help. I am weak through hunger and cold, through want of food and cloathing. My women groan and lament, and tears are in the eyes of all my children. (Frazier 234–35)

As he reminds them in other petitions, help for the Mahicans came from other Natives, not from the states which Aupaumut petitioned and for which he had fought in the American Revolution. The emphasis on reciprocity in the Mahican decalogue implies its absence in Anglo-Americans, who are seen as morally and theologically inferior to their more generous Native neighbors.

Aupaumut's history also implies that White people are unnecessary to the project of Native renewal, even though their habits and customs will affect the Native community. Just as the diplomatic journal emphasizes familial relations as a central political force, these structure the identity of the Muhheakunnuk people in the history. The results of stealing, Aupaumut reminds the reader, are that "you will hurt your name, and disgrace your parents and all relations" (Jones 19). Similarly, marriage partners must be chosen only with the consent of "your parents and all relations" (20). It is through such family structures, not through the intervention of outsiders, that Mahicans can learn to live well. Aupaumut writes that the customs of the Mahicans, which were "handed down to them by their forefathers, and considered as communicated to them by Good Spirit," are repeated by the head of the family to the children (18). The salvation of the Mahicans comes from within the community, not from outside.

Though Aupaumut did record his protest against Anglo-American intrusions in print, he also apparently took the route of Umpachenee a generation before him and succumbed to drinking in his final, frustrating years of unsuccessful petitioning for the rights of his people to the American government. A letter about Aupaumut and his brother from Samuel Kirkland, missionary to the Oneida Indians in upstate New York and a supposed friend of Aupaumut's, suggests as much, and it also confirms Aupaumut's deepest anxieties about the changeableness of Anglo-American support: "For my own part," Kirkland says dismissively, "I have but little dependence upon them. They are, I am afraid, going the way, of all Indians to be consumed by the west-India-liquid-fire. I have entertained great hopes of Capt. Hendrick, till the year past—he begins to fall a prey to that foe of Indians, & it grows fast upon him" (May 31, 1792 NYHS).[47] Kirkland's "friendship" with Aupaumut involves an even greater betrayal, as another letter from Kirkland to Pickering suggests:

> I fear you will be disappointed in your expectations of Capt. Hendrick—I suggested an idea of the kind to you when at Philadelphia lest you should be deceived—I have been most intimately acquainted with him, & a most free and unreserved friendship has subsisted for several years betwixt us & he has done me the honor to publicly declare that—but since his tour to the Westward last summer, he has greatly altered—he has become a lover of the intoxicating draught & duplicity begins to mark many steps of his conduct He becomes less friendly to ye character & cause of the white people. (May 1792 HC)

Thus after establishing a close and trusting relationship with Aupaumut, Kirkland undermines Aupaumut to his superiors, effectively ruining his career as a diplomat. His primary complaint, ironically, is about his supposed "duplicity." If we can give Kirkland's words any credibility, however, it seems that Aupaumut's suspicions about the United States were taking shape before his journey; his foray into the west on behalf of the American government may have simply confirmed his worst fears rather than creating them. His journal, then, provides him with the opportunity to express his sense of betrayal directly to those who are most complicit, and his history expands and completes that expression. Deferred in both the journal and the history, home both as a concept and a physical reality remains elusive for the Mahicans as they struggle to position themselves within constantly shifting alliances.

NATIVE acceptance of Christianity and Anglo-American colonialism were at best mixed in Stockbridge. Handsman and Richmond stress that an examination of the Native record reveals "obvious evidence of Mahican resistance to and persistent concerns about their being missionized and resettled" (3). They emphasize that "unlike the town histories written so frequently after 1850, these Mahican traditions make obvious and thus confront the catastrophic effects of colonialist policies of expansion and occupation. Yet the very fact that such oral histories and cultural memories continued to exist and were being passed on to succeeding generations also attests that the Mahican did not renounce or repudiate their traditions as desired by John Sergeant" (6). Handsman and Richmond look at archeological evidence, oral testimony, and other sources to reconstruct the "Native record"; I maintain that it is embedded even within the Anglo-American narrative. Through Sergeant's journals we can see his perspective as "captive," which is telling in terms of the relationships he developed as a missionary. Even though he was apparently much admired and loved by the Mahicans he served, his construction of his position and identity speak volumes about the tensions that existed between himself and his congregation. Furthermore, Sergeant records evidence of Umpachenee's protest. Although his drinking went unrecognized as anything but a personal shortcoming that illustrated a larger flaw of the entire Native population, Umpachenee did manifest his opposition to Sergeant through the means that were available to him. And the written record also includes Aupaumut's powerful protest. By appropriating a Christian past for the Mahican people, Aupaumut challenges the very basis of Anglo-American superiority. Both his journal and his history suggest that although Aupaumut worked for and with Anglo-Americans, his loyalty to his own people remained strong. Even as he wrote specifically for Anglo-Americans, he demanded their acknowledgment of their own corruption and of their questionable treatment of his people. On the other hand, as he reinscribes his tribe within the dominant colonial paradigm, he aligns himself with the very things he wants most emphatically to reject. Furthermore, his work for the United States government often put him at odds with other Native leaders who were explicitly trying to establish a pan-Indian confederacy. Both his rhetorical and his political strategies distance him from other Native peoples even as he claims to be working in their best interests.

Are we to understand Aupaumut as shrewdly subversive or as a willing accommodationist? Is Umpachenee a romantic rebel or a lamb brought back to the fold? We long to place them, to find the moment in their texts where they unmask themselves, but their positions defy easy interpretation as either "resistant" or "conformist." The Christian Indians of Stockbridge demand a more complex reading of available materials, as much of their identity is written in the interstices of other stories. For Sergeant and Kirkland, the stories of Umpachenee and Aupaumut follow a standard trajectory that marks each individual as a potentially useful ally whose personal flaws ultimately undermine his trustworthiness. As modern readers we long to find marks of rebellion, moments in which their "true" subversiveness give the lie to what may seem a problematic acquiescence to a destructive colonial hierarchy. Ultimately, however, we must reconcile ourselves to the contradictions in their roles; they are *both* rebels and accommodationists, people who move uneasily between the opposite poles of the Christian and the Indian.

# CHAPTER FOUR

# "ONE HEAD, ONE HEART, AND ONE BLOOD"

## Christian Community and Native Identity at Brotherton

✝

We thank you that ye have received us into your Body, so that now we may say we have one head, one heart, and one Blood, and may God keep us united together in very deed untill we Both grow white headed.

—Joseph Johnson to the Oneida Indian council, on the gift of Oneida land
to the Brotherton Indians, January 24, 1774

Groups negotiating their identity in contexts of domination and exchange persist, patch themselves together in ways different from a living organism. A community, unlike a body, can lose a central "organ" and not die. All the critical elements of identity are in specific conditions replaceable: language, land, blood, leadership, religion. Recognized, viable tribes exist in which any one or even most of these elements are missing, replaced, or largely transformed.

—James Clifford, *The Predicament of Culture*

I N 1772, Joseph Johnson, a twenty-year-old Mohegan, returned to his Connecticut home after a year-long sea journey to the West Indies. Once a pupil at Eleazar Wheelock's Charity School for Indians, Johnson had fallen away from his religious training, abandoned school, and turned to drinking and hard living. Returning to the Mohegan community of his childhood, however, he rediscovered Christianity under the religious influence of his fellow Mohegan Samson Occom, also a former pupil of

Wheelock.[1] With Occom and two other Algonquian Wheelock students, David and Jacob Fowler, Johnson embraced the idea of creating a single, unified community of Native Christians out of the converted Algonquians living dispersed throughout New England. Together, these men committed themselves to making such a community a reality.[2] When Eleazar Wheelock, the founder of the school which both had attended, heard the news, his response was an almost delirious joy. Ignoring his estrangement from Occom and Johnson's past apostasy, he wrote that "all the Tribes of christianized Indians in New-England have determined to remove and settle in a Body within the Borders of the Six Nations, the Rev'd. Mr. Occom, and several others, Indian Youths of good Characters, who have been educated in this School, and at present appear promising to accompany them as Preachers." He fervently continued, "GOD grant the Leaven thus put into the Lump may spread far and wide till the whole be leavened" (*Continuation* 1773 41). Even though he was not directly involved in the founding of Brotherton, Wheelock saw the settlement as the culmination of his own lifelong dream of a permanent Native Christian community through which other Natives could be brought to Christianity and therefore (in his view) under English control.

In 1774 Joseph Johnson formally petitioned the Oneida Indians in upstate New York to cede a tract of land to a small group of Algonquian converts from New England. Wheelock gleefully reported the news in his next publication. "The principal *Indians* of the Tribe at *Montauk*, with all the christianized and civilized *Indians* of the several towns in *New-England*... have obtained, and well secured a Tract of choice Land, Fifteen or Twenty Miles square, where they design to settle in a Body, as a civilized and christian People, and cultivate those Lands for their Subsistence" (*Continuation* 1775 15–16). Furthermore, Wheelock announced, "they purpose to have, as far as may be, of their own Sons for Ministers and School-Masters." He proudly repeats that "this has been effected principally, by the Agency of Mr. *Occom* and *Joseph Johnson*" (16). Because of the volatile situation in upstate New York prior to the Revolutionary War, however, the fledgling community was forced to abandon immediate plans for settlement on the Oneida reservation. In 1783 the settlement finally took hold, this time enlarged by the presence of the Stockbridge Indians, but without Johnson, who had died some time around 1776.[3] By 1791 there were about 280 Stockbridge Indians and 250 Brotherton Indians living near Oneida.[4]

Everyone invested in the conversion of Natives to Christianity seemed to agree that this settlement held a great deal of promise. Wheelock wrote optimistically of Brotherton, "These Things being laid together, appear to me (and I am persuaded I shall not be found alone in my Apprehensions) to exhibit the fairest, by far the fairest Prospect of future Success to this great Undertaking, that ever yet opened to View on our Western Wilderness" (16). Joseph Johnson described his plan for Brotherton to a benefactor in New York: "My Design has been for these twenty-one months to lead my New England Brethren into the Western Wilderness where they might Live together in Peace." In this venture, Johnson reported, he had put aside his own temporal interests "to lean upon God, hoping that it was his Pleasure . . . that I might bring about such a Noble Design, as I call it" (December 14, 1774 CHS). Occom wrote: "I am promoting the thing and encouraging the Indians all I can, and if they succeed I shall go with them with all my Heart" (November 10, 1773 CHS). But though all agreed that Brotherton held the promise of better things to come, the writings regarding the settlement suggest that Brotherton meant vastly different things to different people.

Native and Anglo-American missionaries produced stories suffused with theological language to provide narrative coherence to Brotherton; in the process, important differences among their understandings of Native Christian community emerge. As Benedict Anderson and Edward Said have noted, political or cultural identities are structured by narratives, and "national" or communal identity bases itself on mutually agreed-upon narratives of both the past and the future. Anderson argues that "communities are . . . distinguished . . . by the style in which they are imagined" (15). Said further argues that "the power to narrate, or to block other narratives from forming and emerging . . . constitutes one of the main connections between [culture and imperialism]" (xiii). When Native American and Anglo-American missionaries wrote about Brotherton, they revealed their conflicting notions about the shape and structure of a Native Christian community.

The Native American writing that emerges from the early years of the Brotherton settlement, generally in the form of letters, journal entries, and religious confessions, records the attempt by Native missionaries such as Samson Occom and Joseph Johnson to create a Christian community with "one head, one heart, and one Blood," as Johnson described it, from a culturally diverse group of Native Americans living on the margins of Euro-American missionary structures. This metaphorical description of the community as a single living, functioning being is at the center of the Native narrative of Brotherton. The idea that the Native community can be embodied in a single being produces the community's collective history as its autobiography or more properly its autoethnography, which directly confronts Anglo-American missionary assumptions. By using the language and the structure of missionary culture, the writers of Brotherton at once acknowledge and reject their debt to Anglo-American culture.

The writings of the Euro-American missionaries who also participated in the community life of Brotherton provide its biography (or perhaps its ethnography) as they, too, imagine the community through corporeal metaphors. For these missionaries, however, Native subjectivity was inconceivable outside Anglo-American religious and social constructions; like John Eliot, Experience Mayhew, and John Sergeant before them, they could not conceive of a Native Christian community functioning without the watchful guidance of Anglo-Americans. Invested in marking difference, or recording ways in which their Native charges fall short of Anglo-American Christianity, the missionaries ensure their dominance over the community. By writing about Brotherton, they were establishing the parameters of a community that remained distinct from Anglo-American culture but that was absolutely dependent upon it. Rather than promoting Native autonomy, the missionaries asserted their own primacy by emphasizing the need to save the Natives from themselves through discipline and careful monitoring.

As on Martha's Vineyard years earlier, differing versions of Native Christian community coexisted uneasily and the Native writers' version differed greatly from that of the Whites. This time, however, the voices of Native converts were no longer dispersed within a larger narrative structured by an Anglo-American. The Natives of Brotherton were experienced writers and sophisticated negotiators of the colonial world. By speaking for themselves, the Native founders of Brotherton rejected the authority of White missionaries to speak for them, and in the process they reconceptualized the meaning of a Native community along deeply masculinist lines—replacing the infantilizing language of the missionaries with language that emphasized personal agency, action, and control.

## Anglo-Americans and Brotherton

Although Brotherton was founded by Natives as a Native community, missionary societies based in England financed two White missionaries, Samuel Kirkland and John Sergeant Jr., to minister to the Oneida, Brotherton, and New Stockbridge communities. Such societies were the primary source of financial and administrative support for all Protestant missionary work in New England; as such their influence over the lives and careers of both White and Native missionaries was inestimable. Missionaries in New England were required to submit journals to their English benefactors, reporting on the "progress of the gospel" as they saw it among the Natives. Since the premise of the Euro-American missionary endeavor was that Natives could be and in fact must be saved from their innately unstable, sinful ways, the assumption in many of these reports was not only that missionaries always had the Natives' best interests at heart but, more important, that they knew those interests better than the Natives. The writings of Wheelock, Kirkland, and Sergeant attempt to narrate the life of the community from a perspective at once inside and outside that community.

As we have seen in previous chapters, the idea of a constructed community of Christianized Natives was not unique to Brotherton. From John Eliot's seventeenth-century praying towns to John Sergeant's "Indian community" in Stockbridge, the concept informed most attempts to convert Natives to Christianity. The factor that ties these various communities together is the missionaries' and funding agencies' conviction that an Anglo-American missionary must be the guiding force. Though John Eliot and Experience Mayhew encouraged the founding of Native churches with Native ministers, they saw themselves as the linchpin of each community. John Sergeant's ordination sermon, given by Nathanael Appleton, makes this assumption explicit. Directing his comments to the Housatonic Indians among whom Sergeant is to preach, Appleton instructs:

Behold the man, the messenger of the Lord of hosts, that is coming unto you. . . . This is the man that is to shew you the way to salvation; to direct you how you may escape the damnation of hell; and how you may obtain the mercy of our Lord Jesus Christ unto eternal life. See then that you love him, and that you esteem him very highly in love for his works sake; and that you come to him to be instructed by him: that you hearken to his counsels, and observe his directions, and follow his example wherein he follows Christ. And this is the way for you to be happy here, and for ever hereafter; for godliness hath the promise of the life that now is, & of that which is to come. (26–27)

Native salvation, Appleton contends, is absolutely contingent on the missionary, who will show, instruct, direct. In this passage Natives are to be the passive recipients of the "counsels" and "instructions" of their Anglo-American missionary; their happiness in this life and beyond is assured through their obedience to him.

Anglo-American missionaries took their responsibility to reconstruct Native Americans very seriously. In linking religious salvation to fixed settlement, they merged their religious calling with their commitment to the colonial project of establishing a "New England" as God's chosen kingdom on earth. John Eliot required his converts to cease their wandering and settle in permanent, English-style communities, and other missionaries followed this policy as well. John Sergeant too demanded of the Housatonic Mahicans that they forsake their seasonal migrations. Indeed, as a group Anglo-American missionaries tended to emphasize the need for paternalistic control over every aspect of Native life. If Natives are a single body, the missionary implies, that body is a child's body with a child's intellect that must be managed and controlled. The missionary narrative, then, is structured around the interlocking roles of father, teacher, and disciplinarian. With emphasis on the childishness of the adults and the untapped potential of Native children, missionary paternalism and pedagogy center on social and cultural reformation through discipline and control.

At times this control is conceived in violent terms. Samuel Kirkland's language in describing the Natives at Brotherton echoes that of Wheelock, his mentor; citing the language of Psalms 2:9, Kirkland writes to a friend, "Those Heathen (as well as baptized infidels) who will not submit to ye peaceful sceptre of King Jesus—must be subdued and broken with a rod of iron and dasht like ye potter's vessel—if nothing else will do it" (June 30, 1772 HC). Kirkland implies that if Natives won't accept a New Testament Christ, they must then be forced to come to terms with a more violent Old Testament Patriarch. The brutal images of destruction and annihilation in this passage dramatize Kirkland's sense that Natives must be punished for their reluctance to accept God. And even his reference to "King Jesus" involves Native humility, since it implies a political domination that works in favor of the English; Natives must "submit" to his "sceptre" through the terms that are brought to them by English missionaries. The language of both Wheelock and Kirkland emphasizes that Natives must be brought under English political domination to attain salvation.[5]

The primary rationalization for English domination is the assumption that Natives are innately flawed. Again and again the missionaries are struck by what they perceive as the essential instability of the Native character. In his Charity School report, Wheelock writes of his Native pupils: "Nothing has prevented their being imployed usefully, and reputably in various capacities till this day, but their want of fortitude" (*Continuation* 1771 20). And Samuel Kirkland writes, "By searching more into Indian traditions—National temper, past conduct under Providence—with the present state of the different Nations and tribes—I am ready to conclude they are in a peculiar sense and manner under the curse of Heaven—yea, I can resolve the paradox no other way—They appear, as a body, to be given over to strong delusions . . . as they do not like to retain God in their knowledge—they are left to a reprobate or injudicious mind" (June 30, 1772 HC). Kirkland dismisses them "as a body," or as a single entity which can be characterized as "reprobate" and "injudicious." By simultaneously erasing the individual features of Native Christians and emphasizing his own authority to judge them, Kirkland confirms his power as ethnographer as well as his position as the "true" arbiter of God's love. Significantly, both Wheelock's and Kirkland's underlying assumptions about Native inadequacy presume their own centrality—in both religious and cultural terms—to any Native community.

The notion that Native Christian community was inseparable from Euro American political interests shaped eighteenth-century missionary rhetoric. Wheelock makes this point explicitly. He claims, "I can't but hope, and I do hope in God, that . . . we may soon have a string of godly zealous missionaries, among all the numerous tribes from Muskingham to Montreal." These missionaries, he argues, "will be a far better defence to the English provinces against their ravages, and incursions, in case a war should break out, than a double line of forts" (*Continuation* 1772 12). Wheelock's argument thus presents the religious conversion of Natives as the most effective way to protect English settlers. In other words, the work of missionaries is important for its effects on the English, not on the Indians.

The eighteenth century was a particularly volatile time for American colonists, and alliances with the Iroquois were crucial in the balance of power throughout the French and Indian wars and later in the American Revolution. Thus when Wheelock's Mohegan student Samson Occom was sent as a teacher to the Iroquois in 1761, the correspondents of the Society in Scotland for Propagating Christian Knowledge sent along a series of instructions to guide his work. Primary among these was to "use your utmost endeavour . . . to attach them to our sovereign King George the third of Great Britain." Last on the list was the directive to "instruct them in the principles of the Christian Religion" (1762 CHS). From the Anglo-American perspective, Brotherton and New Stockbridge, situated "in the Heart of the Country of the *Six Nations*" (Wheelock *Continuation* 1775 15), seemed perfectly situated to further the political goals of the colonial government. Anglo-American missionaries, as their discussions of Brotherton indicate, cannot conceive of Native community as distinct from their own social and political goals. In the missionary narrative, there is little distinction between boarding schools like Wheelock's and other Native communities, since both operate through a presumption of Native inadequacy. And as is clear from the boarding school analogy, any Native Christian community calls for the strict disciplining and monitoring of Native identity.

## Natives and Brotherton

But the Algonquian leaders of Brotherton were hardly the passive subjects that the Anglo-American missionary establishment was looking for. By giving coherence and value to the project of establishing a "national" identity as Christian Indians, Johnson, Occom, and others challenged the dominant missionary model. Each had been immersed in the values and assumptions of Anglo-American missionary culture, yet each maintained ties with his own community. All were once under the care of Eleazar Wheelock, and several had been students alongside Samuel Kirkland at Moor's Charity School. Furthermore, Kirkland, the Fowlers, Occom, and Johnson had all, at one point in their lives, been sent by Wheelock as missionaries or schoolmasters to the Iroquois.[6] Samuel Kirkland and David Fowler had shared a home among the Oneida for several years; Joseph Johnson had been a schoolteacher at the young age of sixteen for the Oneida under Kirkland's care. But all of them eventually returned to their

Native communities either in protest against Wheelock or to renew their own familial ties.

From the Anglo-American perspective, most of these Natives were failures. Immediately before the establishment of Brotherton, Wheelock writes despairingly of his Indian students: "The most melancholy part of the account which I have here to relate, and which has occasioned me the greatest weight of sorrow, has been the bad conduct, and behaviour of such as have been educated here, after they have left the school, and been put into business abroad" (*Continuation* 1771 18–19). Out of forty students, Wheelock reports, "I don't hear of more than half who have preserved their characters unstain'd, either by a course of intemperance or uncleanness, or both." He continues helplessly, "Some who on account of their parts, and learning, bid the fairest for usefulness, are sunk down into as low, savage, and brutish a manner of living as they were in before any endeavours were used with them to raise them up." Of those who have remained "subjects of God's grace," he relates, "six . . . are now dead" (20). Wheelock is confounded by what seems his students' willful disregard of the lessons he has tried to instill in them. For him any movement away from the rigid racial and religious structures he has established constitutes failure.

But if they seemed failures to Wheelock, the Native pupils of his school seem to have drawn different conclusions about themselves. Both Occom and Johnson, for example, emerged as leaders in Native education and Christian conversion within their own communities.[7] And Dana Nelson has suggested that their establishment of Brotherton was a reaction against Wheelock's teachings and, indeed, the entire colonial missionary project of keeping the "poor Indian" properly submissive (61). By adapting the rhetoric that missionaries had directed at them for years, the founders of Brotherton restructured the idea of the Christian family and rejected the language of Native inferiority; in the process, they declared their independence from Anglo-American missionaries.

For colonial New Englanders, "family" encompassed a series of relationships among all members of a single household including slaves and indentured servants. John Demos emphasizes that servants were "fully integrated into . . . the household" (*Little Commonwealth* 107); he notes that "the prevalent assumptions about family life made little distinction between a natural child and a servant of about the same age . . . the master would perform as a surrogate parent" (108). Familial bonds were strongly hierarchical, with the patriarch controlling and disciplining other family members. This relationship was based on Puritan interpretations of the Old Testament and of Paul's epistles, in which the patriarch was responsible for the moral and religious development of the family unit. In the case of indentured servants who had not reached adulthood, the patriarch was responsible for imparting a trade or an education in exchange for a fixed term of service;[8] during that term, the servant effectively became a member of the family with the same standing as a child or young adult (Axtell, *School* 116).

The crucial exception was the servant who was of a different race from the colonist. African American and Native American servants in colonial family units were considered the property of the patriarch; Anglo-American servants were not (Demos, *Little Commonwealth* 110). Thus even as African American and Native American servants participated in Anglo-American family structures, they did so on very specific terms. Wheelock's description of Occom as a member of his family does not contradict his assumption of Occom's status as an inferior and especially as inferior to his own children; for colonial patriarchs, "family" was understood to involve ownership and obligation, and those concepts fixed the role of Native Americans and African Americans as permanent younger children in the social hierarchy.

Brotherton's Indians employed the language of family as well. The leaders of the Brotherton community were closely connected to one another through family relationships; Samson Occom was the father-in-law of Joseph Johnson, and was also related by marriage to David and Jacob Fowler. But even when individuals were not related, the language of family defined the bonds that connected them. Thus before Johnson's marriage to Occom's daughter Tabitha, Johnson wrote to Occom, "I reverence you as a kind Father, and respect your Hon[orable] wife, as a fond Mother, and your Children dear, as my beloved Brothers and Sisters" (April 5, 1773 CHS).[9] The adjectives are telling: kind fathers receive reverence, honorable wives and mothers receive respect, and brothers and sisters receive love. Personal relationships among family members thus involve a series of obligations based on a descending scale of familial status. Johnson further tells Occom, "Ye have been, as it were, the Support of my drooping heart, when Dejection like a Garment covered it; well I remember the trying times which I went through the last summer, forsaken of friends, &ct: &c :&c: yet was thou pleased to shew me the respect, and consider'd of me, and gave me advice, and Encouraged me" (April 5, 1773 CHS). Family, this passage suggests, implies an intimacy more powerful than mere friendship, which can slip away. Patriarchal relationships in this context involve mutually beneficial exchanges based on clearly established systems of obligation. In another letter Johnson urges Occom: "I hope that you will be pleged to write Large, and free. advise, encourage, Rebuke, and make manifest your Purposes" (October 13, 1773 CHS). The role of the father is active, aggressive; with this series of verbs Johnson suggests the importance of the paternal figure, to whose guidance and support the "son" must always respond. Even in their private correspondence, these two men use the language of patriarchy to shape their relationship, with all its attendant obligations and expectations.

As Wheelock's former students, both Occom and Johnson were well acquainted with their teacher's manipulations of patriarchal language; their own use of such language therefore has obvious connections to his. Indeed, Occom uses Wheelock's language of shame and control specifically as a patriarch in his attempt to discipline his son Benoni, who has fallen in with what his father sees as "Bad Company, which is Ruining and Distructive both Body and Soul" through such evil habits as "Carousing, Drinking, Fiddling, Dancing, Cursing, Swearing, and Blaspheming the Holy Name of God." Occom writes to his son, "You was my only hope, Comfort and Joy, being the only son I depended upon, to manage our Business at Home—You went on very well in your Business, and was in a likely way to prosper in the World; our Neighbours round a bout here, both English and Indians, look'd upon you with pleasure and admiration, especially by our Friends, and You was invied by our Enimies" (June 24, 1780 CHS). Occom emphasizes how intertwined his own life is with his son's, beginning his comments with his own feelings toward his son and then shifting to the perceptions of "our" friends and "our" enemies. He allows no space for a separation between Benoni and himself, suggesting that any relationships with individuals outside the family unit are shared by all its members.

After establishing the potential Benoni represents, Occom continues mournfully:

> But alas, how soon is my hope turned into almost despear, my Comfort into Misery and Grief, and my Joy into Sorrow and mourning, and you have grieved the Hearts of our good Friends and wellwishers; and you have rejoiced the Hearts of our Enimies, and they will say, now we have got Samson Occoms Children in our Company, and they are bad as any of us

and a great deal worse, and especially Nonay, he would not come amongst
us a while ago, but now he is with us, and he does just as we do and worse.
(June 24, 1780 CHS)

Juxtaposing hope and despair, comfort and misery, joy and sorrow, Occom
accentuates the extent of his disappointment. Deploying the language of
shame and the specter of public humiliation, he links his son's misbehavior
to his own reputation, and by doing so accuses his son of willfully betraying him and his cause, just as Wheelock had done to him time after
time.

The letter concludes with the notations, "This was red to my Son 24 of
June 1780 in the hearing of my Family—on the 10 of July he concluded to
stay at Home and go to work peacably on the 12 Day of [illegible] I order
my Son out House for he woud not work steady." For both Wheelock and
his former students, familial language can be wielded as a disciplinary tool.
Both emphasize the far-reaching consequences of any misstep, not only on
the individual but also on the larger family unit. And they make their point
through the public humiliation of the sinner, both through an oral and
written account of the transgression and through the acknowledgment
within the account of the public nature of personal actions. Indeed, the
distinction between public and private vanishes in this exchange; this form
of patriarchy is about regulation, control, and management, and it does
not differentiate between personal hurt and public humiliation. Although
we do not know for whose benefit the notation is appended to the letter,
in a sense it does not matter, since clearly for Occom the private life of his
family is always available for public scrutiny.

But for Johnson and Occom the language of family has political implications that come not only from Wheelock and other missionaries, but
from Native tradition as well. As was evident in Aupaumut's journal, the
formal language of diplomacy in Native cultures of the Northeast is replete
with family terminology. As Native groups negotiated with one another, a
series of hierarchical relations developed based on the masculinized language of family. In this language of patriarchy, personal discipline is not
the primary focus but is rather connected to a larger series of exchanges
that structure alliances between Native groups. Thus, for example, when
the Brotherton community moved to New York, the Oneida explained
the relationships (and obligations) of the new community to their new
neighbors: the Tuscaroras were to be their "elder brothers," as were "the

Onoidas, Kiyougas, Nanticuks, . . . Todelehonas." Furthermore, the Mohawks, Onondagas, and Senecas were to be "fathers" to the new settlement (January 21, 1774 DCC).[10] Those alliances meant very particular things, among which were a series of mutual obligations that are firmly established through tradition.

So the language of Brotherton engages with multiple notions of patriarchy. The language of family echoes Wheelock's merging of the roles of father and disciplinarian and master, and defines the connections among God, Jesus, and all human believers as a series of familial relationships. Both of these notions were very much in keeping with New England Puritan hierarchies. At the same time, the language of family makes use of Algonquian social and diplomatic customs, which focused less on disciplinary mechanisms and more on a series of interlocking obligations and relationships.

Occom's use of patriarchal language with Joseph Johnson and Benoni Occom illustrates the complexities of Native Christian versions of patriarchy. Though Occom's stern manner with Benoni is reminiscent of Wheelock's use of familial language as a disciplinary tool, his interactions with his son-in-law lean more toward the mutual exchange common in Algonquian social structures. Patriarchal language has personal repercussions for Occom, Johnson, and Benoni, and at the same time it structures the political organization of the settlement at Brotherton, not only in terms of its immediate participants but also in terms of its neighbors and allies.

Johnson and Occom simultaneously celebrate Native identity and reject Anglo-American colonial control by invoking a powerful rhetoric of Native manhood. By using the language of the masculine family to define Brotherton, Johnson pulls upon traditional Native language and Christian conventions and, on a more personal level for himself and for Occom, reimagines his position vis-à-vis Wheelock. Instead of situating themselves as obedient and submissive children in Wheelock's patriarchal family, Johnson and his Native brethren unite as a community of equals who are inferior only to God.

This patriarchal rhetoric of Brotherton, which emphasizes manliness within the family, suggests that relations between men take precedence over any relationships involving women. By infusing Brotherton with the rhetoric of manliness, the Native founders of Brotherton express their frustration at class and racial inequality, but this gesture comes at the expense of Native Christian women. In 1773, in his early attempts to establish the community, Johnson sent out a message to six or seven local Native communities with significant numbers of Christian converts, saying, "We beg that ye would by all means send a Man, out of Each Tribe, that they may go with us, and Seek a Country for our Brethren" (October 13, 1773 CHS). The ignoring of women is striking, particularly as the absence of women in a peaceful traveling party might suggest warlike intentions to their Iroquoian hosts.[11] Johnson further urges the participants in the Brotherton venture, "Let us take courage friends, and let us step forward like men . . . be so good as to show yourselves men" (October 13, 1773 CHS).

In this homosocial model of community, even the name "Brotherton" invokes an ideal of manly love. The Christian God is the patriarch of this community, and it is only by trusting completely in God the Father that the community can succeed. Johnson tells those "Brethren" accompanying him in his earliest attempts to establish the community, "Let us put our trust in that God who ruleth in the Armies of Heaven, and doeth his pleasure among the Inhabitants of this lower world. if God be for us, this is Enough. he can comfort us Even in a Wilderness. let us consider of our Condition. let us think of our Children. Let us think of time to come" (October 13, 1773 CHS). The God invoked here by Johnson is absolutely powerful; as one who would provide comfort even in a wilderness, this figure recalls the God of Exodus, whose people were led from slavery and exile in Egypt through a wilderness into safety. Powerful and potentially violent, he is also loving and comforting. And while Kirkland imagines God standing ready to "subdue" and "break" recalcitrant converts, Johnson's God supports them with the "Armies of Heaven." The invocation of "wilderness" in this passage is not without irony. As Native Americans, the settlers were (at least in the minds of the Euro Americans around them) products of wilderness. As Christians, however, they have come to accept the metaphor of wilderness as chaotic and frightening. In referring to Exodus, Johnson invokes a powerful model of community in which the chosen few are saved from the wilderness through their commitment not only to each other but also to the God that controls their destiny. And with God on their side, Johnson's comments suggest, this Native community gains power and agency beyond any other earthly body. By equating Native power with masculinity, Johnson defies Anglo-American visions of Native identity as necessarily subordinate.

Johnson's theological vision of masculinized community is further developed in his negotiations over land with the Oneida. In replying to their offer of land, he tells the Oneida, "We thank you that ye have taken us to be your younger brethren and that ye look upon us to be of the same Blood as yourselves, and we thank you that ye have received us into your Body, so that now we may say we have one head, one heart, and one Blood, and may God keep us united together in very deed untill we Both grow white headed" (January 22, 1774 DCC).[12] The images here recall I Cor. 11–12, in which Paul's letters define both the Corinthians' communal relations to each other and their spiritual debt to Christ, whose body and blood are sacrificed in the name of all humanity. "For as the body is one, and hath many members, and all the members of that one body, being many, are one body: so also is Christ" (I Cor. 12:12). The community, then, is a living creature, whose "members" act in concert both in terms of the Bible and in terms of Johnson's rhetoric. In I Cor. 12:14–21, the "members" are eyes, feet, ears; in Johnson's narrative, they are the head, the heart, and the blood—all of which recall Christ's sacrifice for the future of humanity. In contrast to the dismissive characterizations by Wheelock and Kirkland of all Natives "as a body," Johnson's body of Natives gain power through Christianity. With this Christian rhetoric of the sacramental body, Johnson appropriates what had been until then the language of English entitlement in the New World as a basis for this Native community of chosen men.[13]

To the Oneida, the images from Johnson's speech would have been powerful without the Christian significance of the sacramental body. The images of the single head, heart, and body were common symbols of unity and appeared frequently in Iroquois treaties throughout the colonial period.[14] In a culture based on consensus as a ruling political principle, the promise of unity was powerful indeed. The dual implications of the image of the single head, heart, and mind—at once Christian and traditionally Iroquois—suggest a promising blend of Native and Christian values. But Johnson's rhetoric also suggests a break with Anglo-American colonial power structures. His thanks to the Oneida invokes a series of obligations and hierarchical relations recalling the language of Native political alliance, as does the image of the New England tribes as the "younger brethren" and the Oneida as the "older brethren" growing white-headed together. And in an embattled period of Native-White tensions, the image of a single (Indian) body implies a permanence and security based on the shared desires of the unified Native community. Johnson clearly aligns himself and the Algonquian newcomers with their Oneida "brethren" by invoking the racial language of body and blood. In doing so, he not only recalls a unified Native identity but also implies his separation from Euro-Americans. Despite the insistently patriarchal language of Brotherton, it is as brothers, not fathers and sons, that members of the community interact.

In a letter to a benefactor, Johnson expresses resentment toward Euro-Americans, masked though it is in submissive language:

> Suffer me to ask your Honour, in a humble manner, a Question more. If an Indian is Capable, is faithfull, & is serviceable as an English man in the bussiness . . . Why [is it not] reasonable that an Indian should meet with the same encouragements and be made Equal Sharer of the bounty with the English man Since they are both labouring in one Noble Cause and since it was given freely for the good of the poor Indians and Natives in particular. but forgive my boldness, & familiarity, I desire to keep in Remembrance that I am an Indian & I desire to be submissive before your Honour. (1774 CHS)

Masking his critique in extremely courteous language, Johnson points out that paying Native missionaries adequately would be the most appropriate way to spend money given expressly for "the good of the poor Indians and Natives in particular." His humble manner emphasizes the very discrepancies in rank and prestige that he is questioning, and his suggestion that Indians be "equal sharers" with Englishmen seems a calculated attempt to highlight the poor treatment Natives receive even in matters supposedly designed for their benefit. His anger and bitterness at the injustice of the situation are barely contained beneath the formal rhetorical flourishes of his eighteenth-century epistolary style. He is more forthright in his communications with Occom, when he angrily exclaims, "I am but young. and I am but poor. I am an Indian. If I was the son of some Rich English man perhaps I should be able better to travel the Country up and down at my own Charges.—O that Indians were men!" (May 25, 1774 CHS). His outburst reveals his frustration at his apparent inadequacy as an Indian in terms of White male privilege. While his rhetoric specifically equates maleness with power, it is the racially charged nature of manhood that troubles him in his relations with Euro-Americans.

As they rhetorically structure a masculinized Native community, the leaders of Brotherton insist on more equality in a less hierarchical model of community than that of their Anglo-American missionary counterparts. The condition for this equality, however, is the disempowerment of Native women, and thus the founders of Brotherton find themselves aligned with Anglo-American social model; in the attempt to counter one injustice, Brotherton's leaders replicate another by maintaining rigid gender hierarchies. Their reaction against Anglo-Americans maintains the same structures of power.

## Declaring Independence:
## Brotherton and the Language of Revolution

The efforts of Johnson and Occom to establish an independent Native community coincided with the American colonies' own struggle with England. As the colonies attempted to create an identity that retained what was valuable about English culture yet established separation from England, so the Brotherton Indians struggled to mitigate Anglo-American missionary dominance. Though steeped in Anglo-American culture, Johnson and others nevertheless pulled away from the demands of the increasingly "tyrannical" missionary structure. By accepting Christianity but rejecting White America, the Brotherton community developed systems and structures of Indian identity paralleling models of community emerging from the American Revolution. In particular, their merging of the language of revolution with the language of family marks their attempt to make the American Revolution relevant to the Indian community.

One of the American colonists' primary goals for the Indian populations of the Northeast was to assure their neutrality in the Revolutionary War. Occom agreed, and he worked to keep both Algonquian and Iroquois Natives from participating in the war. In a formal letter to the Oneida, Occom urges tribal leaders to "use all your Influence, to your Brethren So far as you have any connections to keep them in Peace and quietness, and not to entermeddle in these Quarrils among the White People" (1775 CHS). Occom did not remain unpartisan, however. The same letter explains the "Nature of the English Quarrils" in terms that clearly favor the colonists:

> I will now give you a little insight, into the Nature of the English Quarrils, over the great Waters, they got to be rich I mean the Nobles and the great, and they are very Proud and the[y] keep the rest of their Brethren under their Feet, they make slaves of them, the great ones have got all the Land

and the rest are poor Tenants—and the People in this Country live more
upon a leavel and they live happy, and the formor King of England Use to
let the People in this Country have their Freedom and Liberty; but the present King of England wants to make them Slaves to himself, and the People
in this Country don't want to be Slaves,—and so they are come over to kill
them, and the People here are oblig'd to defend themselves, they don't go
over the great Lake to kill them. (1775 CHS)

In seeing the colonists as beleaguered slaves and poor tenants and the English lords as land-hungry, controlling figures who are out to destroy the
lower classes, Occom avoids the economic relationships between his Native
audience and Anglo-American colonists, which often involved Native ser-
vitude. Instead he creates a solidarity of the oppressed, with the English as
the real enemy. The passage concludes, "And now I think you must see
who is the oppressor, and who are the oppressed and Now I think, if you
must join on one way or other you cant join the oppressor, but the oppressed, and God will help the oppressed" (1775 CHS). Ostensibly Occom
is urging the Oneida to stay out of the war; in this he is passing along the
advice of the Anglo-American missionary society and the colonial government of New York. But implicitly he is presenting an analogy between
colonists and Indians, arguing that as oppressed peoples the Indians must
sympathize with the colonists and thereby enter the war in some fashion.

Occom reports that the King of England "wants to make [the English
colonists] Slaves to himself," a reference that has several connotations. Bernard Bailyn has noted that the word "slavery" in this period "was a term
referring to a specific political condition," and that "the degradation of
chattel slaves . . . was only the final realization of what the loss of freedom
could mean everywhere" (234). For Occom, however, slavery was a racial
as well as a political concern. In one of his unpublished sermons, Occom
writes, "I believe many Christians . . . have and do keep slaves, but at this
Time of the Day of the Gospel, they are much Troubled in their Con-
science about it, and great many have freed their Negroes already in these
United States Since these Troubles began, and it is a good work, these
People show themselves to be the True Sons and Daughters of Liberty"
(Sermon book CHS). Fully aware of the racial dynamics embedded in the
political language of slavery, Occom reminds his audience of their participation in a system that claims to valorize freedom yet enslaves an entire
race. By making explicit the connection between the principle of liberty

for which Americans fought and the practice of holding slaves, Occom returns to one of the recurring themes in his own writing: the divisions between "nations," or what today we would call racial groups.

After the war Occom protests: "This Family Contention of the English, has been & is the most undoing war to the poor Indians that ever happen amongst them it has Stript them of everything, both their Temporal and Spiritual Injoyments—It seems to me, at Times that there is nothing but wo, wo, wo, writen in every Turn of the Wheel of God's Providence against us, I am afraid we are Devoted to Distruction and Misery" (c. 1784 CHS). His use of the language of family sets up a dichotomy between the "White People" as one family and "Indians" as another. Occom variously refers to the American Revolution as "This Family Contention of the English," "the English Quarrils," and "these Quarrils among the White People," emphasizing that the American Revolution is not necessarily relevant to Indians, and should be left to those most directly involved. The language through which he makes his point, though, is revealing. By using what we think of as racial terminology ("White People") interchangeably with the language of nationality ("the English"), and by using the language of the family to characterize the war ("Family Contention"), Occom implies a much more permanent distinction between the English and the Indians than a political struggle might imply. His use of these terms also points to his awareness that though the Revolution might sever certain ties between England and the colonies, the "family" connection between the newly formed United States and England is far stronger than any relationship between "Indians" and "White People."

But if revolutionary rhetoric was a means by which Occom differentiated Natives from the English, it was also an effective way for Natives to bring themselves to the attention of the colonists. In 1774, Joseph Johnson shrewdly used the language of revolutionary struggle that was circulating throughout New England to establish a relationship with "all generous, freehearted, and public-spirited gentlemen."[15] He writes:

Unless the Indians use proper Endeavours, to keep in Possession of their Native Liberty, that in short time they will unavoidably be involved, in that wretched state of perfect slavery, which every rational being dreads. Liberty is admired by all noble spirits. and gentlemen, let me with humility tell you, that I have excerted myself, used my utter most endeavours to help my poor Brethren in New England; to bring them out of Bondage, as it were; and to

lead them into a land of Liberty. where they, and their Children might Live
in peace. and to bring about this grand design, I have chearfully given my
all as it were.[16]  (February 21, 1774 CHS)

Having established a connection between the needs and desires of Natives
and those of the colonists, Johnson concludes with a request for financial
assistance to help in "this grand design." Juxtaposing slavery, bondage, and
poverty with liberty, nobility, and rationality, and seeing both Brotherton
and the United States as a "land of Liberty," he characterizes the Native
struggle for sovereignty as one with the colonial struggle.

In a post-revolutionary petition written on behalf of the Brotherton and
New Stockbridge Indians, Occom also uses the language of tyranny, slavery, and freedom. He writes to "the most August Assembly, the Congress
of the Thirteen United States": "We rejoice with you and Congratulate
you that after a long struggle, under the Tyrannic Hand of your invious
Elder Brother, you have broke the Slavish Chaine and the galling yoke,
and by your firmness & steadyness, [illegible] and Great Courage; you have
got your Freedom Liberty and Independence" (1785 CHS).[17] Though this
passage celebrates the newfound independence of the American colonies,
its language also suggests a parallel to the inferior position of Natives. Like
Johnson, Occom implies a link between Brotherton and the newly
founded nation's attempt to break free from tyranny. This passage follows
upon Occom's reminder that his people were here long before the English,
and that they sold their land for almost nothing to accommodate the English settlers. Furthermore, Occom reminds the Congress, the Indians
helped the colonists fight off their King in the recent Revolution. In return,
Occom humbly asks for some small favors for the Brotherton Indians at
Oneida, such as "a Grist Mill" and a "Saw Mill . . . all manner of husbandry tools . . . and a little library" (1785 CHS). The request is couched
in language that at once suggests such small favors are long overdue to the
Indians and implies that one Revolution in which a "Tyrannic Hand" is
overthrown can lead to another.

In a nation ostensibly founded on the principle that "all men are created
equal," Johnson and his peers struggled to establish the fact of their own
manhood as Native Americans. Euro-American missionaries' and funding
agencies' assumption of their own superiority to Native Americans was
central to the education that both Occom and Johnson had received in the
missionary schools of their youth and central to their everyday interactions

with Sergeant and Kirkland. The Natives' deployment of the very language of patriarchy that had been used as an instrument of dominance against them established their objections to that relationship. Furthermore, their appropriation of the language of liberty, freedom, and independence announced their opposition to the infantilizing assumptions of Anglo-American missionaries. By adapting Anglo-American rhetoric to Native traditions of power, the leaders of Brotherton forged dynamic new positions for themselves and their community in the colonial world of New England.

## The Body Out of Joint: Tensions within the Community

Even though they embraced Christianity and Euro-American forms of agriculture, dress, housing, and literacy, the Natives of Brotherton became increasingly suspicious of Euro-Americans themselves. In fact, Occom's and Johnson's writings are suffused with their deep distrust of White people in general and certain individuals more specifically. At the same time, Anglo-American missionaries complained regularly about their Native charges as well as the Native missionaries with whom they worked. As a larger ideological struggle was played out at Brotherton, it manifested itself as a conflict between individuals. Personal animosities became the means through which the broader racial tensions present in the community were expressed.

For example, Samson Occom expresses his growing disillusionment with the missionary establishment through personal attacks against those with whom he has worked. He tells a friend that Samuel Kirkland's work for the United States government during the Revolutionary War was deeply disruptive for the Natives he served as a missionary. He writes, "Mr Kirkland went with an Army against the poor Indians, & he has prejudiced the minds of Indians against all Missionaries, especially against White Missionaries, Seven Times more than anything, that ever was done by the White People" (May 1783 CHS). And he bitterly complains about his former mentor Wheelock's misuse of the funds Occom spent two years collecting in England. He reports to his friend John Bailey, "Doctor Wheelock's Indian Academies or Schools are become altogether unprofitable to the poor Indians—In Short, he has done little or no good to the Indians with all that Money we collected in England, Since we got home . . . there has not been one Indian in that Institution this Some

Time." He concludes cynically, "All that money has done, is, it has made Doctor's Family very grand in the World" (May 1783 CHS). Occom expresses the personal betrayal by Kirkland and Wheelock as a betrayal of all Native Americans. Keenly aware of the political and financial usefulness of Natives to Anglo-American missionaries, Occom sees the effects of various Anglo-American schemes on the Natives they are supposed to benefit as overwhelmingly "destructive" and "unprofitable."

Occom's hostility toward White people was a source of anxiety for Anglo-American missionaries such as Kirkland, who saw it as potentially ruinous to their position in the Native community. In a letter to his supervisor in the American military alleging Occom's role in dividing the community at New Stockbridge and Brotherton, Kirkland's anxiety about racial relations manifests itself in a personal attack on Occom. He warns his supervisor ominously about "Mr Occom, with whose zeal and feelings towards white people, permit me sir to say, you are very much unacquainted" (Kirkland to Pickering, May 1792 HC). He continues:

> There is no Indian, in the compass of my knowledge (Brant only excepted) who has more inveterate prejudices against white people than Mr. Occom. Altho his education & professional calling in most cases restrains them. but in certain companies, & on certain occasions, they will break out & induce him to inculcate sentiments not only derogatory from that national character, which is due to the white people, but injurious to the real interest of the indians, & such as tend to sour their minds & rivet their prejudices. (Kirkland to Pickering, May 1792 HC)

For Kirkland the threat Occom represents is racial on two levels; on one level he openly denigrates the "national character" of White people, and does not give "what is due to white people." On another level, Kirkland claims, Occom hurts Indians as well by turning them against White people.

Kirkland voices even more hostility toward Occom in his journal. He blames Occom for the "unhappy divisions & animosities" among the Brotherton Indians and implies that his own ministrations to these people are what keeps the community from collapsing entirely (1794 HC). He adds in another report: "A great majority of his own people at Brothertown—& also of the Stockbridge Tribe, have told me, it is their opinion, that he has done more injury to the Indians in general, in these parts, than he has done good to them" (letter to Timothy Pickering, May 31, 1792

MHS). Kirkland's words are ironically reminiscent of Occom's own complaint about Kirkland ("Mr Kirkland . . . has prejudiced the minds of Indians against all Missionaries, especially against White Missionaries, Seven Times more than anything, that ever was done by the White People"). Like Occom's, Kirkland's words are at least partially motivated by a desire to present himself in the most flattering light; by personally diminishing his fellow missionary, Kirkland attempts to secure his own position in the community.

Tensions already present between Kirkland and Occom were exacerbated by the arrival in the 1790s of John Sergeant Jr., who had been the minister of the Stockbridge Indians in Massachusetts. As various individuals struggled to attain positions of power, personal tensions with their racial overtones were recorded in such a way as to aggravate divisions in the community. Occom states, "I am Now fully Convinc'd, that the Indians must have Teachers of their own Colour or Nation,—They have very great and reveted Prejudice against the White People, and they have too much good reason for it—they have been imposed upon, too much" (1791 CHS). In August 1787 the New Stockbridge Indians write to him, asking him to become their minister: "We have felt and Experienced the goodness of God, for Raising and fiting one of our own collour, to be Instramental to build up the Cause and the Kingdom our Lord Jesus Christ.—We therefore feel in Duty bound to come to request you, to come and settle with us, and to take the Charge over us, and to live and die with us, in conjunction with Brotherton, if it be agreable to them" (1787 CHS). Natives, this petition suggests, can and must develop their own relationship to God, and a Native preacher is central to establishing that relationship.[18] Thus when Sergeant arrived in upstate New York in the early 1790s fully expecting to renew his ministry to his Native congregation, he was stunned to find that they had accepted "One of their own collour," Samson Occom, as their new spiritual guide. Sergeant set up his ministry nonetheless, and for years Occom, Sergeant, and Kirkland competed for the hearts and souls of converts. At times this competition was barely disguised. For example, Occom writes gleefully to a fellow minister about Kirkland's lack of success. He claims that even though Kirkland preached on Sunday, they preferred listening to Occom: "Mr. Kirkland's People . . . came to our meeting to day, tho' Mr. Kirkland went there this morning, and they knew of his coming." He further states that "they desire, that I might spend some

Sabbaths" preaching to them. He concludes with a statement about the apparent inadequacy of the two White missionaries: "There seems to be a strange inclination among the Indians, to hear the Word of God preached . . . Mr. Kirkland is going away again, and I shall go to his People next Sabbath—Several of them, have great Desire to Join us in full—and some of Mr. Sargeant's people are coming to us also and they will join us in full" (January 8 1791 [2?] STL). By implying that he is the only minister who truly preaches "the Word of God," Occom justifies his attempts to steal away Kirkland's and Sergeant's congregations. In fact, his seemingly innocent comments on the matter suggest that the shifting of congregations is the fault of the other missionaries rather than the result of his own aggressive outreach.

Animosity between Kirkland and Sergeant eventually caused a major rift between the two Anglo-American missionaries as well. And in their battles they used their Native American congregations as ammunition against each other. When Kirkland discovered that Sergeant recommended to the missionary society that he be replaced by a younger, more effective missionary, the suggestion devastated him. He writes in a blinding rage to Sergeant, "My entire removal, or relinquishing my mission, seems to be the main or ultimate object with you." He almost hysterically reminds Sergeant of an earlier incident, in which the "infamous & malicious Charges bro't against me contained in the letter which you and Cap't Hendrick advised the Oneidas to get wrote & directed to the Board of Commissioners in Boston" were "considered by the Board [and] determined . . . *unsupported* and *groundless*." In defending himself, he alludes to Sergeant's own troubles with Occom and the divided New Stockbridge congregation: "In your disputes with Mr Occum & his party, I cautiously avoided any interference" (1794 HC). Astounded by what he sees as Sergeant's betrayal, he reminds his former friend:

> When some of your people in years past, have complained of the meagerness of your sermons (as the Society of Scotland did of your Journals)—I felt a disposition to make matters as easy as possible.—when they said to me, in justification of their complaints & uneasiness with you, that if they could receive as much knowledge & information from two of your Sermons, as they obtained from one of Mr. Occums or mine, they would be contented. I have invariably checked such complaints, & remarked that comparisons were odious, & not profitable. (1794 HC)

Kirkland's petty jibes come from hurt pride. But they recast the pain of personal betrayal as a question of who better represents the Native community. Both missionaries' identities are integrally connected to their sense that they are fully aware of the needs of their congregations. As each suggests the other has failed his congregation, they touch upon the greatest fear of all Anglo-American missionaries—that their years of labor have been in vain, and that Native converts have not received the crucial guidance that Anglo-Americans are morally obligated to provide.

As relationships deteriorated, infighting occurred in all combinations: Occom competed with Kirkland and Sergeant; Kirkland struggled against Occom and Sergeant; Sergeant raged against Occom and Kirkland. Petty quarrels intensified and eventually involved the whole community, and the fighting among the trio destabilized power relations between missionaries and their Native congregations. Each missionary claimed the ultimate authority to speak for the Indians, while the Indians themselves seem to have been incidental to the personal attacks missionaries leveled against each other. Rather than being passive observers, however, the various congregations may have been taking advantage of the situation to get better services and more advantageous treatment. Using the language of each missionary, various petitions circulated, ostensibly from "the Native people." For instance, a petition from the Stockbridge Indians to Samuel Kirkland about the Sergeant-Occom feud pits missionaries against each other: "Our disagreements in our view has in a very considerable measure arisen from Mr. Occom's coming among us not to harmonize with our Minister and to treat him like a Brother; but to draw off a party, and by his preaching and conversation to alionate the affections of our poor ignorant people from white people in general and Ministers in particular. furthermore, we have thought and so believe that Mr Occom has gone out of the line of his duty in meddling too much with our civil government" (June 22, 1792 HC). It is unclear whether Kirkland might have been involved in creating this petition, which echoes so closely his own sentiments about Occom, but the petition does reveal the strategic alliances formed between various congregations and ministers as they sought to maximize benefits to themselves.

Animosities in the new settlements were not just between competing missionaries. With multiple versions of Native identity constantly surrounding them, the populations of Oneida, Brotherton, and New Stockbridge struggled to maintain their own distinctiveness while living in close

proximity. Regardless of the rhetoric of family that suffused the early negotiations between the Oneida and the Brotherton and New Stockbridge
Indians, the new settlers were Algonquian peoples and the Oneida were
Iroquois, and the cultural differences between the two quickly became a
source of antagonism. The Algonquians, accustomed as they were to Euro-
American manners, had adopted much of the condescending attitude of
the White settlers toward western tribes of Native Americans. In a revealing letter to the missionary society, Occom explains the purpose of the
Brotherton Indians in this way: "Their view is if they can find room
[among the western Indians], to embody together both in Civil and Religious State, their Main View is, to Introduce the Religion of Jesus Christ
by their example among the benighted Indians in the Wilderness, and also
Introduce Agriculture amongst them." He adds, "Some Indians are set out
last month, into the Wilderness to Reconnoiter the Wild Indian's Coun-
tries, and to see whether there is any room for our Indians" (November 10,
1773 CHS). Occom's condescension surfaces throughout with respect to
the "benighted" and "wild" Indians as opposed to "our Indians" who will
set an example for proper, civilized living through their understanding of
Christianity.

True to the masculinist assumptions of the Brotherton settlers, Occom
suggests that agriculture will be the solution to the problems of the
Oneida, as if the farming practiced by Iroquois women is invisible to
him.[19] Oneida agricultural practices did not involve investment in heavy
machinery or European technology and so were generally not recognized
by Euro-Americans. Furthermore, as an expression of the Oneida put it,
"Man . . . was made for war and hunting, and holding councils, and . . .
squaws and hedge-hogs are made to scratch the ground" (Belknap and
Morse 20). Many Oneida men found farming to be a humiliating, unnatu-
ral activity; the Belknap-Morse Report explains, "An Oneida Chief . . .
would think himself degraded by driving a team, or guiding a plough"(22).
Accepting the Anglo-American emphasis on both the particular gender
roles of agricultural work and its importance in society would have involved a drastic change for the Oneida. Agriculture was only a small part
of Oneida subsistence practices, and was considered irrelevant to the larger
identity of the Oneida people; another Oneida expression made this point
quite clearly: "The Great Spirit gave the white man a plough, and the red
man a bow and arrow, and sent them into the world by different paths,

each to get his living in his own way" (Belknap and Morse 20). By accepting and repeating the Euro-American position on the importance of agriculture, Occom is separating himself from the Oneida and their practices. In his attempt to forge a new version of Native identity, he finds himself uncomfortably aligned with the Euro-American missionaries he so distrusts. This point was not lost on the Oneida; they were said to "despise their neighbors of Stockbridge and Brotherton, for their attention to agriculture" (23).

Though the Oneida and the Brotherton Indians agreed that the new community was to be based on Native empowerment and cultural integrity, there was little consensus on implementation of these ideals. For the Oneida, Christianity was the basis for community only for part of the tribe; the "pagan" party, or those opposed to Christianity, saw their future in the revival of traditional practices that were often in conflict with Christian beliefs. The Belknap-Morse Report suggests how widespread this belief was in the community; although only eight adults openly considered themselves professed pagans, "the whole nation, notwithstanding their opportunities for religious improvement, are still influenced, in a great degree, by their old mythology" (15). This mythology, the report continues, has various elements, as one of the tribal elders explains:

> Some of them address their devotions to the wind, others to the clouds and thunder, he to the rocks and mountains, which he believed to have an invisible, as well as visible existence, and an agency over human actions . . . He regarded the *Oneida Stone* as a proper emblem or representation of the divinity which he worshipped. . . . [The people] are universally firm believers in witchcraft and invisible agency. They pay great regards to dreams and omens, and attribute most common events to causes with which there can be no natural connexion. (14–15)

Many of the Oneida thus welcomed Native settlers less for their Christianity than for the possibility that a stronger Native presence would buttress the Oneida themselves against the incursions of White settlers. "Community" for many of the Oneida was based on the continuity of past traditions.

Joseph Johnson's early vision of Brotherton, however, rejected the past; for him it represented a time of corruption and degradation that was best forgotten. He explains to his Oneida hosts in the negotiations establishing the settlement:

> Brethren we in New England, or at least many of us are very poor by reason
> of the Ignorance of our Forefathers who are now dead. Brethren ye know
> that the English are a wise people, and can see great ways but some say, that
> Indians cant see but little ways. Brethren, ye also knows that some English
> loves to take the advantage of poor blind Indians. So it was in the days of
> our forefathers in new England . . . whilst our forefathers were blind, and
> Ignorant yea drownded in Liquors, the English striped them yea they as it
> were Cut off our, their Right hands. (January 20, 1774 CHS)

For Johnson, the lives of his forefathers were filled with ignorance, drunkenness, nakedness, and blindness. His anxieties about his associations with
these forefathers surfaces as he corrects his pronoun reference from "our"
to "their right hands"; clearly, he wants to put as much distance as possible
between himself and this horrific past.

At the same time that Johnson criticizes his forefathers, his rage at the
English colonists for taking advantage of the ignorance of Natives emerges
throughout this passage. His ancestors were ignorant, but the English were
consciously malicious and cruel. And though Johnson is careful to establish a rupture between the past and the present of the Native people, English behavior remains constant. His final reference to the English is in the
present tense:

> Now we their Children just opening our Eyes, and knowledge growing in
> our hearts and Just come to our Senses, like a drunken man. I say we now
> begin to look around and we perceive that we are Striped indeed nothing
> to help ourselves. thus our English Brethren leaves us and laugh. So now
> Brethren we leave the English those who have acted unjustly towards us in
> New England, I say we leave them all in the hands of that God who knoweth
> all things. and will reward everyone according to their deeds. whether good
> or Evil. (January 20, 1774 CHS)

He emphasizes in this passage that the future for Natives must involve not
only a rejection of the destructive ways of the Native past, but also a rejection of the English people who have already abandoned them. Indeed
the passage suggests the emergence of a powerful male force: once blind,
drunk, and ignorant, the newly sober Native man now has the knowledge
and the vision through which to live independent of corrupting English
influence.

But even as Johnson rages against Whites and argues for Native empowerment in one document, he uses self-debasing language to get what he

needs from Whites in another. In a letter to an unnamed governor, he begins, "I am an Indian. I am of a Nation little respected in these days. and for good reason." He continues this self-loathing diatribe:

> My forefathers, the Natives of this land, brought this disrespect upon themselves and theirs when your forefathers intreated them as brothers, and received them as thus into their friendships, and in a brotherly manner declared unto them the mind and will of God. they paid no regard to your Worthy Ancestors, nor to their words, but walked, every one according to the imagination of their own wicked and unchristian hearts; and lived in Intemprance. Excess, rioting, and other disolute Practices, these and many others that might be mentioned, their unfaithfulness, Ingratitude, and unhumane Conduct justly brought this disesteem upon them, & also in these days, many are walking in the same beaten track of their forefathers, the Savages, which Confirms Disrespect, & Diss esteem, upon the Indian Nation. (1774 CHS)

Unlike the letter to the Oneida, this one connects the past and present behavior of Natives, suggesting that they are an altogether degraded group. He concludes, "We have reason to mourn for the sins past which our forefathers, and we their children have sinfully committed, is the cause of all these heavey judgments, which my poor Nation is groaning and sinking under" (1774 CHS). Here Johnson takes on all blame, speaking both as an individual and as a representative of his race. Clearly playing up what he imagines prospective donors want to hear, he uses the language of self-hatred to make possible his vision of an independent Native community.[20]

In their writing within the community, Johnson and Occom complicate the meanings of Nativeness and Whiteness. Johnson's attack on the past suggests that "Nativeness" is a mutable term that can mean very different things in the present. A letter written by Occom and other members of the Mohegan tribe also reveals some of the difficulties of defining racial or "national" identity. Occom writes about a situation in which the status of "Ben Mazzeen" as a member of the tribe is in question: "In our overhalling the list of our Tribe we have found one name that we cannot find out where it came from. we find the Families of Mohegan and the Number of the families and their christian or given Names and sir Names but there is one of Moses Mazzeens Family is calld Ben but what Ben no Body can tell it is Moses Mazeens Daughter Hannah's Son and he is Blacker than our Indians and he thinks he is from Guinney peartly" (December 5, 1789

CHS). Even as he is identifiable as the son of a tribal member, Ben Mazzeen is not accepted because of his skin color. Occom continues anxiously: "The whole Tribe objects against him and we cannot tell how his name was put down amongst the Names of the Mohegan Tribe it may be thus the inattention of the Tribe and now we object against his having Right among us—more over if he takes rite amongst us—not only guinney Children but European Children and some other Children will take rite also— and it will also give Liberty to our Daughters to borrow Children from all Quarters" (December 5, 1789 CHS). According to Occom's logic here, Indians exist as a community until they are visibly marked as different from one another. Thus the Mohegan community must remain vigilant against the threat of "guinney" or "European" children passing themselves off as Indian. Such children pose a threat to the very existence of a Native community. The problem is not their lineage but their appearance.

In *Beyond Ethnicity*, Werner Sollors argues that ethnicity as a category exists as defined against the dominant culture. He claims that much ethnic American literature adapts a general rhetoric of American identity to create "seriously divergent models of peoplehood." He continues: "The same ligament constructions that spelled consensus among Americans could also be adapted to formulate secessionist and separatist peoplehoods" (259). Much like Sollor's understanding of ethnicity, Occom and Johnson's versions of Brotherton's racial/ethnic identity exist in opposition to those identities surrounding them. Using language from various sources, Brotherton creates itself in the overlaps and spaces between other identities. Using the language of patriarchy, Brotherton at once defines itself against Anglo-American missionary structures while participating in them. Like the American Revolutionary rhetoric, in which an American identity constitutes itself in opposition to the British "Mother Country," through terms such as "tyranny," "slavery," and "liberty" the Brotherton settlement pulls away from Anglo-American culture, aligning itself with "Indians" rather than "white people." At the same time, in a different context Brotherton rhetorically distances itself from the "savage" or "wild" Indians of Oneida to create an identity that acknowledges its Christianity and at times even embraces its connections to Euro-Americans. Brotherton community identity thus exists at the interstices of other identities. Constantly redefining itself against those around it, Brotherton is powerfully committed to its value as a distinct community.

FOR Johnson and Occom, the bond that united the various Native groups was the empowering possibility of their spiritual salvation through Christianity. The Anglo-American missionaries involved in the venture agreed that the community was built on Christianity, but their understanding of what this meant was quite different from that of the Native missionaries. For Kirkland and Sergeant, Christianizing Natives involved a rather grim process of reducing them to a sense of their innate sinfulness and inferiority as a people. Insisting on their own importance as leaders of the community, Kirkland and Sergeant refused to acknowledge the politically and socially empowering theology of Johnson and Occom.

Even for Christian Indians embarked upon a quest for a Native Christian community, the relationship between Christianity and Nativeness remained unclear. By accepting Christianity but rejecting White America, the Brotherton community developed specifically Native systems and structures of identity based on Anglo-American models, but through their response to the Anglo-American missionary order in which they had been immersed, the Native leaders found themselves drawn into the very paradigms they were attempting to refute. The most vivid example is the gendered rhetorical strategy of these Native writers, which replicates the exclusionary stratifications and hierarchies inherent in colonial structures of power. Another is the demeaning language with which founders of Brotherton refer to other Natives and even, occasionally, themselves. The Native response to missionary condescension falls back onto the very terms it is most trying to reject.

While Johnson held forth the possibility of a dynamic community with the strength and power of full "manhood," the financial and material needs of the Brotherton Indians often went unmet. As Kirkland, Occom, Sergeant, and Wheelock struggled over who could best represent the community, several years of famine nearly decimated the community. By 1818 the first wave of settlers left upstate New York to move to Wisconsin, where, after a series of other dislocations, the descendants of the Brotherton and Stockbridge Indians live today. Conflict cut short what might have been a radically new type of community, a hybrid of various needs and desires. The tensions between the autobiographical accounts of Occom and Johnson and the biographical accounts of Wheelock, Kirkland, and Sergeant can tell us a great deal about the complex process of declaring independence within a multicultural, postcolonial society.

# EPILOGUE

# A Son of the Forest and
# a Preacher of the Gospel
## Narratives of Captivity and Conversion

†

In the academy scholars now want "an Indian point of view." And Indians want and need to talk, to tell their stories. But what constitutes "an Indian point of view"? By what and whose definition is a point of view "Indian"? How might an Indian's story in turn define "Indian"? What of an Indian's story that is not "Indian"?

—Greg Sarris, *Keeping Slug-Woman Alive*

Where racist, nationalist, or ethnically absolutist discourses orchestrate political relationships so that . . . identities appear to be mutually exclusive, occupying the space between them or trying to demonstrate their continuity has been viewed as a provocative and even oppositional act of political insubordination.

—Paul Gilroy, *The Black Atlantic*

IN 1992, Barry O'Connell republished the works of an obscure nineteenth-century Christian Indian in a collection entitled *On Our Own Ground: The Complete Writings of William Apess, a Pequot*. O'Connell's publication was a literary event of quite some significance. It forced many of us engaged in the study of American literature to reevaluate our assumptions (if we had any at all) about Christian Indians and the nature of radical religious and political thought among nineteenth-century New England Indians. The introduction to this collection situates William Apess in his time and in our own. O'Connell acknowledges, "Apess's militant consciousness is not only surprising in its modern ring but puzzling both to the common assumption that most Indians had disappeared from southern New England by the nineteenth century and to knowledgeable scholars who know something, though still much too little, about the scattered and impoverished New England Indians in this period" (xv). Other critics including David Murray, Arnold Krupat, Laura Murray, and Maureen Konkle have analyzed Apess's rhetoric, arguing for his sophisticated manipulation of the language of colonial domination surrounding him. Hailed as a radical, Apess has been praised for his unique challenge to European assumptions about Native Americans. But literary scholars' accolades, while well deserved, deny the extensive tradition of Native American Christian writing that existed well over a century before Apess.

Apess's accomplishments were certainly remarkable. Native Americans in the nineteenth century (and to a certain extent still today) were often regarded as authentic only as they fit into preconceived generic constructions of Euro-American observers; by publishing his own writing without the intervention of an editor, Apess undermined the terms of such observers. Challenging Euro-American beliefs about exactly who and what Indians were and what they wanted, William Apess demanded that White New Englanders reevaluate their privileged social position, a position he insisted came at the expense of the original inhabitants of the land. By doing so, he garnered for himself a reputation—both in his own time and in ours—that obscured much Native protest writing before his. But the attacks that he leveled against Anglo-American Christians were part of a tradition of Native Christian writing that dates back at least to Eliot's first converts. Apess constructs a textual identity out of several of the discourses available to Christian Indians. The extensive writings of this culturally marginal figure suggest the hybridity inherent in his life and in the lives of the Christian Indians before him.

Along with his full-length autobiography *A Son of the Forest,* Apess produced political documents concerning the Mashpee Revolt, a missionary tract/biography/autobiography called *The Experiences of Five Christian Indians of the Pequot Tribe,* and what many consider his most famous contribution to American letters, a speech entitled "Eulogy on King Philip." Though the chronology of Apess's work is disputed, several important themes run throughout his writing. Specifically, he engages throughout with particular notions of Native community and history, and he connects White people's moral with their economic injustice toward Native Americans. Most important, Apess emphasizes the role of Christianity in establishing a true Native identity. In this way he participates in an extensive tradition through which Native Christians write themselves into Anglo-American Protestantism not as pawns of a White establishment but rather as active participants in a system that allows them their own particular identity.

In *The Experiences of Five Christian Indians of the Pequot Tribe* Apess is poised between his role as a convert and his position as a missionary. As missionary, he writes brief biographical accounts of his converts just as the Anglo-American missionaries John Eliot, Experience Mayhew, John Sergeant, and Samuel Kirkland did before him. But in an important shift he includes himself as a convert along with four other Indians. In doing so he emphasizes the interrelations of the roles of missionary and convert. Just as Joseph Johnson, Samson Occom, and to a certain extent Hendrick Aupaumut did, he approaches those he refers to as his "brethren" (other Native Americans) as precisely that—individuals of coequal status to whom he must present Christianity as a community resource, not a means of eradicating culture.

In "Eulogy on King Philip" Apess looks to the past, as did Johnson and Aupaumut generations earlier, to better understand the present. In this document Apess adapts revolutionary rhetoric, as Johnson and Occom did at Brotherton, to his own purposes. Apess argues for King Philip's status as a true revolutionary hero, one to rival George Washington; thus he writes Native Americans and their struggle into the history of America, not as villains or tragic victims but as heroes to be celebrated.[1] For Apess, Native Christians must celebrate their Nativeness, however that is constructed. By honoring King Philip not as an acknowledged Christian but as a Native hero, Apess aggressively rejects the notion that Native Christians must become White; for him it is specifically as Native Americans that they become good Christians, and King Philip serves as an example of a true Christian who simply does not call himself one. This is much the same argument of Aupaumut's Mahican history, in which he ascribes Christian values and structures to his own people, in this way claiming Christianity as an indigenous system. Apess's writing, then, does not mark a departure from the previous writing of Native Christians but rather can be seen as a culmination of it.

Much of Apess's life is shrouded in invisibility. He was born into the

Pequot tribe, a people marked by the English colonists' violent attempt through the Pequot War in 1636 to erase them as a historical and legal entity. Living on the margins of colonial and later American society, the Pequots remained largely invisible to others as they struggled to maintain a presence along the Connecticut-Massachusetts border.[2] Other than his own narratives about his life and family, there is little official record of his early existence. He was born in the last few years of the eighteenth century to William and Candace Apes, went to live with his grandparents after his parents separated, and eventually was taken from them to live with a White family in the small town of Colchester, Massachusetts. In this early separation from his Native family Apess was not so different from many of the Natives we have encountered in previous chapters. James Printer, for example, was sent by his family to learn a trade among Anglo-American colonists, and Tobit Potter of Martha's Vineyard, the child described by Experience Mayhew, was bound out to an Anglo-American family as a servant until he became unwell and was sent home to die. Similarly, Joseph Johnson was sent as a child to Eleazar Wheelock's Charity School. As in each of these previous cases, despite the separation Apess maintained ties throughout his life with his Native community.

Like other Natives raised by Whites, Apess turned to Christianity early. Brought up by his masters in Congregationalism, he was not consistently faithful but instead struggled with alcohol and debauched living as a young man (much as Joseph Johnson did fifty years before him). Apess eventually converted to Methodism and wrote the story of his life in a narrative that is steeped in the conventions and rhetoric of the Christian conversion narrative. Like Christian Indians before him, Apess not only found personal salvation through his religious affiliation but came to envision it as the means through which all Natives could come to terms with their racial identity.

In his extended autobiography, *A Son of the Forest* (1829), Apess uses the metaphor of captivity to shape the narrative of his life. Like John Sergeant, Apess uses the structure of the captivity narrative to emphasize the dramatic racial confrontations that characterize his life. But though Sergeant uses the conventions of captivity to rationalize the alienation he feels as a missionary to a Native community, Apess's first use of captivity language establishes his alienation from his own people as a child. And in contrast to Sergeant's wholehearted acceptance of the conventions of captivity as an explanatory model for race relations, Apess's use of the trope critiques the conventions of the Anglo-American captivity narrative as fraudulent.

Brought up in the homes of well-respected Anglo-Americans, the youthful Apess is terrified by encounters with his own people. In a telling moment early in his narrative, the child's fear of Indians leads him to misconstrue a situation in which imaginary Natives pose a threat to him. As he goes berry-picking in the woods with his White family, they are joined by young women whose skin, Apess reports, was "as dark as that of the natives" (10). "I broke from the party with my utmost speed, and I could not muster courage enough to look behind until I had reached home" (11). When he returns to town to warn everyone of what turns out to be a nonexistent Native threat, he creates a story along the traditional lines of the captivity narrative, in which Indians are savages and Whites their innocent victims. He tells his readers, "By this time my imagination had pictured out a tale of blood." When his master asks about what has happened, Apess tells him "that we had met a body of the natives in the woods, but what had become of the party [the family members Apess was with] I could not tell" (11).[3]

The older Apess ruefully tells us that "the great fear I entertained of my brethren was occasioned by the many stories I had heard of their cruelty toward the Whites—how they were in the habit of killing and scalping men, women, and children" (11). In particular, the berry-picking episode evokes the drama and horror of captivity stories, in which the cruelty of the Native is offset by the innocence and fragility of the White victim. The child Apess finds himself in a peculiarly racial no-man's-land, in which he must protect his White family from people he fears absolutely, but who are like him. The narrator's adult voice emphasizes the powerful effect of White versions of Indianness on the child Apess, who fears and hates people of his own color and prefers to align himself with White people. At the same time, his mock-captivity-narrative points to the role of fear and hysteria in vilifying Native Americans, a role so powerful that it even turns Native Americans against themselves.

According to the adult Apess narrating the story, the young Apess has misunderstood the real threat of captivity, which comes from the White family who is willing to sell him into bondage as an indentured servant. Apess concludes the story, "But the Whites did not tell me that they were in a great majority the aggressors—that they had imbrued their hands in the lifeblood of my brethren, driven them from their once peaceful and happy homes. . . . If the Whites had told me how cruel they had been to the 'poor Indian,' I should have apprehended as much harm from them" (11).[4]

From this point on, the adult Apess inverts the traditional captivity narrative to point to his own victimization at the hands of his savage White masters. Apess is outraged at the seeming randomness of the injustices against him—injustices that are heaped upon him because of his race. It is not only the fact that his indenture can be bought and sold without his knowledge and approval that disturbs him; what rankles even more is "to be sold to and treated unkindly by those who had got our fathers' lands for nothing" (16). Thus it is specifically as a Native American that he objects to the power of his masters. But in Apess's narrative, the captivity narratives' racial categories are inverted; instead of the typical innocent White victim of Native injustice, here the innocent young Indian is victimized by the incomprehensible brutality of White people. In the case of his indenture, he claims to have truly experienced captivity at the hands of his White masters, unlike his youthful experience of a false captivity at the hands of purported Natives.

Along with their social and racial injustice, the religious intolerance of his masters is very disturbing to Apess. He explains that as a child he was numbed by the formality and rote quality of his masters' Presbyterian prayer. He concludes, "I could fix no value on [their] prayers" (15). Apess criticizes Presbyterian prayer because it demands only his physical presence, not his participation, and thus stifles his expression; he clearly feels alienated and silenced. Here Apess openly condemns the Anglo-American protestant tradition established by the likes of Eliot, Wheelock, and Kirkland, who expect docile converts for whom they can define and delimit Christianity. Apess represents himself as trapped—spiritually, emotionally, and physically—in a world that allows him no voice or identity. His use of the term "value" further stresses the element of captivity, where both spiritual and physical redemption are connected to economic exchange.

The links among race, religion, and finance are echoed in Joseph Johnson's 1774 outburst about his lack of financial stability, which comes as a result of his poor treatment as an Indian. The writings of Apess, Occom, and Johnson are filled with the bitterness that comes from their belief in their own value as Christians and Indians even as White society consistently undermines them. Johnson and Occom eventually form their own religious community with uneasy alliances to Anglo-American Congregationalist missionary culture. But for Apess, redemption from the injustices of his masters lies in his conversion to an alternative religious group—the Methodist Church, which stands in marked contrast to his masters' formal, unemotional tradition. Apess is drawn to Methodism through the camp meeting, one of the more expressive and enthusiastic of religious gatherings. Russell E. Richey points out that "the camp meeting was a ritual recovery of . . . openness, inclusiveness, and flexibility" (23). Indeed, unlike the decorous Presbyterian prayer sessions, camp meetings were enthusiastic, vibrant, multiracial community affairs that emphasized spontaneity and emotional excess.[5] Apess is welcomed into the larger community and asked to pray in his own voice, not simply to repeat words that have no meaning to him.

Alienation from Congregational and Presbyterian forms of worship can be seen in much of the literature concerning Native converts. As Natives attempt to create their own forms of worship, they are often condemned by representatives of the Puritan missionary hierarchy. We see this, for example, in Timothy Woodbridge's 1735 criticism of Native forms of worship. And if the condemnation is not overt, it is certainly the source of a great deal of uneasiness, as we saw in both Mayhew's and Eliot's reactions to the practices of their Native converts that were not immediately comprehensible to them. Rather than being forced to choose between Christianity and Nativeness, Apess has available to him forms of worship that allow him to integrate both.

For Apess, the distinction between his religious and his racial oppression is insignificant, and the metaphor of captivity makes this absolutely clear: if captivity is racially based, and release from captivity is through a religious awakening, then religion becomes implicated in racial identification. Emphasizing inclusion, spontaneous and emotion-laden prayer, and personal testimonials, Methodism, in its incarnation during the Second Great Awakening, stood in sharp contrast to the more structured, formal worship of denominations that had extensive roots in the culture of the New England elite.[6] For Native Christians before Apess, there were few sanctioned alternatives to the forms of worship dictated by the Congregational elite, so they integrated Native cultural traditions to give shape and meaning to their Christianity. For Apess, however, Methodism becomes the very structuring principle of his Nativeness; it does not alienate him as a socially or racially inferior being but rather demands his active participation.[7] Methodism gives him the voice and the language through which to tell his story as a Christian and an Indian.

In the process of finding his voice as a Christian Native American, Apess rejects the role defined for Native converts by White missionaries since the time of John Eliot—that of the docile, humble beneficiary of the superior White religious establishment. Congregational and Presbyterian denominations perpetuated models of Native Christianity emphasizing obedience, humility, and acquiescence. The common thread of several of these denominations' missionary narratives is a tragic early death that cuts off a deeply spiritual—and remarkably docile—young life. The clear implication is that Christianity is not intended as a way to live for Natives—it is instead a way to die.[8] And as we have also seen, Native writers were unwilling to accept the limited role determined for them by Anglo-Americans. For Apess, too, far from representing a quiet acquiescence to Euro-American civilization, Christianity is a means through which Natives could express not just equality with Whites but even supremacy. By appropriating the dominant discourse as Native autoethnographers of previous generations had done, Apess demands for himself and his people a place in American society.

Like Hendrick Aupaumut, Joseph Johnson, and Samson Occom before him, Apess uses religious rhetoric to critique and even rewrite his tenuous position in American society. For him and his Native Christian forebears, Christianity cannot be understood as a Euro-American religion, since it is for them the very basis of their ethnicity as Native Americans. As Apess tries to forge a Native Christian identity, he envisions a radical empowerment for his brethren on a racial as well as a religious level. Sandra Gustafson argues that Apess's writings "chart his journey away from a primarily Methodist identity and toward an ethnically defined identity" ("Nations" 33).

In several of his works Apess advocates a commonly held Euro-American theory of Native American origins as the basis for his superiority as a Christian to Anglo-American Christians.[9] This theory, often referred to as the "lost tribes theory," was the basis for some of the early missionary efforts to convert Native Americans in New England in the seventeenth century.[10] Essentially, this theory proposed that Native Americans were descendants of one of the lost tribes of Israel and therefore of Semitic origin.

Because the biblical books of Daniel and Revelation foretold the conversion of the Jews as a sign of the coming of the millennium, this theory gave missionaries both the rationale and the incentive to convert the Natives to Christianity.[11] It also absorbed Native Americans into a Christian world view that made them comprehensible to Euro-Americans, who were otherwise faced with a population whose mysterious origins threatened to call into question the explanatory value of the Bible.[12] Largely forgotten after the seventeenth century, the theory was resurrected, according to Roy Harvey Pearce, around 1815 by Whites to rationalize renewed missionary impulses to civilize the Natives (61–62).

The earliest critics of the lost tribes theory were Native Americans. Gregory Dowd cites several instances in which unconverted Natives rejected the teachings of missionaries by arguing that if the Bible had been intended for their use, it would have come directly to them, not to Europeans. Dowd argues that the idea of a separate creation for Whites, Blacks, and Indians was a commonplace among Native tribal peoples by the eighteenth century. To accept the teachings of the missionaries that all races had one origin, according to Dowd, often implied a rejection of a sense of Native pride or unity (30–31). For already Christianized Indians such as Hendrick Aupaumut, however, the single-creation theory opened a space for Natives to fully engage with Christianity. Rather than rejecting Christian orthodoxy, Aupaumut and Apess both embraced it, integrating it into Native American history.

In his writing about travels among other tribes as well as in his history of the Mahican people, Aupaumut integrates what seem to be divergent traditions, in the process radically redefining Christianity and its place in both Native and Anglo-American cultures. Apess begins his own revision of Anglo-American religious assumptions modestly, telling us that he lays no claim to greatness, even though he is descended from a Pequot king. He says, "We are in fact but one family; we are all the descendants of one great progenitor—Adam" (4). Thus, it would seem, Apess is emphasizing to his readers not only the common origins of all people—a claim firmly based in the teachings of Christianity—but also by implication the essential humanity of Native Americans—a claim that needed restatement for many nineteenth-century readers. Further on he is even more insistent, saying, "It is my opinion that our nation retains the original complexion of our common father, Adam. This is strongly impressed on my mind"

(34). It is the Native Americans, not the Euro-Americans, who have re-tained the "original complexion" of Adam. And being more closely linked to Adam, Native Americans are by implication closer to God, since Adam was made in His image. Like Native Christians before him, Apess turns Anglo-American religious assumptions back on themselves to argue for his own particular authority as a Native American Christian.

Extending his manipulation of Anglo-American religious assumptions, Apess openly advocates the lost tribes theory in the appendix to his autobi-ography. But for him this theory, rather than confirming the primacy of White Christians, radically alters the hierarchy of racial value that mission-aries and White Christians assumed. He states that when he studies the "many ancient usages and customs" of the Native tribes in this country, he is "led to believe that they are none other than the descendants of Jacob and the long lost tribes of Israel" (53). In advocating the theory, Apess fur-ther buttresses his argument for the superiority of Native Americans. As descendants of the Israelites, Natives are the chosen people of God. By inverting a theory originating in the dominant culture, Apess has appro-priated the language and the logic of dominance, arguing for his own supe-riority in terms that have their roots in the culture that least wants to hear such arguments.

Apess's inversion of a classically racist Euro-American theory does away with the Anglo-American assumption that Christianizing Natives must in-volve eliminating their culture, since their culture would necessarily al-ready be within a Christian framework. Apess grounds his sense of his own ethnicity in a theory that is sanctioned by the dominant society. But he goes much further than that. He claims for Natives a truer or closer under-standing of Christianity by using the very language of the dominant cul-ture. This gesture, much like that of Hendrick Aupaumut in his late eighteenth-century history and journal, turns Anglo-American religious theories on their heads and makes them serve his own purpose, which is to question the authority that White people claim as possessors of the Truth, and to replace it with his assurance of his own superiority.

Like Aupaumut, Apess uses history to come to terms with contempo-rary race relations. Aupaumut uses tradition and ritual to invoke a Native past and Apess reinterprets classic texts of Anglo-American history such as Rowlandson's narrative to re-envision the colonial past of both Natives and Anglo-Americans. Making his point most vehemently in his "Eulogy on

King Philip," Apess inverts the civilized/savage dichotomy by listing the historical injustices heaped upon Native Americans by so-called civilized Whites. Indeed, for Apess, Native Americans were inherently better Christians through their actions than the pilgrims who had access to the Bible but whose actions were unjust and hypocritical. For both Apess and Aupaumut, the reinterpretation of history to include Natives in Christian history and Christianity in Native history also authorizes contemporary Native critiques of Anglo-American behavior. Apess exclaims (with more than a tinge of irony), "How much better it would be if the Whites would act like civilized people" (33). Apess attacks corrupt missionaries who profit from the Natives they are supposed to be helping, and points out that because of this situation Natives find themselves in a position to respond to missionaries with these words: "'Your doctrine is very good, but the whole course of your conduct is decidedly at variance with your profession—we think Whites need fully as much religious instruction as we do'" (33). Apess has radically shifted the roles of missionaries and Indians. It is in fact the Indians who must explain the truth to the missionary, not the other way around.

In laying claims to moral and cultural superiority, Apess is part of an extended tradition of Christian Indian critiques of Anglo-American claims of superiority. The writings that emerged from the Brotherton settlement express the frustration of several Christian Indian missionaries who were consistently underpaid and underemployed by an Anglo-American missionary culture; Aupaumut's work, too, expresses similar frustrations at the racial and cultural inequities he and his people faced at the hands of Anglo-American government and religious institutions. In fact, it becomes clear from an examination of the writings of Christian Indians as early as the seventeenth century that the image of the docile Indian convert was a fiction of White missionary culture from the very start of Anglo-American missionary settlements.

For Apess, the Native identity he embraces is constituted by his vision of the Methodist church, and the Christianity of the Methodist church is inseparable from the very concept of Nativeness. This connection of seemingly divergent (and even oppositional) identities leaves him like other Native Christians before him in a position that is perhaps best defined by its constantly shifting parameters or in-betweenness. Indeed, the cultural mutability of Apess's position is connected, just as it was for Aupaumut, the Brotherton Indians, and to a certain extent the inhabitants of Eliot's praying towns, with the literal phenomenon of geographical displacement or upheaval. Despite John Eliot's fervent desire to link Native Christianity to fixed, permanent space, the history of Native Christians in America is the history of migration, mutability, and removal. As both a preacher and an exhorter, Apess travels from place to place, drawing crowds of disenfranchised people like himself, much in the tradition of the typical Methodist circuit rider. In fact, Apess's narrative is defined by migration and movement as he travels throughout Connecticut, New York, Maine, Rhode Island and Massachusetts, preaching to both Whites and "colored people," as he calls his largely Native American and African American audiences. As the journals of Occom, Johnson, and Aupaumut make clear, however, his migratory lifestyle was one in which Native Christians had long participated; well before Methodist circuit riders became popular, Native American missionaries traveled throughout the area to reach dispersed pockets of Native Christians. Indeed, it can be argued that Native Christianity is defined by the constant deferral of home, or the constant movement, both geographical and cultural, of a fragmented people.

Once again confirming the strong connection in his mind between Nativeness and Christianity, Apess asserts that the most fulfilling experiences of his career as a Christian were at the Pequot reservation at Groton. Holding regular meetings and conversing with his pious Aunt Sally George, Apess tells us simply, "These seasons were glorious" (40). As Apess sees it, Methodism has given him a means of expressing an identity that he comes to believe is truly Native. Methodism releases him from his captivity and brings him back into a community of his brethren, where he is free to tell his story in a way that can make his experience coherent for him. As a Methodist, Apess is finally comfortable enough with his identity as a Native American to embrace his tribe and his extended family. This homecoming and the connection he draws between his racial and religious identity are foreshadowed fifty years earlier in Joseph Johnson's record of his return to his Connecticut home, where he joins the religious community of Samson Occom and other Christian Indians from the area.

But it eventually becomes impossible for Apess to embrace his own Nativeness unproblematically, for it is intertwined with the Methodist church. Even as he locates the Methodist church as the real source of his

Native identity, that connection is less clear for other Methodists. Apess notes that in his travels "crowds flocked out, some to hear the truth and others to see the 'Indian'" (51). He is a novelty, a figure to be marveled at as an Indian more than as a missionary preaching saving doctrine. As a servant he is unremarkable, and his Indian identity is of no consequence to anyone. As a minister, however, his Indianness is strange, unusual. As people come out to view him, they emphasize the discrepancy between his Indianness and his position as a minister. In the process of coming to terms with his indeterminate status, they attempt to fix his identity as a "mere" Indian to be treated with disdain by throwing things at him as he attempts to speak (44). The same tension existed in Native communities from John Eliot's seventeenth-century praying towns to John Sergeant's mid-eighteenth-century experiment at Stockbridge to the late-eighteenth-century community at Brotherton. In all these situations Anglo-American missionaries were unable to see past Indianness as a weakness, while Native Christians struggled to formulate an independent Native Christian identity based on the strength of Native community structures. Just as Apess struggles to be heard by a crowd who can't get past his Indianness, so Native missionaries before him were silenced by the assumptions of Anglo-Americans who didn't accept that they had anything important to say.

Though the Methodist church was liberal in comparison to the Presbyterians and Congregationalists of the early nineteenth-century, Apess's language was nonetheless restricted and censored by the Methodist hierarchy. Although Apess methodically lists the order of his promotions in his autobiography, he also notes the problems he encounters as he attempts to gain church sanction for his speaking. When he lectures without a license from the church, he is condemned for his forwardness and told to wait (45). Eventually he does receive his exhorter's license (48), but when he applies to the church for a license to preach, he is denied. It is not until 1829 or 1830 that he finally is licensed. In the first edition of his autobiography, Apess implies that this delay is due to racism on the part of the Methodist hierarchy, though he removes this claim in the second edition. What is clear from his few comments on the matter, though, is that the White community can't conceive of Apess as both a Native and a minister. Apess remains a captive to the White community even as his conversion promises him a life of freedom. Paradoxically, as he struggles to name his ambiguous status, he is silenced by the very institutions through which he has acquired his voice. Much in the same way as the Christian Indians before him, however, he finds a way to speak even as he is censored.

Paul Gilroy has argued for the importance of modern theorizations of "creolization, metissage, mestizaje, and hybridity." Gilroy points out that "from the viewpoint of ethnic absolutism, this would be a litany of pollution and impurity." But he emphasizes that "these terms are rather unsatisfactory ways of naming the processes of cultural mutation and restless (dis)continuity that exceed racial discourse and avoid capture by its agents" (2). As the dominant culture became progressively more invested in cultural purity, separation, and removal, Apess found himself attempting to forge an identity that was mixed and hybrid and willing to encompass a multiplicity that was at once personal, ethnic, and religious—precisely the identity that Gilroy's theorizations attempt to describe. Apess and the Christian Indians writing 150 years before him were consciously engaged in the process of defining or explaining their tenuous cultural positions. Working against an Anglo-American absolutist ideology that threatened to erase them, Native Christians wrote in the margins, in fragments, and even in other people's books. This writing defies our common strategies of reading, inviting us to reimagine the spaces in between and the elusive identities that may be written there.

# NOTES

## Introduction

1. Roger Williams's famous *Key into the Language of America* (1643) did contain a list of Algonquian words, but it was closer to a phrase book than any systematic attempt to "convert" the language into a written form.

2. This material is translated and reprinted in Goddard and Bragdon. Reading marginalia for information about readers has been most famously done in Davidson, which analyzes the gendered reading patterns of colonial readers.

3. The classic study of such texts is Berkhofer, *White Man's Indian*. In his study Berkhofer emphasizes the distinction between Native Americans as real individuals with real lives and "the White Man's Indian"—"a White invention [that] still remains largely a White image, if not a stereotype"(3). This image, he claims, is confused in the minds of most Euro-Americans with the "real" Indian. Deloria points out that many Americans feel confident speaking with great authority about all Indians based on almost no evidence; he writes sarcastically, "anyone and everyone who knows an Indian or who is *interested,* immediately and thoroughly understands them" (5). Repercussions of this assumption are quite serious; Little points out that as recently as the 1970s a particular land deed was challenged as a forgery on the basis that "no Indian could write in 1668" (12).

4. See Axtell, "Some Thoughts" which questions what constitutes missionary success and/or failure, and for whom; Axtell also surveys recent scholarship for various opinions on the failure or success of early American missions.

5. The exception here is Samson Occom, whose autobiographical narrative has gained some recognition, and whose published sermon on the death of Moses Paul has been treated in Elliott (see Chapter 4 for more on Occom's writing).

6. Ruoff, *American Indian Literatures* and "American Indian Authors," credits William Apess with having published the first Native American autobiography. O'Connell, *Our Own,* also cites Apess as the first published Native American autobiographer.

7. For more on Pratt's formulation of her concept of autoethnography, see "Transculturation."

8. Bragdon, "Vernacular," and Goddard and Bragdon provide similar illustrations of syncretism as they show the ways in which Native documents indicate a continuation with Native oral traditions rather than a break from them. This evidence suggests that even as Natives appropriated such Euro-American written forms as the conversion narratives, they brought to these forms elements of their own world view. See also Goddard, "Stylistic Comparison."

9. See Lepore, *Name* and "Dead," for a different perspective on the "uses" of literacy for Native converts. She argues that the impact of literacy on particular individuals and even on Native language in early New England was almost entirely destructive and resulted in assimilation rather than the maintenance of Native identity.

10. Keller-Cohen argues that the strong connection between oral and written forms, which becomes apparent in colonial punctuation and spelling, is often overlooked by modern critics, who see only randomness rather than vernacular patterns in grammatical variations in colonial writing. She points out that "a set of linguistic strategies was used to engage the reader or to talk to the reader as though the reader and writer were face to face," and she cites such examples as textual representations of dialogues and even direct references to "reader" or "dear reader" (168).

11. See Gray, *"Indian Language"* esp. chaps. 2 and 3, for more on colonial missionaries' beliefs about Native languages.

12. John Sergeant, missionary at Stockbridge from 1734 to 1749, felt much the same way about the language of the Mahicans. We are told by his biographer, Samuel Hopkins, that he "found it to be a dry, barren and imperfect dialect, and by no means sufficient to convey to his hearers the knowledge of divine things; for the Indians being utter strangers to religion, their language wanted terms expressive of divers things; he was oblig'd therefore to supply that defect by introducing English words, such as Jesus, Christ, etc, which in time by frequent use, the Indians well understood. By this help he so perfected their defective language as to render it tolerably sufficient for his purpose" (166–67).

13. See Gustafson, "Performing," for an alternative description of the place of textuality and orality in Puritan and Native cultures. Gustafson points out that both oratory and textuality have an important place in Euro-American cultural traditions, but that Puritan suspicion of "rhetoric" expresses itself in early American missionary efforts as a dismissal of Native customs and oratory styles. Gustafson further argues that Eliot's text-based missionizing falls into disuse in the evangelical waves of the First Great Awakening, when oratory gains an increased status both religiously and more generally in Euro-American culture. See esp. 240–77 for an extended analysis of oratory and textuality in early American culture.

14. See Berkhofer, "Political" 357–82. See also Merrell; Salisbury, *Manitou;* White; and Richter.

15. See translations of early Massachusett texts in Goddard and Bragdon; Samuel Kirkland's papers in the Hamilton Collection also include some documents that are not written in English.

16. In particular, see Cheyfitz, chaps. 1 and 6, and David Murray, introd. Greenblatt makes a similar point. Missionaries such as John Eliot, Experience Mayhew, and Samuel Kirkland were all conversant in the language of their converts. Their use of Indian languages thus provides an interesting counterpoint to Cheyfitz and Murray but does not ultimately undermine the value of their analysis. Eliot, for example, may have been conversant in the Massachusett language,

but most modern scholars agree that the bulk of the translation of "Eliot's" Indian Bible was done by Natives who were given little credit for the job.

17. Spivak clearly differentiates between literate subjects who have accommodated themselves to the colonial order and the "subaltern" or the heterogeneous category of nonliterate, tribal peoples who do not have the means to express themselves in a colonial system that will not accommodate them.

18. As archaeologists and ethnologists would be quick to point out, though, the absence of written documentary evidence does not imply total erasure; a rich cultural history can be recreated through material evidence and by assessing orally perpetuated tribal histories.

19. Not all critics are uncomfortable about Native affiliations with the dominant culture. Moon argues disparagingly that scholars who are drawn to narratives by more "traditional" Native Americans often prefer works in which "a traditional Native lifestyle comes into conflict with that of the burgeoning White population to the detriment of the natives who act out a tragedy of displacement and disappearance" (52). He claims that by ignoring works by less traditional Natives, such critics miss the radical critiques of dominant power structures that more acculturated writers often produce. David Murray contends that it is "the ruling out of bounds . . . of a natural or unmediated Indianness as a resource to fall back on which is the most interesting thing about [this] writing, but that this does not necessarily make [the autobiographer] a white mouthpiece" (58). Indeed, notes Murray, by abandoning the longing for an essentialized ethnic subjectivity, critics can turn to the complex and fascinating work of "cultural brokers" who live on the margins of multiple cultural systems. And as Jaskoski indicates, a close examination of such writers provides rich and exciting results. Jaskoski says in her preface, "The works examined in the essays collected here must be seen . . . as always involved in a dynamic negotiation across many boundaries, barriers, gaps, and silences" (xii). Such an approach is particularly suited to the fragmented writings of the Native "autobiographers" I examine.

20. This book focuses on the Society for the Propagation of the Gospel, familiarly known as the New England Company. This society was actually several legal entities. Winship gives a particularly useful exposition of the shifting identities of this society (see vi–vii). The New England Company, organized in 1649, was created by an act of Parliament "for the promoting and propagating the Gospel of Jesus Christ in New England." It ceased to exist legally in 1660, but in 1662 a royal charter was issued to the effect that "there be, and forever hereafter shall be, within this our kingdom of England, a Society or Company for propagacion of the Gospell in New England, and the parts adjacent, in America." In 1701 the authorities of the established church organized the Society for the Propagation of the Gospel in Foreign Parts, known as the SPG. In 1787, when the SPG largely turned its attention from America, New England established "the Society for Propagating the Gospel among the Indians, and others, in North America." For more on the New England Company, see also Kellaway.

21. According to McCallum, "there is no evidence that Wheelock ever visited

the Indians in their remote settlements in the Province of New York or that he ever visited any body of Indians in Connecticut" (15).

22. For more on the captivity narrative's popularity throughout the eighteenth century, see Sekora 94–95; Derounian-Stodola and Levernier, chaps. 1 and 6, and Slotkin 144–45. According to Pearce, "by 1800 the narrative of Indian captivity had become a staple source for thrilling and shocking details of frontier hardships. The Indian of the captivity narrative was the consummate villain, the beast who hatcheted fathers, smashed the skulls of infants, and carried off mothers to make them into squaws" (58).

23. For a broader overview of English Protestant missions, see Beaver; Berkhofer, *Salvation;* and Bowden.

## Chapter One

1. Richard Cogley has pointed out that Eliot's rejection of Native cultural practices was not universal; he did approve of Native traditional medicine, which he considered efficacious (personal correspondence).

2. See Amory 39n on the cultural implications of the Indian Bible for Native converts. He argues that the impact of the Massachusett Bible was enormous— that it dramatically changed social and cultural expectations and caused significant upheavals in the ways local tribes interacted with each other and even in the ways in which they were able to communicate as they converted to Christianity. Amory points out that extrapolating the importance (or lack thereof) of the Indian Bible from extant copies which were owned by Whites (and to whom they were probably little more than an oddity or an interesting artifact) does not begin to do justice to the cultural impact of the book on Native Americans.

3. Most of these tracts were reprinted in volume 4 of the third series of the *Collections of the Massachusetts Historical Society* (1834). The first (not published by the MHS) is *New England's First Fruits* (1643). See works cited for a complete listing with publication dates. For more detail on the publication history of these tracts, see Kellaway 22–24.

4. Eliot himself was very aware of his own importance in terms of the future missionizing of Natives. He intones at one point: "The work which we now have in hand will be as a patterne and Coppie before them, to imitate in all the Countrey, both in civilizing them in their order, government, Law, and in their Church proceedings and administrations; and hence great care lyeth upon me to set them right at first, to lay a sure foundation for such a building, as I foresee will be built upon it, and in this matter I greatly need to pray" (*Strength* 7).

5. See also Peyer, *Tutor'd Mind* 34–40, for reasons for Native acceptance of praying towns. He argues that in addition to very pragmatic reasons, Natives could continue a "close-knit kinship-based village life and a communally oriented economy" that in many ways mirrored their traditional patterns.

6. The rules for Indian towns—including lice-biting—were published twice in the Eliot tracts (*Day-Breaking* 22; *Clear Sun-shine* 4–5). There were as many as

twenty-nine rules to live by, most of which were a combination of "civility"—regulations about lice-biting, cutting of hair, knocking at doors, allowable games and ceremonies—and "Christianity" rules against adultery, fornication, and murder, and an injunction to obey the Sabbath. The rules published by Eliot are from two different towns, Musketaquid and Nonatum.

7. Eliot may have felt proprietary about the Massachusett language, but his command of the language was apparently less than fluent as he needed translators throughout his career.

8. Recent books on King Philip's War have added greatly to the insights in Leach. For example, Lepore, *Name,* emphasizes the war's impact on Anglo-American colonists' sense of their identity as distinct from that of both the Native inhabitants of the Americas and the Spanish conquistadores. See also Bourne and James Drake. For an excellent collection of contemporary accounts of King Philip's War (including Mary Rowlandson's captivity narrative), see Slotkin and Folsom.

9. See Cronon, *Changes,* and Jennings, *Invasion* chap. 8.

10. English portrayals of John Sassamon and his position vis-à-vis both King Philip and John Eliot leave a lot of questions unanswered. Was Sassamon one of Philip's advisors or someone the Native leader hated and distrusted from the start? Why did Sassamon betray Philip and the larger Indian goal? Was Sassamon truly an ally of the English, and did this necessarily pit him against Philip? Lepore attempts to answer some of these questions both in "Dead" and in greater detail in *Name.* Although the record is sparse, Lepore suggests that Sassamon, raised and educated in one of Eliot's praying towns and in fact one of Eliot's interpreters, may have had a falling out with Eliot in the late 1650s. Since his signature appears on various treaties between the colonies and King Philip, Lepore suggests he probably switched sides to act as interpreter and scribe for Wampanoag sachems Alexander and later Philip ("Dead" 494). She warns, however, "that it is difficult to know if Sassamon's work for Philip at this time represents a genuine change of heart in relation to the English or whether, essentially acting as a spy for Eliot, he infiltrated Philip's council in order to convert him" (495). Lepore concludes, "it seems most likely that Sassamon remained troubled and confused about to whom he most owed his allegiance" (500).

11. On an incident in which seven Christian Indians were attacked by Englishmen for being outside of their allotted territory, see Pulsipher.

12. For more on Daniel Gookin, see Galinsky.

13. This attack had been foreseen by two Native informants, Job Nesuton and James Quannapohit, but the colonists were slow to act on the uncorroborated words of Natives.

14. Aid came in many different forms. Some gave food and shelter to Joseph Rowlandson as he struggled to reclaim his family. Others, however, with less concrete opportunities for help, resorted to displays of outrage. In fact, according to Daniel Gookin, some English settlers were so incensed by this attack, as well as an

attack on nearby Medfield, that many were led to cry, "'Oh, come, let us go . . . and kill all the Praying Indians.'" Gookin continues, bitterly, "They could not come at the enemy Indians, for they were too crafty and subtle for the English; therefore, they would have wreaked their rage upon the poor unarmed Indians our friends" ("Historical Account" 494).

15. The original letter is in the Massachusetts Archives. This and the following letters are reprinted in Samuel Drake.

16. Peter Jethro was the son of Old Jethro, a Nipmuck Indian who was apparently one of John Eliot's early converts. Daniel Gookin claims that Old Jethro (or Tantamous) was not really a convert but lived in a praying town anyway ("Historical Account" 473). Samuel Drake adds that when colonists wanted to bring in several Indians toward the close of the war for questioning in Boston, "Old Jethro's spirit could not brook the indignity offered by those English who were sent to conduct the praying Indians to Boston, and in the night he escaped, with all his family, into his native wilds. His son Peter had been so long under the instruction of the English, that he had become almost one of them. He deserted his father's cause, and was the means of his being executed with . . . other Nipmuk sachems" (267).

17. This letter is reprinted in Meserve, and is also contained in Samuel Drake 274. Gookin also cites part of this letter in *Historical Account.*

18. According to Bragdon, "the sachem was a representative of the community with a pivotal or transformative role. He or she faced inward, to the community, regulating interpersonal relations, land allocations, and disputes, and saw to the redistribution of surplus resources. The sachem was intimately connected to others through ties of affection and kinship, and to the continuity of the sachemship through descent and marriage. At the same time, the sachem mediated contacts between the world outside of the community, just as the powwaw and priest . . . mediated the group's contact with the supernatural. The sachem entertained visitors, coordinated a cadre of messengers and information gatherers, and personally visited all communities within his or her territories. He or she also served as a delegate to councils of more influential sachems" (*Native People* 153). For more on the social and political role of the sachem in early southern New England, see Salisbury, *Manitou* 35–40, and Simmons, *Spirit* 12–14.

19. See Bourne chap. 5 for more on the relationship of Mary Rowlandson's captivity to King Philip's War.

20. It is possible that this James is the same boy in the account books of Henry Dunster, president of the struggling Harvard College. If this is in fact the same boy, he went on to enroll in Master Elijah Corlet's Cambridge Grammar School in 1645–46 (Szasz, *Indian Education* 114). Amory points out, that this is unlikely, however, since "the Nipmucks did not 'submit' to English jurisdiction until 1649, and would hardly have entrusted their children to an open enemy" (41).

21. Salisbury suggests that Native translators were far more significant than had previously been acknowledged ("Red Puritans," 42n62); Szasz claims that "for too many years this Indian contribution to the publications has been ignored"

(*Indian Education* 115), suggesting that without Cockenoe, Nesuton, and Printer, none of the works for which Eliot has become so famous would exist.

22. Hubbard notes, "He had attained some skill in printing, and might have attained more, had he not, like a false villain, ran away from his master before his time was out" (94). Undoubtedly he ran away to join King Philip's War.

23. For more on James Printer's life, see Samuel Drake 114–15. See also Lepore, *Name* chap. 5 for a different interpretation of Printer's actions.

24. Also in Meserve, this letter is reprinted in Samuel Drake, 331 and Forbes. For a slightly different version, see Palfrey.

25. This note, reprinted in Gookin's history, was stuck on a post of the bridge leaving Medfield. The original has been lost.

26. In comparing the two ransom letters, Meserve notes that "James's letter seems to indicate the better vocabulary and a more adequate grasp of the language . . . [specific] words in the context given together with his general sentence construction present evidence of James's more thorough background in the study of English" (270).

27. He is referred to in *A True Account* as "one *Jumet* called a Printer, as having been employed about the work of the Press in *Cambridge:* a Revolter he was, and a fellow that had done mischief, and staid out as long as he could, till the last day but one of a Proclamation set forth, to encourage such Indians as had a desire to return to the *English*" (5). Increase Mather explains the proclamation and Printer's return in a little more detail in his *Brief History:* "Whereas the Council at *Boston* had lately emitted a Declaration, signifying, that such Indians as did within fourteen days come in to the English, might hope for mercy, divers of them did this day return from among the *Nipmucks.* Amongst others, *James* an Indian, who could not only read, and write, but had learned the Art of Printing, notwithstanding his Apostasie, did venture himself upon the mercy and truth of the English Declaration which he had seen and read, promising for the future to venture his life against the common Enemy. He and the other now come in, affirm that very many of the Indians are dead since this *War* began, and that more have dyed by the hand of God, in respect of Diseases, Fluxes, and Feavers, which have been amongst them, than have been killed with the Sword" (39).

28. Hubbard 81 also claims that it was through the intercession of the Christian Indians that Rowlandson was ransomed.

29. This debate went on not only among the English, who were deeply suspicious of the idea of Indians becoming Christians, but also among the Native populations that were introduced to Christianity but maintained that it had nothing to do with them since it was only for White people. For more on this attitude, see Ronda, "We Are Well."

## Chapter Two

1. My aim here is not to question the sincerity of Native conversions or to examine the theological implications of Native conversions. For more on these issues, see Cohen, Naeher, Van Lonkhuyzen, and Axtell, "Indian Conversions".

2. White ix–xvi, 50–93, has formulated a theory of "the middle ground" in which cultures interact through a series of strategic "misunderstandings" that eventually form the basis for a shared culture.

3. Since it was often hard to convince appropriately skilled individuals to spend their time and energy in such a poorly paid field, schools on Martha's Vineyard had an erratic history.

4. For more on this accident, see Hare 112–15. See also Thomas Prince's supplement to Mayhew's *Indian Converts,* esp. 292–92. According to some accounts, Mayhew was accompanied by an Indian preacher brought up in Mayhew's own home, who was the son of one of the first converts to Christianity, Miohqsoo. This young man, who also disappeared at sea, was to have helped him discuss the mission on the Island.

5. Gookin repeats a story about Quakers who tried to turn the Natives of Martha's Vineyard from the Puritan teachings of Thomas Mayhew. One of the Natives who spoke English reportedly said, "You are strangers to us, and we like not your discourse. We know Mr. Mayhew, that he is a good and holy man; but you we know not . . . we cannot receive your counsel, contrary to our own experience, and the advice and exhortations of our ancient and good teachers. Therefore we pray you, trouble us no further with your new doctrines; for we do not approve it" ("Historical Collections" 203). The trust Mayhew had acquired from the Wampanoag population based on his secular guidance seems to have affected their willingness to accept his religious teachings as well.

6. Originally his older brother, Matthew, who was trained as a minister, was expected to follow in his father's and grandfather's footsteps. Matthew Mayhew's education was undertaken at the expense of the Society for the Propagation of the Gospel; it soon became clear, however, that he was more interested in temporal affairs, and he turned to politics, abandoning missionary work completely. His brother John became a pastor in 1673 and took over the missionary work that his brother had left (Banks 1: 237–46). Matthew's contribution to the missionary effort of the Mayhew family was not insignificant, however; in 1695 he published *The Conquests and Triumphs of Grace: Being A Brief Narrative of the Success which the Gospel Hath had among the Indians of Martha's Vineyard.*

7. See Prince's account of his death, supplement to *Indian Converts* 305–6.

8. For more on the Mayhew family, see Banks 1: 213–57. See also Prince's supplement to *Indian Converts.*

9. Bowden explains that the missionary work of the Mayhew family "probably harbored some patriarchal condescension, but it also produced undoubtedly beneficial results among the people who responded" (112). He neglects to mention what, specifically, those results might have been.

10. Other texts include Mayhew family letters, published tracts such as the Eliot tracts, and Matthew Mayhew's 1695 account.

11. Bragdon describes the loss of land as a result of the "concerted efforts on the part of the English to dispossess the Indians, and to circumscribe their mobility and independence" ("Native Economy" 32).

12. Far more prevalent on Nantucket, whaling was also pursued to a lesser extent on Martha's Vineyard.

13. Simmons suggests that "a shift in authority in favor of the English was a precondition for Indian populations to be open to religious persuasion and that the more implicit and less threatening this shift, the more favorably Indian subjects responded to religious assimilation" ("Conversion" 216). He believes that because of this dynamic, the religious conversions on Martha's Vineyard were "the most successful in . . . thoroughness and permanence" (215).

14. On Native literacy and education on Martha's Vineyard as represented in Mayhew's *Indian Converts,* see Monaghan, "'She loved.'"

15. Samuel Sewell, on a visit to Martha's Vineyard in 1714, could find only two young men who could read English; most were literate only in Massachusett. (Kellaway 243–44).

16. See Goddard and Bragdon, which contains some of Mayhew's translations as well as the original documents.

17. In Edward Winslow's 1649 missionary tract, John Eliot gives an example of the working of grace on a particular Native convert by recounting her life story. This narrative may well have been the model for Mayhew's much later collection, as in many ways they follow similar conventions. For example, Eliot writes, "And though of the living I will not say much, yet of the dead I may freely speak" (*Glorious Progresse* 6); Mayhew also writes only of those converts who have already died. The woman in Winslow's tract appears again in the appendix, where her life shows "reall and undenyable evidences of the work of grace" (26). The attempt to reveal the workings of God's grace on the lives of individual converts is obviously very much the point of Mayhew's later work.

18. See, for example, Cotton Mather, *Magnalia,* and, later, *Parentator,* the life of his father Increase Mather.

19. Gookin speaks for many of his peers when he denigrates the Indian churches: he says that Indians should be educated in English so that "they will hereby be able to understand our English ministers, who are better fitted to instruct them in substantial and orthodox divinity, than teachers of their own nation, who cannot in reason be imagined to be so sufficient, as if they were learned men" ("Historical Collections" 221).

20. Experience Mayhew, it seems, is following in a family tradition of putting himself forward as the best representative of the Natives of Martha's Vineyard. In a letter from Thomas Mayhew Sr. to Daniel Gookin in 1674, the "Patriarch to the Indians," as he is fondly referred to by his biographer, Thomas Hare, states: "Many can read and write Indian: very few, English; none, to great purpose; not above three or four; and those do it brokenly. Myself and my two grandsons can speak the language of this island." He concludes this letter with an apology for being so brief, and welcomes further correspondence, "for I am always considering of persons and things, being well acquainted with the state and condition of the Indians" (Gookin, "Historical Collections" 205).

21. See the brief discussion of Eliot's 1685 publication, *The Dying Speeches of*

*Several Indians,* in David Murray 34–35. Murray argues that the dying speeches of Native Americans provided a safe and comforting vision of an essentially doomed race that could be controlled and manipulated.

22. See also Salisbury, *Manitou* 44–46, which emphasizes the role of ritual in the redistribution of wealth.

23. A contemporary observer's description points out some of the differences between the wigwam and the English-style house:

> They make a fire in the centre of the house; and have a lower hole in the top of the house, to let out the smoke. They keep the door into the wigwam always shut, by a mat falling thereon, as people go in and out. This they do to prevent air coming in, which will cause much smoke in every windy weather. If the smoke beat down at the lower hole, they hang a little mat in the way of a skreen, on the top of the house, which they can with a cord turn to the windward side, which prevents the smoke. . . . I have often lodged in their wigwams; and have found them as warm as the best English houses. In their wigwams they make a kind of a couch or mattresses, firm and strong, raised about a foot high from the earth; first covered with boards that they split out of trees; and upon the boards they spread mats generally, and some times bear skins and deer skins. These are large enough for three or four persons to lodge upon: and one may either draw nearer or keep at a more distance from the heat of the fire, as they please; for their mattresses are six or eight feet broad. (Gookin, "Historical Collections" 150)

Bragdon, "Probate," notes that the simplicity of the Native home remained even after the wigwam had been replaced; she points out that Natives of similar economic status to Anglo-Americans tended to have much more sparsely furnished homes.

24. Such gender divisions seem to have been present before the arrival of the English. See Bragdon, "Gender" 576–79; Russell 96–103; and Salisbury, *Manitou* 39–41.

25. See Cotton Mather, *Family,* which emphasized the relationship between discipline and family prayer. Mather warns against any "undutiful" behavior of children toward their parents, saying darkly, "*Undutiful Children,* for the *Sin of Contempt* they cast on their Parents, are often *Cursed* by God" (44).

26. See Salisbury, *Manitou* 35, 42–45, for the role of reciprocity in traditional Native groups of southern New England.

27. See Simmons, *Spirit* 37–38, for more on English views of powwows. See also Thomas Mayhew's description of the work of the powwows in the Eliot tract *Tears of Repentance* 4–6; he does not question the power of the powwows, but he does stress that God's power is stronger than that of the "imps" of the powwows. Matthew Mayhew writes of the cultural relativity of the powwows. One man, Mayhew tells us, claimed he could only help those who believed in his particular

God. His wife, Mayhew reports, "was accounted a Godly Woman, and lived in the practice and profession of the *Christian Religion,* not only by the approbation, but the incouragement of her Husband. . . . He declared he could not blame her, for that she served a God that was above his; but that as to himself, his gods continued kindness, obliged him not to forsake his service" (18–19).

28. Other sermons by Natives emphasize this point as well. Waban's fast-day speech at Natick in 1658 refers to Matt. 9.12–13, in which Christ is compared to a physician:

> What should we doe this day? goe to Christ the Phisitian; for Christ is a Phisitian of souls; he healed mens bodies, but he can heal souls also: he is a great Phisitian, therefore let all sinners goe to him. Therefore this day know what need we have of Christ, and let us goe to Christ to heale us of our sins, and he can heale us both soul and body  (Eliot tracts, *further Accompt* 9)

Similarly, Wutasakompavin, or Poliquannum, refers to Christ's healing of the leper, saying, "This sick man came to Christ and worshipped him . . . which . . . was so pleasing to Christ, as that he presently touched him and healed him. . . . so let us this day cry to Christ, and worship him, and if we do it in faith then he will heal us" (19).

29. Bragdon points out that "women could be sachems and powwaws" (*Native People* 177); Gookin also claims that both men and women can be sachems ("Historical Collections" 154).

30. Several writers have pointed out that older women in Native societies were often well practiced in the art of healing. My argument here has more to do with the link between religion and curing than with any particular healing abilities. See Russell 37–38.

31. For more on the idea of synecdoche and metonymy as useful ways of engaging Native Americans and their relationship to autobiography, see Krupat, *Ethnocriticism* 201–31.

32. See Ronda, "Generations."

## Chapter Three

1. The impact of Hopkins's account is suggested by its abridgment and republication four years later by Benjamin Franklin in Philadelphia, who follows Hopkins's account with the following suggestion about certain local Native groups:

> whether [they] might not be collected, provided with Lands, and settled in Townships on our Frontiers (in the same Manner as those at Stockbridge are) and in that case be as great a Security to our Province as the Stockbridge Indians have been to that Part of New England; and whether we might not, by establishing a Trade with them, in a just and equitable Manner, draw other Tribes into our Alliance, and thereby extend our Trade, secure our Frontiers, and open a Way for bringing in the Everlasting Gospel of

CHRIST to the Heathen Nations, we submit to the serious Consideration of the Public. (14)

2. Brasser describes the sites: "Typically the core of each homeland was five-to-ten-square miles in extent and contained one or two important settlement places, often located at long-used fishing sites. Here clan ceremonies and elders' councils were held. Extensive corn fields were nearby, as were sacred sites such as cemeteries, memory piles, and sweat lodges used for curing. Throughout the core area and surrounding spaces of each homeland stood dozens of wigwams, alone, or in pairs, or in small hamlets not very different in size from a traditional meeting place. The people who lived in each homeland were joined to one another and to their kin in other homelands by enduring social and economic relations organized and mediated through a system of matrilineal descent" (6–9).

3. Centered in the area around Albany, the Mahicans had settlements throughout New York and southern New England.

4. See Dunn for more on Dutch interactions with the Mahicans. By the eighteenth century the Mahicans lived in close proximity to Dutch colonists. One of the first complications in the settlement of Stockbridge was eliminating the land claims of several Dutch claimants, including Jehoiakim Van Valkenburgh (Field 241).

5. See also Jones 81 and Calloway 86.

6. See Haefeli and Sweeny for details of the attack on Deerfield and the tribes involved.

7. There is some uncertainty about the political authority of these Native figures. Though English records place Konkopot at the head of everyone, it is unclear if this was the case. One possibility is that Umpachenee's group was Mahican and therefore "newer" to the area, while Konkopot's group were native Housatonics and of longer existence in the area; Umpachenee would then have deferred to Konkapot out of courtesy (Mandell 7–8). According to Brasser, Umpachenee "may have been the chief of the local Mahican immigrants . . . and it is most probable that he became the Nation's Chief Sachem in the 1740's." Konkapot, Brasser suggests, was the leader of the native Housatonic tribe by intermarriage (32).

8. See Stephen Williams's addition to Appleton's sermon, in which he addresses the 'Houssatonnocs' directly (26–27); see also Hopkins and Jones.

9. Hopkins tells us: "It was upon Mr. Sergeant's desire that those families were admitted. The ends he had in view were not only that he and Mr. Woodbridge might have the comfort of their neighborhood and society, but especially to civilize and Anglicize the Indians, and be a help to them in their secular affairs" (58).

10. Mandell 22; the quote is from *Journals* 17: 42.

11. See Miles 58–62, particularly on the manipulations of Ephraim Williams, patriarch of a steadily growing family in Stockbridge and cousin to the powerful

Williams clan that dominated Connecticut's political and social activities in the eighteenth century.

12. Miles explains: "Whereas Ephraim Williams had seven living children, Timothy Woodbridge and Joseph Woodbridge, eight each, and Josiah Jones, five, Indian families averaged only two children" (50–51).

13. Children were baptized and adults were brought into full communion, were censored, and generally took part in the Christian community of Stockbridge (until their departure for New York in the 1780s). See "Church records, 1776–1819" and "Records of the Church of Christ in Stockbridge, from June 1759 until Aug. 1819: Taken Principally from manuscripts left by Dr. Stephen West," STL.

14. West's tenure was from June 13, 1759, to August 27, 1818.

15. See Frazier (187–90) for more on the division of West's church; Calloway (91) dates the division of the church at 1775. The two Sergeants' views on Native languages were quite different; the father, we are told by his biographer, "found it to be a dry, barren and imperfect dialect, and by no means sufficient to convey to his hearers the knowledge of divine things" (Hopkins 166–67). The son, on the other hand, believed that the language of the Natives "is not so barren, but that every doctrine of the gospel can be communicated to them in their own language" (Morse 114).

16. See Calloway 105–6.

17. For a full account of the Williams family's captivity and aftermath, see Demos, *Unredeemed*.

18. See Demos, *Unredeemed* 118–98 for a description of her first visit. She returned several times to visit New England but did not ever return permanently (201–2; 207–13; 227–29).

19. This sister is undoubtedly Jemima Richards, listed in the appendix to the third edition of John Williams's narrative as still captive in 1758. The appendix, interestingly enough, is written by Stephen Williams himself.

20. This letter is the frontispiece to the 1911 reprint of Hopkins; the recipient is unidentified.

21. See *Letter.* As sincere as this plan may have been, Sergeant had trouble implementing it. Almost immediately, he complains to a friend that "thro' a childish fondness for home" the girls he wants to educate alongside the boys are ruining his plans since "they would not be contented to stay long enough where I sent them, to obtain any good by it" (82). For more on Sergeant's school, see Axtell, "Scholastic."

22. "New heart" is a common Christian metaphor for conversion. Sergeant does not say the same for Konkapot, whose heart was apparently already prepared for God.

23. This question is similar to Wabbakoxet's question as reported by John Eliot: "Seeing the English had been 27 yeers (some of them) in this land, why did we never teach them to know God till now? had you done it sooner, said hee, wee

might have known much of God by this time, and much sin might have been prevented, but now some of us are grown old in sin, etc." (*Cleare Sun-shine* 23–24). Umpachenee's question is more pointed in its references to land, but the suspicion is the same. David Brainerd reports a similar level of suspicion in his mission in New Jersey. He writes of the Delaware Indians in 1746:

> When I've attempted to recommend Christianity to their acceptance, they have sometimes objected, that the *white* People have come among them, have cheated them out of their Lands, driven them back to the Mountains, from the pleasant Places they us'd to enjoy by the Sea Side, etc. That therefore they have no Reason to think the *white* People are now seeking their Wellfare; but rather that they have sent me out to draw them together under a pretence of Kindness to them, that they may have an Opportunity to make slaves of them as they do of the poor *Negroes,* or else to ship them on Board their Vessels, and make them fight with their Enemies, etc. (211)

24. This hostility between traders and missionaries was apparently a common problem. John Brainerd, brother of David Brainerd, reports from New Jersey in 1753 that "wicked Men, Emissaries of Satan; who trade among the *Indians* . . . had persuaded them that I was sent by crafty Men with a View to bring them into a Snare, and finally deprive them of their Country and Liberties" (10).

25. For more on drinking habits of Anglo-Americans, see Rorbauch.

26. See Mancall, chap. 1, which explains many of the Euro-American stereotypes of Native American drinking behaviors.

27. Samuel Danforth's 1710 sermon, "The Woful Effects of Drunkenness" was one of a very few documents translated into the Massachusett language.

28. For references to "civilizing" Natives as the most effective way to "Christianize" them, see Hopkins 58, 84. See also Axtell, *Invasion,* on the relationship between "civilizing" and "Christianizing" in Puritan missions generally. Missionaries often brought the financial and structural ability to coordinate large projects such as mills and forges in communities of Native converts. Stockbridge itself contained a grist mill, and after the Stockbridge tribe emigrated to New York they were given annuities to build a sawmill and a smith's shop and to purchase agricultural tools (Belknap and Morse)—no doubt to replace those they had left behind in Massachusetts. See 1794 "Treaty with the Oneida," arts. 2–4 (Kappler 38). It is hardly accidental that such treaty arrangements were made under the supervision of two missionaries, John Sergeant Jr. and Samuel Kirkland. Similarly, Eleazar Wheelock's first order of business when he establishes his "Indian School" in New Hampshire is to build a sawmill and a grist mill to bring income to the school (Wheelock, *Continuation* 1772).

29. This particular journal, at the Beinecke Rare Book and Manuscript Library at Yale, is one of the rare extant examples of John Sergeant's handwritten journals.

30. This idea is repeated on the tour of the mission house in Stockbridge given today. We are told that a small hallway at the back of the house was designed by Abigail to keep Indians from the rest of the house.

31. For run-ins between Williams and Natives, see Miles 49 and Axtell, "Scholastic" 61. A 1748 petition from the Stockbridge Indians to the Massachusetts court reveals their frustrations over "the disposition and conduct of Col Williams" as his manipulations led to their loss of "more than one hundred days work in cutting drawing timber and erecting fence" on land they were told would be theirs. The Stockbridge Indians dryly report: "Your petitioners were ordered very much to their surprise to desist from going on with their design for no other reason that your petitioners can possibly conjecture than that the aforesaid land lay ajoining to the aforesaid Williams's land and is good and therefore is more proper for him then for your petitioners" (DC 37:5, 1–2).

32. For more on Umpachenee's death, see Frazier 89–90.

33. On the school in Stockbridge, see Frazier 190–91; for a brief biography of Aupaumut's early years, see Love 239. Benjamin Coates, author of the foreword to Aupaumut's journal, suggests that Aupaumut was educated at a Moravian school near Stockbridge; more recent scholarship suggests that he was educated in Stockbridge proper. See Coates 64–65; Taylor 436; Ronda and Ronda 44–45.

34. See Frazier 99.

35. Before the revolution Edwards "was a Commissioner, associated with Silas Deane, to the Indians on the Western border of Massachusetts . . . he spent his wealth and exhausted his credit in aiding the Government through the war" (William Edwards 20).

36. Jonathan Edwards Jr., son of the minister of Stockbridge, reports similar interracial friendships. In a description of the Stockbridge Indians' language, Edwards explains the basis for his expertise as follows: "When I was but six years of age [1752], my father removed with his family to *Stockbridge*. . . . The Indians being the nearest neighbours, I constantly associated with them; their boys were my daily schoolmates and play-fellows. Out of my father's house, I seldom heard any language spoken, beside the Indian" (84–85). Edwards was about ten years old when Aupaumut was born.

37. For more on the role of the Stockbridge Indians in the American Revolution, see Calloway 85–107 and Ronda and Ronda 47.

38. For more on Aupaumut's connection to the Americans, see Taylor 431, 434–37.

39. For more on the politics of the western confederacy and its ties to the English, French, and Americans, see White 413–68 and Dowd 90–115.

40. A Munsee chief wishes "to hear some news" as Aupaumut enters his village, and Aupaumut happily tells him some ("Short Narration" 84). Similarly, a Delaware sachem says to Aupaumut, "I should be glad to hear some news from the east" (89).

41. Counselman argues that treaties, along with captivity narratives, are the only "literature" (that is, written texts) indigenous to the New World, and not "the expression of a transplanted, imitative culture" (749).

42. Brasser points out that "although the Mahican had ceased to be a major power factor, they maintained a respectful status among the eastern and midwestern tribes" (23).

43. For more on the relationship between history and Native American narrative, see Trafzer.

44. The simple fact of this text's existence suggests that it was written for White readers; the tribe itself would have passed such information along orally. Aupaumut's text is fragmentary; three versions currently exist, all incomplete. The most complete version is in Jones 14–23. She tells us, "Dr Dwight seems to have had access to a perfect copy; but the one here given has lost its first and its last leaf, and no traces of their contents have yet been discovered except what can be gathered from his "Travels." The History, as we have it, was sent from New York, and is said to have been written, 'doubtless, by Capt. Hendrick Aupaumut.'" She explains her reasons for not changing the wording of the document: "Its false syntax is *valuable,* rather than objectionable," since it illustrates the uses of language (14).

The second version is the "Extract from an Indian History," *Massachusetts Historical Society Collections,* ser. 1, vol. 9 (1804). This version seems to contain the missing beginning, although it is unclear if the earliest part of this version is the work of an editor since the fragment as it is reprinted has been edited for grammar and spelling. The fragment stops three pages into the Jones version, cutting off a good deal of the rest of the history.

The third version is in the *First Annual Report of the American Society for Promoting the Civilization and General Improvement of the Indian Tribes within the United States.* Also heavily edited, it begins, "The following abstract of the traditionary history of the origin and ancient customs of the Muhheakunnuk tribe of Indians, written about 30 years ago, by Capt. Hendrick, their present Chief, transcribed from his Mss. And transmitted to Rev. J. Morse, by Rev. John Sergeant [Jr.], missionary to this tribe, July, 1822." It then explains, "The two first pages of the Mss. Are wanting. Mr. Sergeant, who had formerly read them, gives, from recollection, the following as the *substance* of their contents" (41). It then starts where the Jones version begins, but it has been corrected so that the text has fewer idiosyncratic elements. The text is substantially cut, leaving out descriptions of kinship alliances and governmental structures.

45. The MHS version says, "At this period the tribe, to a considerable extent, was civilized" (41).

46. The Jones version says, "A famine compelled them . . . to disperse themselves throughout the regions of the wilderness after sustenance—and at length lost their ways of former living, and apostatized" (15); the *First Annual* version states that "while they lived on the western river, an extraordinary famine hap-

pened, which obliged them to separate and spread themselves in the wilderness of the east, for sustenance. During this dispersion they changed their former modes of living, lost the habits pertaining to civilization, and apostatized from the religion of their fathers" (41).

47. Kirkland to General Israel Chapin (NYHS, B. V. O'Reilly, vol. 8, #18). Material quoted courtesy of the New-York Historical Society.

## Chapter Four

1. For Johnson's version of his life to this point, see McCallum 150. See also his various accounts of his conversion reprinted in McCallum 142–148, as well as his journal (EWP); see also the book of sermons by Occom and Johnson, containing what is probably Johnson's actual conversion narrative (CHS). Laura Murray's collection of Johnson's writing, *To Do Good,* is another excellent source of historical and cultural detail.

2. There is some contention about the genesis of this community. Szasz suggests the idea was Wheelock's. Most historians agree that the community was primarily Occom's idea. See Love, chap. 12.

3. For more on Hendrik Aupaumut and Stockbridge Indians, see chapter 3. For more on the events surrounding the founding of Brotherton, see Szasz "Samson Occom"; Love; Peyer, "Samson Occom"; McCallum; and Laura Murray, *To Do Good.*

4. This estimate was provided by Samuel Kirkland, missionary to the Oneida and also once a pupil of Wheelock's, in Belknap and Morse.

5. For a richer and more nuanced view of Kirkland's years among the Oneida, see Pilkington.

6. For specific information about which of Wheelock's students went where as missionaries and schoolmasters, see McCallum 24–27.

7. Several excellent biographical studies examine various elements of Samson Occom's life. See, for example, Blodgett; Burr; Szasz, "Samson Occom"; and Peyer, "Samson Occom."

8. For more on New England family relations, see Morgan, *Puritan;* Demos, *Little;* and Earle.

9. In October 1773 Johnson asks for Occom's permission to marry Tabitha, his daughter. The letter suggests that as close as they all were, Occom had previously expressed misgivings about such a marriage: "My design is to ask for your daughter again, and my firm resolution is by your consent to have her. My heart is fixed upon her, and believe me I say, upon no other at present, and I have promised by my all to have her, and she also has promised to give herself to me if Possible. So I humbly beg that no Denial be given hereafter. Seeing that we truly Love each other" (October 1, 1773 CHS).

10. DC Mss. 774121. Oneida Nation. An answer the Oneida Indians gave to the speech of Joseph Johnson. Dartmouth College and The Connecticut Historical Society both have important letters and documents pertaining to the founding

of Brotherton. In several cases, these documents differ only in a few words or phrases. For example, both Dartmouth and The Connecticut Historical Society have petitions signed by Joseph Johnson and others urging the New England Indians to participate in the venture to upstate New York. Both collections also have slightly different versions of Johnson's speech to the Oneida Indians from January 1774 and the response of the Oneida council, from which the above quote is taken. I indicate the origin of each particular citation when relevant.

11. See Taylor 446.

12. DC Mss 774120. "Joseph Johnson's speech to the Onoida Indians."

13. See, for example, John Winthrop's famous use of the language of the body to emphasize the sacred purpose of the Massachusetts Bay Settlement in his sermon, "A Model of Christian Charity."

14. See Fenton, "Structure" 13 and Fenton, "Glossary" 122. For an overview of Iroquois treaty protocol, see Richter chaps. 2, 3.

15. Bailyn establishes the very public nature of political rhetoric through his examination of the pamphlets and broadsides that emerged in the decades leading up to the American Revolution; see in particular chaps. 1, 3, and 6.

16. Apparently such petitions circulated through several cities; the Connecticut Historical Society has several versions of the same petition written to different cities such as Albany and Boston.

17. This passage is similar to another petition written by Occom for the Mohegans of Connecticut:

> We are very glad and Rejoice with you that you have at last got your Freedom Liberty and Independence, from under the heavy and gauling yoke of your Late King, who has tryed very hard to make you Slaves, and have kill'd great many of you, but by your steadiness Boldness, and Great Courage, You have broke the yoke and the Chain of Slavery." (nd CHS)

18. Though it is tempting to conclude that the community embraced Occom wholeheartedly, it is more likely that Occom himself orchestrated and possibly even wrote the petition. Regardless, the petition does point to the ways in which tensions in the community quickly became racially charged.

19. At Oneida, according to Belknap and Morse, "Agriculture is in its infancy, labour being performed almost wholly by the women" (20). While clearly reflecting the assumptions of Euro-American culture about the inadequacy of women working in the fields, this quote also acknowledges the fact of Oneida agricultural activity.

20. Laura Murray 19–20 argues that "in order to obtain money or land or protection, Johnson had to produce humility" since "as an Indian Johnson was expected to be humble before white people." Murray argues that Johnson was particularly adept at this rhetorical strategy.

## Epilogue

1. For more on "Eulogy on King Philip," see Gustafson, *Nations;* Laura Murray, "Aesthetic"; and Dannenberg.

2. For more on the history of the Pequots in nineteenth-century New England, see Trigger, McBride, and Campisi.

3. For an alternative reading of this passage, see Moon 50–51; see also David Murray 59.

4. David Murray suggests that Apess is consciously complicating racial identities as he explores "the whole idea . . . of an Indian being in danger from whites when he ventures into the forest" as "both a historical truth and an ironic reversal of white fears" (59).

5. Hatch explains that "those who led the meeting made overt attempts to have the power of God 'strike fire' over a mass audience; they encouraged uncensored testimonials by persons without respect to age, gender, or race; the public sharing of private ecstasy; overt physical display and emotional release; loud and spontaneous response to preaching; and the use of folk music" (50).

6. On the distinctions between Methodists and the New England Puritan elite, see Gustafson, "Nation" 31–32.

7. Tiro suggests the importance of Methodism for Apess by pointing out the double reference in the title of his autobiography, "a son of the forest," which identifies Apess "not only as an Indian, but also as a product of that hallmark of American Methodism, the 'plain-folks camp-meeting.'" Tiro further acknowledges Apess's selective use of the term "brethren," which he uses to refer to both Methodists and Native Americans (655).

8. For nineteenth-century examples of this missionary ideology, see Cornelius; *Memoir of John Arch;* and Anderson.

9. In addition to *A Son of the Forest,* see Apess's short sermon, "The Increase of the Kingdom of Christ: A Sermon" (1831), in which he asks rhetorically,

> If, as many eminent men with apparently high presumption, if not unquestionable evidence, believe, the Indians of the American continent are a part of the long lost ten tribes of Israel, have not the great American nation reason to fear the swift judgments of heaven on them for nameless cruelties, extortions, and exterminations inflicted upon the poor natives of the forest? (106)

See also "The Indians: The Ten Lost Tribes" (1833), in which Apess confirms that Natives are descended from the ten lost tribes, "that nation, peculiarly and emphatically blessed of God" (113).

10. John Eliot and Edward Winslow were the most significant proponents of this theory in New England. For more information about seventeenth-century

theories of Native American origins, see Bercovitch chap. 3; Cogley; and Huddleston.

11. Bercovitch has pointed out that this theory was not prevalent in New England since it went against the Puritans' vision of themselves as the new Israelites and the notion of Native Americans as doomed or Satanic figures (75n).

12. For more on the precedents of this theory, see Gustafson, "Nations" 37–39.

# WORKS CITED

## Primary Sources

Apess, William (Pequot). *On Our Own Ground: The Complete Writings of William Apess, A Pequot.* Ed. Barry O'Connell. Amherst: University of Massachusetts Press, 1992.

Appleton, Nathanael. *Gospel Ministers Must be Fit for the Master's Use . . . A Sermon Preached at Deerfield, August 31, 1735 at the Ordination of Mr. John Sargent.* Boston, 1735.

Anderson, Rufus B. *Memoirs of Catherine Brown a Christian Indian of the Cherokee Nation.* Philadelphia: American Sunday School Union, 1824.

Aupaumut, Hendrick (Stockbridge). "Extract from an Indian History." *Massachusetts Historical Society Collections* 1st ser., vol. 9. 1804. 99–102.

———. "History." *Stockbridge, Past and Present: Records of an Old Mission Station.* By Electa Jones. Springfield, Mass.: Samuel Bawles, 1854. 15–23.

———. "History of the Muhheakunnuk Indians" *First Annual Report of the American Society for Promoting the Civilization and General Improvement of the Indian Tribes of the United States.* New Haven, 1824.

———. "A Short Narration of My Last Journey to the Western Contry." 1791. *Historical Society of Pennsylvania Memoirs,* vol. 2, pt. 1. 1827. 76–131.

Barber, John Warner. "Boston Post Boy." 1739. *Historical Collections.* Worcester, Mass., 1839.

Brainerd, David. *Mirabilia Dei inter Indicos, or the Rise and Progress of a Remarkable Work of Grace Amongst a Number of the Indians in the Provinces of New-Jersey and Pennsylvania, Justly Represented in a Journal Kept by the Order of the Honourable Society (in Scotland) for Propagating Christian Knowledge. With some general Remarks.* Philadelphia, 1746.

Brainerd, John. *A Genuine Letter from Mr. John Brainard, Employed by the Scotch Society for Propagating the Gospel, a Missionary to the Indians in America, and Minister to a Congregation of Indians, at Bethel in East Jersey, to his Friend in England, Giving an Account of the Success of his Labours, as well as the Difficulties and Discouragements that attend his Mission among those Savages.* London, 1753.

*A Brief and True Narration of the Late Wars Risen in New-England: Occasioned by the Quarrelsome disposition, and Perfidious carriage of the Barbarous, Savage, and Heathenish Natives There.* London, 1675.

Burr, Esther. *The Journal of Esther Edwards Burr 1754–1757.* Ed. Carol Karlsen and Laurie Crumpacker. New Haven: Yale University Press, 1984.

Church, Benjamin. *Entertaining Passages Relating to Philip's War. So Dreadfull a Judgment: Puritan Responses to King Philip's War, 1676–1677.* Ed. Richard Slotkin and James K. Folsom. Middletown, Conn.: Wesleyan University Press, 1978.

Cornelius, Elias. *The Little Osage Captive.* 1822.

Danforth, Samuel. *The Woful Effects of Drunkenness.* Boston, 1710.

Easton, John. *A Relation of the Indyan Warr, by Mr Easton of Rhoad Island, 1675.* Reprinted in *A Narrative of the Causes which led to King Philip's War, of 1675 and 1676.* Ed. Franklin B. Hough. Albany: J. Munsell, 1858.

Edwards, Jonathan Jr. "Observations on the Language of the Muhhekaneew Indians." *Massachusetts Historical Society Collections,* ser. 2, vol. 10. 1823. 84–105.

Eliot, John. *The Indian Grammar Begun: or, An Essay to bring the Indian Language into Rules, for the Help of such as Desire to Learn the same, for the furtherance of the Gospel among them.* Cambridge, 1666.

Eliot Tracts:

> *A Brief Narrative of the progress of the Gospel amongst the Indians in New-England, in the year 1670.* John Eliot. 1671.
>
> *The Clear Sun-shine of the Gospel breaking forth upon the Indians in New England.* Thomas Shepherd. 1648.
>
> *The Day-Breaking, if not the Sun-Rising of the Gospel with the Indians in New England.* [John Wilson?]. 1647.
>
> *A further Accompt of the progress of the Gospel amongst the Indians in New-England and Of the Means used effectually to advance the same.* 1659.
>
> *A further Account of the progress of the Gospel Amongst the Indians in New-England being a Relation of the Confessions made by several Indians.* 1660.
>
> *The Glorious Progress of the Gospel, amongst the Indians in New England.* Edward Winslow. 1649.
>
> *A Late and Further Manifestation of the Progress of the Gospel amongst the Indians in New England.* 1655.
>
> *The Light appearing more and more towards the perfect Day.* Henry Whitefield. 1651.
>
> *New England's First Fruits.* 1643.
>
> *Strength out of Weaknesse; Or a Glorious Manifestation of the further Progresse of the Gospel among the Indians in New England.* 1652.
>
> *Tears of Repentance; Or, a further Narrative of the Progress of the Gospel Amongst the Indians in New-England.* John Eliot. 1653.

*A farther Brief and True Narration of the Late Wars Risen in New-England, Occasioned by the Quarrelsome Disposition and Perfidious Carriage of the Barbarous and Savage Indian Natives There. With an Account of the FIGHT, the 19th of December last, 1675.* London, 1675.

Gookin, Daniel. "An Historical Account of the Doings and Sufferings of the Christian Indians in New England." 1677. Reprinted in *Archaeologia Americana: Transactions and Collections of the American Antiquarian Society* 2 (1836): 423–534.

———. "Historical Collections of the Indians of New England." 1674. Reprinted in *Massachusetts Historical Society Collections,* ser. 1, vol. 1. 1792. 141–229.

Hopkins, Samuel. *Historical Memoirs Relating to the Housatonic Indians.* 1753. Reprinted in *Magazine of History with Notes and Queries,* extra no. 17 (1911).

Hubbard, William. *A Narrative of the Troubles with the Indians in New England, from the first planting thereof in the year 1607, to this present year 1677. But chiefly of the late Troubles in the two last years, 1675. and 1676.* Boston, 1677.

Hutchinson, Richard. *The Warr in New-England Visibly Ended. King Philip the barbarous Indian now Beheaded, and most of his Bloudy Adherents submitted to Mercy, the Rest fled far up into the Countrey, which hath given the Inhabitants Encouragement to prepare for their Settlement.* London, 1677.

*Journals of the House of Representatives of Massachusetts.* Vol. 17. Boston: Massachusetts Historical Society 1919–1981. 42.

Kappler, Charles J., ed. *Indian Treaties, 1778–1883.* Mattituck, N.Y.: Amereon House, 1972.

Mather, Cotton. *An Epistle to the Christian Indians.* Boston, 1706.

———. *A Family Well-Ordered Or an Essay to Render Parents and Children Happy in one another.* Boston, 1699.

———. *India Christiana.* Boston, 1721.

———. *Magnalia Christi Americana: or, The Ecclesiastical History of New England, From its First Planting, in the Year 1620, unto the Year of Our Lord 1698.* Vol. 1. Hartford: Silas Andrus and Son, 1853.

———. *Parentator.* Boston, 1724.

Mather, Increase. *A Brief History of the War with the Indians in New England.* London, 1676.

———. *Relations of the Troubles which have hapned in New England by reason of the Indians there.* London, 1677.

Mayhew, Experience. *Indian Converts.* London, 1727.

Mayhew, Matthew. *The Conquests and Triumphs of Grace: Being A Brief Narrative of the Success which the Gospel Hath had among the Indians of Martha's Vineyard.* London, 1695.

McCallum, James D., ed. *Letters of Eleazar Wheelock's Indians.* Hanover: Dartmouth College Publications, 1932.

*Memoir of John Arch, A Cherokee Young Man.* Boston: Massachusetts Sabbath School Society, 1836.

Morse, Jedidiah. *A Report to the Secretary of War of the United States, On Indian Affairs, Comprising a Narrative of a Tour Performed in the Summer of 1820.* New Haven, 1822.

Morse, Jedidiah, and Jeremy Belknap. "Report of a Committee of the Board of Correspondents of the Scots Society for Propagating Christian Knowledge, Who Visited the Oneida and the Mohekunuh Indians in 1796." *Massachusetts Historical Society Collections,* ser. 1, vol. 5. 1798. 12–32.

*News From New-England, Being a True and Last Account of the present Bloody Wars carried on betwixt the Infidels, Natives, and the English Christians, and Converted*

*Indians of New-England, declaring the many Dreadful Battles Fought betwixt them: As also the many Towns and Villages burnt by the merciless Heathens. And also the true Number of all the Christians slain since the beginning of that War, as it was sent over by a Factor of New-England to a Merchant in London.* London, 1676.

Pilkington, Walter, ed. *Journals of Samuel Kirkland: Eighteenth-Century Missionary to the Iroquois, Government Agent, Father of Hamilton College.* Clinton, N.Y.: Hamilton College, 1980.

Prince, Thomas. *Some account of Those English Ministers who Have Successively presided over the Work of Gospelizing the Indians on Martha's Vineyard, and the adjacent Islands.* London, 1727.

Rowlandson, Mary. *The Sovereignty and Goodness of God . . . A Narrative of the Captivity and Restoration of Mrs. Mary Rowlandson.* Cambridge, 1682.

[Saltonstall, Nathaniel.] *A Continuation of the State of New-England; Being a Farther Account of the Indian Warr, and of the Engagement betwixt the Joynt Forces of the United English Colonies and the Indians, on the 19th of December 1675. With the true Number of the Slain and Wounded, and the Transactions of the English Army since the said Fight. With all other Passages that have here hapned from the 10th of November, 1675 to the 8th of February 1675/6.* London, 1676.

[———.] *A New and further Narrative of the State of New-England, Being a Continued Account of the Bloudy Indian-War, From March till August, 1676. Giving a Perfect Relation of the Several Devastations, Engagements, and Transactions there; As also the Great Successes Lately obtained against the Barbarous Indians, the Reducing of King Philip, and the Killing of one of the Queens, etc.* London, 1676.

[———.] *The Present State of New-England, with respect to the Indian War. Wherein is an Account of the true Reason thereof, (as far as can be Judged by Men.) Together with most of the Remarkable Passages that have happened from the 20th of June, till the 10th of November, 1675.* London, 1676.

Sergeant, John. *A Letter from the Rev'd Mr. Sergeant of Stockbridge, to Dr. Colman of Boston; Containing Mr. Sergeant's Proposal of a more effectual Method for the Education of Indian Children; to raise 'em if possible into a civil and industrious People; by introducing the English Language among them; and thereby instilling into their Minds and Hearts, a more lasting Impression, the Principles of Virtue and Piety.* Boston, 1743.

Thompson, Benjamin. *New-Englands Tears for her Present Miseries: Or, A Late and True Relation of the Calamities of New England Since April last past. With an Account of the Battel between the English and Indians upon Seaconk Plain: And of the Indians Burning and Destroying of Marlbury, Rehoboth, Chelmsford, Sudbury, and Providence.* London, 1676.

*A True Account of the Most Considerable Occurrences That have hapned in the Warre Between the English and the Indians in New-England, From the Fifth of May, 1676, to the Fourth of August last; as also of the Successes it hath pleased God to give the English against them.* London, 1676.

Webster, Charles. *The Confessions, Covenants, and Standing Rules of the Church in Stockbridge, together with a notice of the Officers, and Catalogue of the Existing Members.* Stockbridge, 1827.

Wharton, Edward. *New England's Present Sufferings Under Their Cruel Neighbouring Indians.* London, 1675.

Wheeler, Thomas. *A Thankefull Remembrance of God's Mercy To Several Persons at Quabaug or Brookfield: Partly in a Collection of Providences about them, and Gracious Appearances for them: And partly in a Sermon Preached by Mr Edward Bulkley, Pastor of the Church of Christ at Concord, Upon a day of Thanksgiving, kept by divers for their Wonderfull Deliverance there.* Cambridge, 1676.

Wheelock, Eleazar. *A Continuation of the Narrative of the Indian Charity School, in Lebanon, in Connecticut. . . .* Boston, 1765.

———. *A Continuation of the Narrative. . . .* Hartford, 1771.

———. *A Continuation of the Narrative. . . .* [n.p.], 1772.

———. *A Continuation of the Narrative. . . .* Hartford, 1773.

———. *A Continuation of the Narrative. . . .* Hartford, 1775.

———. *A Plain and Faithful Narrative.* Boston, 1763.

Williams, John. *A Faithful narrative of Remarkable Occurences in the Captivity of the Reverend John Williams.* 3d ed. Boston, 1758.

Williams, Stephen. "A Letter to a Gentleman then in Boston." In *Gospel Ministers Must be Fit for the Master's Use . . . A Sermon Preached at Deerfield, August 31, 1735 at the Ordination of Mr. John Sargent.* By Nathanael Appleton. Boston, 1735.

Williams, Roger. *Key into the Language of America.* Boston, 1643.

Winthrop, John. "A Model of Christian Charity." *Winthrop Papers*, vol. 2. Ed. Stewart Mitchell. New York: Russell and Russell, 1968. 282–95.

## Secondary Sources

Amory, Hugh. *First Impressions: Printing in Cambridge, 1639–1989.* Cambridge: Harvard University Press, 1989.

Anderson, Benedict. *Imagined Communities: Reflections on the Origin and Spread of Nationalism.* London: Verso, 1983.

Axtell, James. *The Invasion Within: The Contest of Cultures in Colonial North America.* New York: Oxford University Press, 1985.

———. "The Scholastic Frontier in Western Massachusetts." *After Columbus: Essays in the Ethnohistory of Colonial North America.* New York: Oxford University Press, 1988. 58–72.

———. *The School Upon a Hill: Education and Society in Colonial New England.* New York: Norton, 1974.

———. "Some Thoughts on the Ethnohistory of Missions." *After Columbus: Essays in the Ethnohistory of Colonial North America.* New York: Oxford University Press, 1988. 47–57.

———. "Were Indian Conversions Bona Fide?" *After Columbus: Essays in the Ethno-*

*history of Colonial North America.* New York: Oxford University Press, 1988. 100–121.

Bailyn, Bernard. *The Ideological Origins of the American Revolution.* Cambridge, Mass.: Harvard University Press, 1967.

Banks, Charles Edward. *The History of Martha's Vineyard.* Vol. 1. Edgartown: Dukes County Historical Society, 1966.

Beaver, R. Pierce. "Protestant Churches and the Indians." *History of Indian-White Relations.* Vol. 4 of *Handbook of North American Indians.* Ed. Wilcomb Washburn. Washington, D.C.: Smithsonian Institution, 1988. 430–37.

Bercovitch, Sacvan. *The American Jeremiad.* Madison: University of Wisconsin Press, 1978.

Berkhofer, Robert F. Jr. "The Political Context of a New Indian History." *Pacific Historical Review* 40 (1971): 357–82.

——. *Salvation and the Savage: An Analysis of Protestant Missions and American Indian Response, 1787–1862.* University of Kentucky Press, 1965.

——. *The White Man's Indian: Images of the American Indian from Columbus to the Present.* New York: Knopf, 1970.

Bhabha, Homi K., ed. *Nation and Narration.* New York: Routledge, 1990.

Blodgett, Harold. *Samson Occom.* Hanover: Dartmouth College Publications, 1935.

Bourne, Russell. *The Red King's Rebellion: Racial Politics in New England 1675–1678.* New York: Atheneum, 1990.

Bowden, Henry Warner. *American Indians and Christian Missions.* Chicago: University of Chicago Press, 1981.

Bowden, Henry Warner, and James P. Ronda. *John Eliot's Indian Dialogues: A Study in Cultural Interaction.* Westport, Conn.: Greenwood, 1980.

Bragdon, Kathleen. "Gender as a Social Category in Native Southern New England." *Ethnohistory* 43:4 (1996): 573–92.

——. "Linguistic Acculturation in Massachusett: 1663–1771." *Papers of the Twelfth Algonquin Conference.* Ed. William Cowan. Ottawa: Carleton University, 1981. 121–32.

——. "Native Economy on Eighteenth-Century Martha's Vineyard and Nantucket." *Actes du Dix-Septieme Congres des Algonquinistes.* Ed. William Cowan. Ottawa: Carleton University, 1986. 27–40.

——. *Native People of Southern New England, 1500–1650.* Norman: University of Oklahoma Press, 1996.

——. "Probate Records as a Source for Algonquian Ethnohistory." *Papers of the Tenth Algonquin Conference.* Ed. William Cowan. Ottawa: Carleton University, 1979. 136–41.

——. "Vernacular Literacy and Massachusetts World View, 1650–1750." *Algonkians of New England: Past and Present.* Ed. Peter Benes. Boston: Boston University, 1991. 26–34.

Brandt, Deborah. *Literacy as Involvement: The Acts of Writers, Readers, and Texts.* Carbondale: Southern Illinois University Press, 1990.

Brasser, Ted J. *Riding on the Frontier's Crest: Mahican Indian Culture and Culture Change.* Ottawa: National Museums of Canada, 1974.

Breen, Timothy. "Creative Adaptations: Peoples and Cultures." *Colonial British America: Essays in the New History of the Early Modern Era.* Ed. Jack P. Greene and J. R. Pole. Baltimore: Johns Hopkins University Press, 1984.

Breitwieser, Mitchell R. *American Puritanism and the Defense of Mourning: Religion, Grief, and Ethnology in Mary White Rowlandson's Captivity Narrative.* Madison: University of Wisconsin Press, 1990.

Brereton, Virginia Lieson. *From Sin to Salvation: Stories of Women's Conversions, 1800 to the Present.* Bloomington: Indiana University Press, 1991.

Brumble, H. David III. *American Indian Autobiography.* Berkeley: University of California Press, 1988.

Caldwell, Patricia. *The Puritan Conversion Narrative: The Beginnings of American Expression.* Cambridge: Cambridge University Press, 1983.

Calloway, Colin G. *The American Revolution in Indian Country: Crisis and Diversity in Native American Communities.* New York: Cambridge University Press, 1995.

Campisi, Jack. "The Emergence of the Mashantucket Pequot Tribe, 1637–1975." *The Pequots in Southern New England: The Fall and Rise of an American Indian Nation.* Ed. Laurance M. Hauptman and James D. Wherry. Norman: University of Oklahoma Press, 1990. 117–40.

Cheyfitz, Eric. *The Poetics of Imperialism: Translation and Colonization from* The Tempest *to* Tarzan. New York: Oxford University Press, 1991.

Clifford, James. *The Predicament of Culture: Ethnography, Literature, and Art.* Cambridge: Harvard University Press, 1988.

Coates, Benjamin. "Foreword to Aupaumut's journal." *Historical Society of Pennsylvania Memoirs,* vol. 2, pt. 1. 1827. 63–74.

Cogley, Richard W. "John Eliot and the Origins of the American Indians." *Early American Literature* 21:3 (1986/87): 210–25.

Cohen, Charles. "Conversion among Puritans and Amerindians: A Theological and Cultural Perspective." *Puritanism: Transatlantic Perspectives on a Seventeenth-Century Anglo-American Faith.* Ed. Francis J. Bremer. Boston: Massachusetts Historical Society, 1993. 233–56.

Cook-Lynn, Elizabeth. "American Indian Intellectualism and the New Indian Story." *American Indian Quarterly* 20.1 (1996): 57–77.

Cooper, Marilyn. *Writing as Social Action.* Portsmouth: Heinemann, 1989.

Counselman, Lawrence Wroth. "The Indian Treaty as Literature." *Yale Review* 17 (July 1928): 749–66.

Cressy, David. "The Environment for Literacy: Accomplishment and Context in Seventeenth-Century England and New England." *Literacy in Historical Perspective.* Ed. Daniel Resnick. Washington, D.C.: Library of Congress, 1983.

Crosby, Constance. "The Algonkian Spiritual Landscape." *Algonkians of New England: Past and Present.* Ed. Peter Benes. Boston: Boston University, 1991. 35–41.

Cronon, William. *Changes in the Land: Indians, Colonists, and the Ecology of New England.* New York: Hill and Wang, 1983.

Dannenberg, Anne Marie. "'Where, then shall we place the hero of the wilderness?': William Apess's *Eulogy on King Philip* and Doctrines of Racial Destiny." *Early Native American Writing: New Critical Essays.* Ed. Helen Jaskoski. New York: Cambridge University Press, 1996. 66–82.

Davidson, Cathy N. *Revolution and the Word: The Rise of the Novel in America.* New York: Oxford University Press, 1986.

Deloria, Vine Jr. *Custer Died for Your Sins: An Indian Manifesto.* 1969. Norman: University of Oklahoma Press, 1988.

Demos, John. *A Little Commonwealth: Family Life in Plymouth Colony.* New York: Oxford University Press, 1970.

———. *The Unredeemed Captive: A Family Story from Early America.* New York: Knopf, 1994.

Derounian, Kathryn Zabelle. "The Publication, Promotion, and Distribution of Mary Rowlandson's Indian Captivity Narrative in the Seventeenth Century." *Early American Literature* 23 (1988): 239–61.

Derounian-Stodola, Katherine, and James Levernier. *The Indian Captivity Narrative, 1550–1900.* New York: Twayne, 1993.

Dowd, Gregory Evans. *A Spirited Resistance: The North American Struggle for Unity, 1745–1815.* Baltimore: Johns Hopkins University Press, 1992.

Drake, James D. *King Philip's War: Civil War in New England, 1675–1676.* Amherst: University of Massachusetts Press, 2000.

Drake, Samuel. *The Book of the Indians of North America.* 11th ed. Boston, 1851.

Dunn, Shirley W. *The Mohicans and Their Land 1609–1730.* Fleischmanns, N.Y.: Purple Mountain, 1994.

Earle, Alice Morse. *Child Life in Colonial Days.* 1899. Stockbridge, Mass.: Berkshire, 1993.

Edwards, William. *Timothy and Rhoda Ogden Edwards of Stockbridge, Mass., and Their Descendants: A Genealogy.* Compiled by William Edwards. Cincinnati: Robert Clarke Co., 1903.

Elliott, Michael. "'This Indian Bait': Samson Occom and the Voice of Liminality." *Early American Literature* 29 (1994): 233–53.

Fenton, William. "Glossary of Figures of Speech in Iroquois Political Rhetoric." *The History and Culture of Iroquois Diplomacy: An Interdisciplinary Guide to the Treaties of the Six Nations and Their League.* Ed. Francis Jennings. Syracuse: Syracuse University Press, 1985.

———. "Structure, Continuity, and Change in the Process of Iroquois Treaty Making." *The History and Culture of Iroquois Diplomacy: An Interdisciplinary Guide to the Treaties of the Six Nations and Their League.* Ed. Francis Jennings. Syracuse: Syracuse University Press, 1985.

Field, David D. "A History of the Town of Stockbridge." *A History of the County of Berkshire, Massachusetts.* Pt 2. Pittsfield, Mass.: S. W. Bush, 1829.

Fitzpatrick, Tara. "The Figure of Captivity: The Cultural Work of the Puritan Captivity Narrative." *American Literary History* 3.1 (1991): 1–26.

Forbes, Allan. *Some Indian Events of New England.* Boston: State Street Trust Company, 1934.

Franchot, Jenny. *Roads to Rome: The Antebellum Protestant Encounter with Catholicism.* Berkeley: University of California Press, 1994.

Frazier, Patrick. *The Mohicans of Stockbridge.* Lincoln: University of Nebraska Press, 1992.

Galinsky, Hans. "'I cannot join with the multitude'—Daniel Gookin (1612–87), Critical Historian of Indian-English Relations." *Mythos und Aufklarung in der Amerikanischen Literatur/Myth and Enlightenment in American Literature.* Ed. Deiter Meindl and Friedrich Horlacher. Erlangen, Germany: 1985.

Gilroy, Paul. *The Black Atlantic: Modernity and Double Consciousness.* Cambridge: Harvard University Press, 1993.

Goddard, Ives. "A Stylistic Comparison of Two Mashpee Petitions from 1752 (in Massachusett) and 1753 (in English)." *Algonkians of New England: Past and Present.* Ed. Peter Benes. Boston: Boston University, 1991.

Goddard, Ives, and Kathleen Bragdon, eds. *Native Writings in Massachusett.* 2 vols. Philadelphia: American Philosophical Society, 1988.

Goody, Jack, and Ian Watt. "The Consequences of Literacy." *Literacy in Traditional Societies.* Ed. Jack Goody. Cambridge: Cambridge University Press, 1968.

Gray, Edward Gordon. "Indian Language in Anglo-American Thought, 1550–1820." Diss. Brown University, 1996.

Greenblatt, Stephen J. "Learning to Curse: Aspects of Linguistic Colonialism in the Sixteenth Century." *First Images of America: The Impact of the New World on the Old.* Ed. Fredi Chiappelli. Vol. 1. Berkeley: University of California Press, 1976. 561–80.

Gustafson, Sandra. "Nations of Israelites: Prophecy and Cultural Autonomy in the Writings of William Apess." *Religion and Literature* 26.1 (1994): 31–53.

———. "Performing the Word: American Oratory, 1630–1860." Diss. Cornell University, 1993.

Haefeli, Evan, and Kevin Sweeney. "Revisiting *The Redeemed Captive:* New Perspectives on the 1704 Attack on Deerfield." *William and Mary Quarterly* 52.1 (1995): 3–46.

Hall, David. *Cultures of Print: Essays in the History of the Book.* Amherst: University of Massachusetts Press, 1996.

———. *Worlds of Wonder, Days of Judgment: Popular Religious Belief in Early New England.* Cambridge: Harvard University Press, 1989.

Handsman, Russell G., and Trudie Lamb Richmond. "Confronting Colonialism: The Mahican and Schaghticoke Peoples and Us." Essay for seminar at the School of American Research, Santa Fe, N. M. April 1992. STL.

Hare, Lloyd. *Thomas Mayhew: Patriarch to the Indians.* New York: Appleton, 1932.

Hatch, Nathan O. *The Democratization of American Christianity.* New Haven: Yale University Press, 1989.

Holstun, James. "John Eliot's Empirical Millenarianism." *Representations* 4 (1983): 128–53.

Huddleston, Lee E. *Origins of the American Indians: European Concepts, 1492–1729.* Latin American Monographs 11. Austin: University of Texas Press, 1967.

Hulme, Peter. *Colonial Encounters: Europe and the Native Caribbean, 1492–1797.* London: Methuen, 1986.

Jaskoski, Helen. *Early Native American Writing: New Critical Essays.* New York: Cambridge University Press, 1996.

Jennings, Francis. *The Invasion of America: Indians, Colonialism, and the Cant of Conquest.* New York: Norton, 1976.

Jones, Electa. *Stockbridge, Past and Present: Records of an Old Mission Station.* Springfield, Mass.: Samuel Bowles, 1854.

Kellaway, William. *The New England Company, 1649–1776.* London: Longman's, 1961.

Keller-Cohen, Deborah, ed. *Literacy: Interdisciplinary Conversations.* Cresskill, N.J.: Hampton, 1994.

Konkle, Maureen. "Indian Literacy, U.S. Colonialism, and Literary Criticism." *American Literature* 69 (1997): 457–86.

Krupat, Arnold. *Ethnocriticism: Ethnography, History, Literature.* Berkeley: University of California Press, 1992.

——. *For Those Who Come After: A Study of Native American Autobiography.* Berkeley: University of California Press, 1985.

——. *The Voice in the Margin: Native American Literature and the Canon.* Berkeley: University of California Press, 1989.

Leach, Douglas E. *Flintlock and Tomahawk: New England in King Philip's War.* New York: Macmillan, 1958.

Lepore, Jill. "Dead Men Tell No Tales: John Sassamon and the Fatal Consequences of Literacy." *American Quarterly* 46 (1994): 479–512.

——. *The Name of War: King Philip's War and the Origins of American Identity.* New York: Knopf, 1998.

Little, Elizabeth A. *The Writings of Nantucket Indians.* Nantucket: Nantucket Historical Association, 1981.

Lockridge, Kenneth. *Literacy in Colonial New England.* New York: Norton, 1974.

Love, William DeLoss. *Samson Occom and the Christian Indians of New England.* Boston: Pilgrim Press, 1899.

Lurie, Nancy Oestreich. "The World's Oldest On-going Protest Demonstration: North American Indian Drinking Patterns." *Pacific Historical Review* 40.3 (1971): 311–32.

Mancall, Peter C. *Deadly Medicine: Indians and Alcohol in Early America.* Ithaca, N.Y.: Cornell University Press, 1995.

Mandell, Daniel. "Change and Continuity in a Native American Community: Eighteenth-Century Stockbridge." M.A. thesis. University of Virginia, 1982.

Maracle, Brian. *Crazywater: Native Voices on Addiction and Recovery.* New York: Penguin, 1993.

McBride, Kevin. "The Historical Archaeology of the Mashantucket Pequots, 1637–1900: A Preliminary Analysis." *The Pequots in Southern New England: The Fall and Rise of an American Indian Nation.* Ed. Laurance M. Hauptman and James D. Wherry. Norman: University of Oklahoma Press, 1990. 96–116.

McQuaid, K. "William Apes, Pequot: An Indian Reformer in the Jackson Era." *New England Quarterly* 50.4 (1977): 605–25.

Merrell, James. *The Indians' New World: Catawbas and Their Neighbors from European Contact through the Era of Removal.* Chapel Hill: University of North Carolina Press, 1989.

Meserve, Walter T. "English Works of Seventeenth-Century Indians." *American Quarterly* 8.3 (1956): 265–76.

Miles, Lion G. "The Red Man Dispossessed: The Williams Family and the Alienation of Indian Land in Stockbridge, Massachusetts, 1736–1818." *New England Quarterly* 67.1 (1994): 46–76.

Monaghan, E. Jennifer. "Literacy in Eighteenth-Century New England: Some Historiographical Reflections on Issues of Gender." *Making Adjustments: Change and Continuity in Planter Nova Scotia, 1759–1800.* Ed. Margaret Conrad. Fredericton, Nova Scotia: Acadiensis, 1991. 12–44.

———. "Readers Writing: The Curriculum of the Writing Schools of Eighteenth-Century Boston." *Visible Language* 21.2 (1987): 168–212.

———. "'She loved to read in good Books': Literacy and the Indians of Martha's Vineyard, 1643–1725." *History of Education Quarterly* 30.4 (1990): 493–521.

Moon, Randall. "William Apess and Writing White." *Studies in American Indian Literatures* 5.4 (1993): 45–54.

Morgan, Edmund. *The Puritan Family.* New York: Norton, 1966.

———. *Visible Saints.* Ithaca, N.Y.: Cornell University Press, 1965.

Morrison, Dane. *A Praying People: Massachusett Acculturation and the Failure of the Puritan Mission, 1600–1690.* New York: Peter Lang, 1995.

Murray, David. *Forked Tongues: Speech, Writing, and Representation in North American Indian Texts.* Bloomington: University of Indiana Press, 1991.

Murray, Laura. "The Aesthetic of Dispossession: Washington Irving and Ideologies of (De)Colonization in the Early Republic." *American Literary History* 8.2 (1996): 205–31.

———. "'Pray, Sir, Consider a Little': Rituals of Subordination and Strategies of Resistance in the Letters of Hezekiah Calvin and David Fowler to Eleazar Wheelock, 1764–1768." *Studies in American Indian Literatures* 4.2–3 (1992): 48–74. Reprinted in *Early Native American Writing: New Critical Essays.* Ed. Helen Jaskoski. New York: Cambridge University Press, 1996. 15–41.

——, ed. *To Do Good to My Indian Brethren: The Writings of Joseph Johnson, 1751–1776.* Amherst: University of Massachusetts Press, 1998.

Naeher, Robert James. "Dialogue in the Wilderness: John Eliot and the Indian Exploration of Puritanism as a Source of Meaning, Comfort, and Ethnic Survival." *New England Quarterly* 62.3 (1989): 346–68.

Nelson, Dana. "'(I speak like a fool but I am constrained)': Samson Occom's Short Narrative and Economies of the Racial Self." *Early Native American Writing: New Critical Essays.* Ed. Helen Jaskoski. New York: Cambridge University Press, 1996. 42–65.

O'Connell, Barry. "William Apess and the Survival of the Pequot People." *Algonkians of New England: Past and Present.* Ed. Peter Benes. Boston: Boston University, 1991. 89–100.

Ong, Walter. *Orality and Literacy: The Technologizing of the Word.* New York: Methuen, 1982.

Palfrey, John Gorham. *The History of New England.* Vol. 3. Boston: Little, Brown, 1865–1890.

Pearce, Roy Harvey. *The Savages of America: A Study of the Indian and the Idea of Civilization.* Baltimore: Johns Hopkins University Press, 1953. Reprinted as *Savagism and Civilization: A Study of the Indian and the American Mind.* Baltimore: Johns Hopkins University Press, 1965.

Peyer, Bernd. "Samson Occom: Mohegan Missionary and Writer of the Eighteenth Century." *American Indian Quarterly* 6.3–4 (1982): 208–17.

——. *The Tutor'd Mind: Indian Missionary-Writers in Antebellum America.* Amherst: University of Massachusetts Press, 1997.

Pratt, Mary Louise. *Imperial Eyes: Travel Writing and Transculturation.* New York: Routledge, 1992.

——. "Transculturation and Autoethnography: Peru 1615/1980." *Colonial Discourse/Postcolonial Theory.* Ed. Francis Barker, Peter Hulme, and Margaret Iversen. New York: St. Martin's, 1994. 24–46.

Pulsipher, Jenny Hale. "Massacre at Hurtleberry Hill: Christian Indians and English Authority in Metacomet's War." *William and Mary Quarterly,* 3d ser., 53.3 (1996): 459–86.

Richardson, Leon Burr. *An Indian Preacher in England.* Hanover, N.H.: Dartmouth College Publications, 1933.

Richey, Russell E. *Early American Methodism.* Bloomington: Indiana University Press, 1991.

Richter, Daniel. *The Ordeal of the Longhouse: The People of the Iroquois League in the Era of European Colonization.* Chapel Hill: University of North Carolina Press, 1992.

Ronda, James P. "Generations of Faith: The Christian Indians of Martha's Vineyard." *William and Mary Quarterly,* 3d ser., 38 (1981): 369–94.

——. "'We Are Well as We Are': An Indian Critique of Seventeenth-Century Christian Missions." *William and Mary Quarterly* 34 (1977): 66–82.

Ronda, James P., and Jeanne Ronda. "'As They Were Faithful': Chief Hendrick Aupaumut and the Struggle for Stockbridge Survival, 1757–1830." *American Indian Culture and Research Journal* 3.3 (1979): 43–55.

Rorbauch, William. *The Alcoholic Republic: An American Tradition.* New York: Oxford University Press, 1979.

Ruoff, A. LaVonne Brown. "American Indian Authors, 1774–1899." *Critical Essays on Native American Literature.* Ed. Andrew Wiget. Boston: G. K. Hall, 1985. 191–202.

———. *American Indian Literatures: An Introduction, Bibliographic Review, and Selected Bibliography.* New York: Modern Language Association, 1990.

———. "Three Nineteenth-Century American Indian Autobiographers." *Redefining American Literary History.* Ed. A. LaVonne Brown Ruoff and Jerry W. Ward. New York: Modern Language Association, 1990. 251–69.

Russell, Howard S. *Indian New England before the Mayflower.* Hanover, N.H.: University Press of New England, 1980.

Said, Edward. *Culture and Imperialism.* New York: Vintage 1993.

Salisbury, Neal. *Manitou and Providence: Indians, Europeans, and the Making of New England, 1500–1643.* New York: Oxford University Press, 1982.

———. "Red Puritans: The 'Praying Indians' of Massachusetts Bay and John Eliot." *William and Mary Quarterly* 31 (1974): 27–54.

———, ed. *The Sovereignty and Goodness of God.* Boston: Bedford Books, 1997.

Sarris, Greg. *Keeping Slug-Woman Alive: A Holistic Approach to American Indian Texts.* Berkeley: University of California Press, 1993.

Scribner, Sylvia, and Michael Cole. *The Psychology of Literacy.* Cambridge: Harvard University Press, 1981.

Sedgwick, Sarah Cabot, and Christina Sedgwick Marquand. *Stockbridge, 1739–1939: A Chronicle.* Great Barrington, Mass.: Berkshire Courier, 1939.

Sekora, John. "Red, White, and Black: Indian Captivities, Colonial Printers, and the Early African-American Narrative." *A Mixed Race: Ethnicity in Early America.* Ed. Frank Shuffleton. New York: Oxford University Press, 1993. 92–104.

Sewell, David. "'So Unstable and Like Mad Men They Were': Language and Interpretation in American Captivity Narratives." *A Mixed Race: Ethnicity in Early America.* Ed. Frank Shuffleton. New York: Oxford University Press, 1993. 39–55.

Shea, Daniel B. *Spiritual Autobiography in Early America.* Princeton: Princeton University Press, 1968.

Simmons, William S. "Conversion from Indian to Puritan." *New England Quarterly* 52.2 (1979): 197–218.

———. *Spirit of the New England Tribes: Indian History and Folklore, 1620–1984.* Hanover, N.H.: University Press of New England, 1986.

Slotkin, Richard. *Regeneration through Violence: The Mythology of the American Frontier, 1600–1860.* Middletown, Conn.: Wesleyan University Press, 1973.

Slotkin, Richard, and James Folsom. *"So Dreadfull a Judgment": Puritan Responses to King Philip's War, 1676–1677*. Middletown, Conn.: Wesleyan University Press, 1978.

Sollors, Werner. *Beyond Ethnicity: Consent and Descent in American Culture*. New York: Oxford University Press, 1986.

Spivak, Gayatri. "Can the Subaltern Speak?" *Marxism and the Interpretation of Culture*. Ed. Cary Nelson and Lawrence Grossberg. Urbana: University of Illinois Press, 1988.

Szasz, Margaret. *Indian Education in the American Colonies, 1607–1783*. Albuquerque: University of New Mexico Press, 1988.

——. "Samson Occom: Mohegan as Spiritual Intermediary." *Between Indian and White Worlds: The Cultural Broker*. Norman: University of Oklahoma Press, 1994. 61–78.

Taylor, Alan. "Captain Hendrick Aupaumut: The Dilemmas of an Intercultural Broker." *Ethnohistory* 43.3 (1996): 431–57.

Tiro, Karim. "Denominated 'SAVAGE': Methodism, Writing, and Identity in the Works of William Apess, A Pequot." *American Quarterly* 48.4 (1996): 653–79.

Trafzer, Clifford. "Grandmother, Grandfather, and the First History of the Americas." *New Voices in Native American Literary Criticism*. Ed. Arnold Krupat. Washington, D.C.: Smithsonian Institution Press, 1993. 474–87.

Trigger, Bruce, ed. *Northeast*. Vol. 15 of *Handbook of North American Indians*. Washington, D.C.: Smithsonian Institution Press, 1978.

Ulrich, Laurel. *Good Wives: Image and Reality in the Lives of Women in Northern New England, 1650–1750*. New York: Random House, 1982.

Van Lonkhuyzen, Harold. "A Reappraisal of the Praying Indians: Acculturation, Conversion, and Identity at Natick, Massachusetts, 1646–1730." *New England Quarterly* 63 (1990): 396–428.

Vaughan, Alden. *New England Frontier: Puritans and Indians, 1620–1675*. New York: Norton, 1979.

Vaughan, Alden T., and Edward W. Clark. *Puritans among the Indians: Accounts of Captivity and Redemption 1676–1724*. Cambridge: Harvard University Press, 1981.

Washburn, Wilcomb, ed. *History of Indian-White Relations*. Vol. 4 of *Handbook of North American Indians*. Washington, D.C.: Smithsonian Institution Press, 1988.

Watkins, Owen. *The Puritan Experience*. New York: Routledge, 1972.

White, Richard. *The Middle Ground: Indians, Empires and Republics in the Great Lakes Region, 1650–1815*. Cambridge: Cambridge University Press, 1992.

Winship, George Parker. *The New England Company of 1649 and John Eliot*. Boston: Plimpton, 1920.

Wong, Hertha. *Sending My Heart Back across the Years: Tradition and Innovation in Native American Autobiography*. New York: Oxford University Press, 1992.

# INDEX